Brendan
Foster

Brendan Foster

BRENDAN FOSTER
AND
CLIFF TEMPLE

Heinemann : London

William Heinemann Ltd
15 Queen Street, Mayfair, London W1X 8BE

LONDON MELBOURNE TORONTO
JOHANNESBURG AUCKLAND

First published 1978

434 26910 7 (*Hardback*)
434 26911 5 (*Paperback*)

Printed and bound in Great Britain by
Morrison & Gibb Ltd, London and Edinburgh

One

Long before I even reach the stadium I can hear waves of noise overflowing from the walls and floating reluctantly away on the still, warm air. Well, it isn't really a stadium; just a small wooden stand on one side of the track, and mounds of earth where, one day, seats will be installed. But although I have raced at the Olympic Games, the Commonwealth Games and the European championships, this is something different. In fact, it still seems almost impossible to believe it is happening at all.

I am in Gateshead, just a mile or so from home, and yet preparing to run an important race in front of 10,000 spectators and millions of television viewers on a brand new, all-weather Tartan track. In the past my clubmates and I have always had to travel down to London, or up to Edinburgh, for anything like this. Gateshead, our home town, just across the River Tyne from Newcastle, is where we set out from, or return to, or do our training round. Racing-wise, nothing ever actually *happens* here; it is simply a base. Until today.

For months we have been telling everyone that on August 3rd, 1974, we are going to stage the biggest and best athletics meeting ever seen in the north-east to celebrate the opening of our new track. My mind jumps back to that civic reception which Gateshead Council threw for me the previous winter to celebrate a successful 1973 season, and how, semi-intoxicated after I had joined my family and friends in a few celebration drinks, I had risen to my feet and told everyone present that if, as we had heard rumoured, Gateshead Council went ahead and laid the all-weather track, then I would have a go at setting a world record on it.

They were brave, easy words to speak when you have had a few beers in good company, and when the occasion you are talking about seems way ahead, lost in the mists of time. But time passes, mists clear, and now with the promised track having been down all of ten days I am beginning to seriously question whether Old Big Mouth has put his foot in it again. I feel sure he has.

The recent weeks have been a mad frenzy of activity, completely alien to the way I like to build up to any race. For a start, Gateshead Council had appointed me their Sports and Recreation Officer two weeks earlier. But I have been involved with this meeting long before that. Everyone at our club, Gateshead Harriers, has been: Stan Long, the club distance running coach, a welder by trade, who ten years before had talked me into becoming an athlete; Lindsay Dunn, who had been an idol of mine when I first joined, and was later to become a regular training partner and mentor; John Caine, himself an international runner whose career had been ruined by leg injury; and all the others. They are all here today in their best suits, organising this, organising that. It is Gateshead Harriers' tea-party.

It has been a hell of a strain. There have been problems with officials, athletes, transport, facilities, the lot. We have managed to get a sponsor, Rediffusion, but television coverage was not definite until the last minute. Everyone seemed to have some crisis which they wanted to hand over to me, and all the time I have been trying to prepare for the race I know that I have lost a large chunk of training through a hamstring injury at the beginning of the summer. In May, when I was trying to prepare for the race I know that I have lost a large chunk of training even training. The BBC turned us down. Finally ITV, rarely able to show any athletics in Britain, bought the pig in the poke, and I knew we were assured of the publicity we needed.

Last night I had just shut off. I had taken the telephone off the hook and gone to bed early, so all that is left for me to do now is to run. All? It seems the hardest part of it. As I warm up outside the stadium I can hear the crowd cheering as a local boy, Dave Gibbon, beats New Zealander Dick Quax in the mile.

But my mind is in a turmoil, as flashes of past and present race across the horizon. I remember those bleak days running round Brighton Racecourse when I was at Sussex University, trying to make the university cross country team and wondering why I did not seem to be getting any better. Has Andy Carter arrived on the 12.30 train?

I remember training days when I seemed to be flying along with wings on my feet, and others when I could barely put one ton-weighted foot in front of the other. Or when it poured with rain throughout a Sunday morning twenty-miler. Where is Ainsley Bennett? He's due to run the 100 metres at 2.30, and he's not here yet.

A small boy carrying a football flashes across my mind. He wanted to be a professional footballer because it was like a religion in these parts, but he became

2

a runner instead. I was that boy. Down the road Sunderland are playing Newcastle United at Roker Park in the Texaco Cup, yet here we still have people trying to force their way into our packed ground. If I disappoint them today, having promised them so much, will they ever come to watch athletics at our new track again?

Back in Brighton, back in time, I throw my running shoes down in disgust after finishing an exhausted 163rd in the British Universities cross country championship. I wonder if the food is all right at the athletes' hotel?

Nearly time for my race, the 3000 metres. More doubts cross my mind. Have I given it enough thought? Have I trained too hard this week? Am I tired? How much have the organisational problems taken out of me? Above all, can I really get close to the world record? Can I, having said it so casually all those months before, come out on a given day in a given place at a given time and run 3000 metres faster than anyone else in history? I try to dismiss that last thought; it is getting too close to revealing the illogicality of the situation.

Instead, I go through the tunnel and into the arena. I see faces I know – Stan, Lindsay, John – all busy with their own duties. I see the bald-headed young American Dick Buerkle, and I suddenly remember that I am in a race, not a time trial, and there are others in it who will be trying to beat me. I see Mike Baxter, the tall Leeds runner, and I remember that I have at least one ally. Mike, himself an international athlete, but coming back from injury, has offered to make the pace in the opening half of the race, keeping it on a world record schedule. He has an important role to play, and briefly my mind goes back four years to when I was studying in Leeds and training regularly with Mike. He knows how important it is to me to run well today in front of my own people.

I look up in the stands. I can see my wife, Sue, and my Mum and Dad, and various members of the Gateshead Council, who agreed to spend £140,000 on laying the new track. I see a lot of faces I don't know, I see television cameras, I see journalists from the national newspapers, lured to a town they had to look up on a map by the promise of a performance which even now I am having my doubts about.

The announcer is telling the crowd about the existing records for the distance: '. . . and the world record is held by Emiel Puttemans of Belgium, with 7 minutes 37.6 seconds.' To many of the crowd it is just a set of figures, but I know that it means running one mile in around 4 minutes 5 seconds, and then continuing at the same pace for almost another mile.

A whistle, and the starter calls us to the line. At the gun Mike Baxter goes straight into the lead, and already we are running hard, and the field is stretching

As Mike Baxter makes the pace, the stopwatch is the enemy. (Newcastle Chronicle & Journal).

rather than bunching. We go through the first lap in 60 seconds, and the second lap only fractionally slower. But then I feel that Mike is tiring and the third lap drops to 62.2 seconds. In the next, I see Mike's hand waving me past, and I realise he is telling me that he can do no more. So I go on alone, and try to pick up the pace, as the rumbling cheers of the crowd seem to become more highly pitched.

I feel the sweat running off my forehead and into my eyes. My throat is dry, but my tongue feels a tang of salt. I have passed the halfway mark, 1500 metres, in 3 minutes 49 seconds, slightly slower than I wanted, and inside the track John

4

Caine is shouting to me, 'It's too slow! It's too slow!'. I try to pick it up again, and by 2000 metres the timekeeper is calling 'five minutes, four seconds', so I have only missed breaking the UK record for that distance by less than a second.

But there are still two-and-a-half laps to go, and my next circuit slumps again: 62.2 seconds. The crowd are going berserk, and although they are outside the track I feel I could almost reach out and touch them, as they seem to lean into me, urging me to go faster, still faster. I know I have the race won; the rest of the field are well back, and the temptation to slow down and just win is enormous.

But I know as well as everyone else that there is a record beckoning, and I get round. The bell clangs. Just once more. The time is 6:37.6, so if I can summon up a sub-60-seconds final lap, I can do it. I hear applause and cheering, I see arms waving, programmes flapping, like a wild sea. And I know I am running faster than a 60-second pace.

Into the home straight with just 100 metres to run . . . fifty . . . twenty . . . and a great shout goes up as I cross the line. Someone nods to me and holds up a stopwatch. At that moment I don't care what the exact time on it reads. It is enough to know that here in Gateshead I have broken a world record. I run a lap in the opposite direction, waving to the crowd, and among the first hands I shake

I've won the race, but have I broken the record?

is that of Mike Baxter, who set up the fast early pace. And I shake hands with Stan Long, who has devoted his life to athletics and whose open door for Gateshead Harriers members led both directly and indirectly to what has happened today.

The time, I hear later, is 7:35.2 seconds, and Lindsay tells me that this is the same as running seven-and-a-half laps at 60.7 seconds for each one, without stopping. If I had known that was what it needed to break the record, I would never have started the race, I'm sure!

I go home and have a cup of tea. I still feel light, not tired at all, so I go out and run another four miles, which takes my week's mileage to 101. The following month the European championships are taking place in Rome, and that is the next target. But for today I am satisfied. It is like a dream come true, as I tell journalists after the race. One of them later writes that this seems too hackneyed a phrase to describe such an emotional occasion. Well, what does he expect after a world record? Shakespeare?

*A moment to savour the success for Gateshead, but I must
get back to training quickly.* (Newcastle Chronicle & Journal).

Two

The north-east of England, where I was born and bred, has a character all of its own. We don't go round wearing mufflers and cloth caps, as some southerners would have you believe, and nor is 'When the Boat Comes In' televised live. But nevertheless there is an undeniable insularity which has evolved among people who have, in general, not expected a great deal from life. If Tyneside was an island, I don't think people there would be terribly bothered, even if you needed a passport to get in and out.

Names like Hebburn and Jarrow still evoke an image of depression, unemployment, and greyness, an image hardened by the Jarrow Marches of the 1930s. In fact, the area is nowhere near as bad as that external image, and the north-east has changed a great deal in recent years, simply because there are some more optimistic people who have worked hard to change it.

It used to be the wealth-producing area in Britain, but it was the landowners, the mineowners and the shipowners who were the aristocracy, while the people who created the wealth for them, the working class, did not benefit a great deal from their labours. From those historical roots there is still a feeling that other people sometimes take advantage of north-easterners. It may be more of a feeling than an actuality, but I can now understand why locally people like to label me as the 'people's' champion. It is because anyone from this area who does well at anything gets a little extra recognition, as it means that you have broken through the invisible wall which some people insist exists between the north-east and success.

It was in Hebburn, County Durham, some five miles from Newcastle, that I was born, on January 12th, 1948. Both sides of my family have an Irish background, having come over to work in the Tyneside shipyards in the late nineteenth century. My parents, Frank and Margaret, were both born in Hebburn themselves, but the local towns have strong Irish centres and Ceilidh clubs.

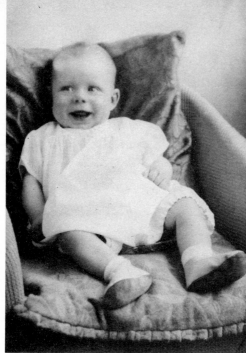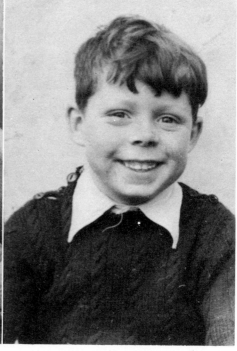

Aged six months – I wouldn't fancy
running far in those shoes!

Teeth and hair make all the difference.
Aged 5.

My Dad used to work in the rents and rates office of the local council and was always a sporting fanatic, particularly where Newcastle United were concerned. He was a good footballer himself, while my Mum was always talented at netball and running at school. The north-east has a tradition of keen sporting interest anyway, so I grew up in a very sports-conscious environment.

But always there was this underlying feeling that you were never likely to get the breaks because you lived in a place where fortune so often turned a blind eye. We always knew about the good players from the north-east who should have played for England but somehow didn't. We always knew about the good players from Hebburn who should have played for Newcastle United, but somehow didn't. Or about the lad down the road who should have made a great soccer player, but had to go down the pits instead because he was fourteen and his family needed the financial support. Some of the stories we heard were true; some of them probably not. But it all gave strength to the idea that people from this area never had a fair chance. And although things have changed drastically now, there are still people who think that way.

I went to a Catholic junior school, St Aloysius, in Hebburn, and I was in the Wolf Cubs, but the activity I took most seriously then was being an altar boy in the church. This meant that I had to get up very early in the morning – around

6.30 – to be serving on the altar at the church by seven. We lived in Ann Street, Hebburn, a row of terraced houses on the south bank of the River Tyne, and I remember leaving the house in all kinds of weather, running up the bank, and off to the church. It was only about three-quarters of a mile away, but seemed like three miles then. Every day of the week I did it, and sometimes in the summer the sun was beginning to warm the grey roofs of the huddled houses and the air was as fresh as it was likely to be all day in such an industrial area. On other days it would be pitch dark and bitterly cold as the winter wind blew off the icy black river, and I would leave a trail of footprints as I padded silently across the previous night's fresh fall of snow. It was a ritual for me, every day, year in and year out, and perhaps because of this early-formed habit I now still manage to drag myself out of bed to go training first thing every morning.

Those were happy days, living at 31 Ann Street, even though it was so very cold in winter, and all the doors had curtains behind them to try to keep the warmth in. When you wanted a bath (or, rather, when Mum decided it was time for a bath!) it was out with the old tin tub in front of the fire, which had to be filled from a series of heated kettles. None of the houses had running hot water.

Ann Street was a neighbourly place, where everyone knew everyone else, and there were always plenty of kids of your own age to play with. Most of the families in the area were large ones, part of the post-war 'baby boom', and I am the oldest of six myself. But the community spirit was typical of Hebburn itself, and indeed of the whole north-east. I think that people now keep themselves a bit more to themselves, sitting around the television, but then TV was a luxury few people in our street could even think about affording. Entertainment and friendship was still no further away than your front door.

I spent much of my time with two brothers, Don and Wally Stevenson, and we used to go everywhere together. We played cricket and football all day long in a field at the bottom of the street, and there was no vandalism in those days. I remember that there was a big hill of sand nearby, ballast from the ships, and it was ideal for playing on. We would climb up it, jump down it, or throw bricks into the Tyne from the top of it. Whatever Herb Elliott was doing with sandhills in Australia around that time, preparing to break the world mile record, we were also doing it in Hebburn for quite different reasons. There were also pill-boxes – those thick-walled concrete defence posts – which had been left over from the war, but we knew little of that. They were merely great places for hide-and-seek as far as we were concerned.

We lived only a few hundred yards away from the shipyard gates, and I remember the buzzer blowing every morning at 7.30, and all these men hurrying through the gates. Then at 5 o'clock the buzzer sounded again, the gates flew open, and they all came running out, their heads down, off home as quick as they could.

I was very lucky, because if I had been born five years earlier I would certainly have been working in the shipyards too. And that would have meant no athletics, because you cannot work manually every day from 7.30 to 5 o'clock and then go out training for long distance running afterwards. You are just too exhausted. Lots of the boys I was at school with went on to the shipyards, but at least there are now systems for taking exams there, and advancing your education.

Years ago, sport was the privilege of the upper classes. The working classes were too busy earning their living and, especially in athletics, it was towards Oxbridge that the British teams usually looked for its members, because students were the only people who had the time and leisure to train properly. They could also afford to take time off to go to the Olympic Games, which a working man with a family to support or assist just could not do.

I feel quite strongly that everyone in Britain today should be given the opportunity to find and develop their own sporting talent. Although PE is included in every school's timetable, too often it seems to become simply an excuse for the teacher to throw the children a football and tell them to get on with a game of soccer. There is no sense of 'teaching' the youngsters sport, and the activities they are allowed to try are frequently only the ones which interest their particular teacher. If a school does not have athletics among its sports, then it does not mean that none of the pupils has any ability in athletics. It just means that the staff responsible are not interested in athletics, and that therefore any budding athlete who attends that school will probably never discover his talent. I have often said that I might be potentially the greatest table tennis player the world has ever known, but as I never had an opportunity as a boy to play table tennis, I never found out. There are probably many people in Britain who are much better runners than I am, but because they did not get the chance to develop their ability, that talent lies dormant.

So I consider myself fortunate to have been able to develop my running ability when so many others in Britain can only sit and wonder what they might have been able to achieve. Recently a tapestry was presented to an art gallery in Gateshead, based on a photograph of me in Montreal. It was made by a Scotsman, Archie Brennan, and underneath there is a quote of mine which appeared in a national newspaper. It simply says: 'I am not even the greatest distance runner in Gateshead'. It sums up my feeling that the athletes at the top of the pile in Britain are not necessarily the best, but just the best of those who have been given the opportunity to get to the top, through favourable circumstances.

10

The Gateshead Tapestry.

In Hebburn, with a population of 30,000, the one sport which did flourish when I was a boy was soccer, and one of the town's proudest days came in 1957 when two Hebburn-born men faced each other in the FA Cup Final at Wembley. One of them was the Manchester United goalkeeper Ray Wood, who often visited one of his best friends who lived next door to us, and the other was Aston Villa's captain, Johnny Dixon. For the record, Villa won 2–1.

When I was at junior school we had a lad there called Geordie Armstrong, who went on to play for Arsenal, and was a member of the famous team which won the League and Cup double in 1971. He was a local hero even as a boy, and when he played for the Jarrow, Hebburn and Felling Schoolboys team they would get crowds of 3000 or 4000 turning out to watch. I remember the day he was presented with his schoolboys' soccer cap by the Headmaster, and the whole school gathered, with the partitions specially opened, to see the presentation. That memory sticks out a mile; locally it was the sign of a potential god.

A father was always measured by how good his son was at soccer. I enjoyed football a great deal, particularly playing for the school team, because it meant you got out early two or three nights a week. We played at Hebburn Park, about one-and-a-half miles from the school, and we would get changed at school and then march in formation to the park, right through the middle of the local shopping centre. It was all right going out, but when we came back we were covered in mud, so all the shoppers gave us a very wide berth. I quite enjoyed the trek, because if you were considered good, you got to go in front and carry the ball, and because I was in the school team, I was often granted this 'honour'.

I took football very, very seriously at the time, and often the mood of the whole weekend was influenced by how we got on in our match. I played in the school team for three years, from the time I was nine, and even got selected for the Jarrow, Hebburn and Felling Schools team, which to someone of that age was like being picked to play centre forward for England.

In 1955 Newcastle United reached the FA Cup Final at Wembley, and my Dad, who followed them everywhere and had been to their semi-final against York, decided to go. But he had to get a ticket, and the way they were being distributed was that if you went to the last home Newcastle match at St James's Park before the Cup Final you could put your ticket in a hat, and if it was drawn out afterwards, then you could buy a Cup Final ticket. I was seven, and Dad took me, my five-year-old brother Frank, and a friend, to the match, hoping to increase his chances of a ticket, and he promised me that if he got two tickets he would take me to Wembley with him. It was the first real soccer match I'd ever been to, and Jackie Milburn, who was a god in those parts, was playing. But I was broken-hearted

12

On holiday in Whitley Bay with brother Frank. At least we saw the FA Cup Final on TV.

when I found that Dad had only managed to get one Cup Final ticket.

On the afternoon of the Final I remember being out in the road in Ann Street about a quarter of an hour before kick-off, with my brother Frank, as we forlornly kicked a ball to each other. Then I heard a voice behind me suddenly say, 'All right, lads, let's be having you', and I turned round to see my Uncle Bob, who lived quite close to us.

He and my Auntie Mary had one of the few TV sets in the area, and he had come to collect Frank and I to take us off to watch the match on television. The day was made even happier when Newcastle beat Manchester City 3–1, to win the FA Cup for the third time in five years, and Jackie Milburn ('Wor Jackie'), who had been in all three winning sides, scored one of the goals.

(I eventually did get to see Newcastle 'live' at the FA Cup Final, but it took another nineteen years. In 1974 I was invited to run in a special 3000 metres race round the pitch before the kick-off of the Newcastle v Liverpool final, and borrowed a black and white striped vest – Newcastle's colours – for the occasion. It was a great pleasure to win that race in front of 100,000 spectators, many of them loyal Newcastle supporters who gave me immense encouragement. Unhappily the day ended in tragedy for them when Liverpool won the game 3–0. But at least I saw the match, and was able to take my Dad, and my brothers Frank and Pete as well.)

Apart from being Fairy Godfather to a couple of tiny, dejected Newcastle fans that day in 1955, my Uncle Bob was also indirectly responsible for an early fleeting

13

ST. ALOYSIUS BOYS' SCHOOL, HEBBURN

Athletics Certificate

NAME   BRENDAN   FOSTER

EVENT   220 Yards   (Junior   Sports   )

YEAR   1959

SIGNED   *J. Golden Headmaster*

My first athletics award. The winning time is lost in history –
thank goodness.

involvement with athletics. He was the groundsman at a place called Leslie's
Sports Ground, where every year they had a big athletics meeting. In 1957 the star
attraction at this meeting was Derek Ibbotson, the Yorkshireman who, the day
before, had broken the world mile record with 3:57.2 at White City, London.
Despite pouring rain, Leslie's Ground was absolutely packed, and all the streets
for miles around were lined with cars and buses and coaches, for it seemed everyone
in Hebburn wanted to be there that day.

Ibbotson, who came from Huddersfield, was the most famous athlete in Britain
at that time, and I can remember catching my first glimpse of him, jogging round
and round the sports field in a baggy white tracksuit. All he was doing, of course,
was just warming up for his race, but we kids didn't know anything about such
exercises in those days. We just used to go out and race, without even bothering
to warm up, and I remember thinking 'Whatever is he doing? Doesn't he realise
he's got to race in a minute? He'll be worn out!'

My youthful concern for his well-being proved unfounded, however, and he had
little difficulty in winning his two miles race, despite the long journey from London.
As Uncle Bob was in charge of the changing rooms, I was in there, helping with the
teas, and I managed to get Derek's autograph. I've never forgotten that, and when
I told him the story a couple of years ago he was tickled pink. He said, 'Fancy that,

a snotty-nosed kid in Hebburn, and look where you are now!'

At the time, of course, my interest was only in soccer, and it was not until five years later, when I was about fourteen, that I had my first race on, appropriately enough, the same Leslie's Sports Ground where Derek Ibbotson had run. It was a 440 yards inter-schools event, and I collapsed after the heat, even though I had got through into the final. My Dad was fussing around, saying, 'He's not running any more', but I did run, and finished second in the final to qualify for the Durham Schools championships. But that is jumping ahead a little bit.

Yet the strange thing is that even when I was very young I had this feeling that one day I was going to be outstanding at something, even if I didn't know what. I made a five-pound bet with a lad who used to share a desk with me at school, Joe Joyce, that one day I would run in the Olympic Games, although at that time there was no indication that I was going to be anything more than a reasonable schools runner. I didn't see Joe at the 1972 Munich Olympics, but he sent me a telegram after I had been selected, saying, 'You only did it to win that bet!' Then in 1976 he actually came to Montreal to see me run in my second Olympics, and sure enough he paid up that five pounds.

I had passed my 11-plus exam, and in 1959 went to a brand new grammar school, St Joseph's at Hebburn. It was so new it wasn't even finished when we started there, and for the first couple of weeks we had to sit on the floor because the desks had not yet arrived. But we did not tell people about that, because we felt it was such an honour to go there, and to tell them about the lack of desks would have spoiled it all. The school was an expression of faith in the town by the Catholic community who got together with the Bishop to raise the money to build it. It was to serve the whole of County Durham, so only about four kids from each town went there, and if you did you were quite well known locally. But as it was literally a community school, you were expected to show that you were worth your place.

We went to school on the first day in our brand new uniforms of grey caps, blazers, shorts, socks and black shoes, which made us feel a little self-conscious because no one else in Hebburn ever wore school uniforms.

I was a plump kid then, a little fatty, with a round face and rosy cheeks, which everyone considered to be a sign of health. I still have a sweet tooth, probably because when I was young my parents used to let me have all the goodies they could afford, and even now I have to be careful because despite all the training my weight can still shoot up.

At school I played soccer, ran cross country, played basketball, and got involved in every sport I could. Soccer was the one in which we were all most interested, of course, and my life at that time just consisted of sport and study, both of which

First day at St Joseph's, complete with the much-prized uniform. September 1959.

I took seriously. In athletics and cross country I was always finishing fourth or fifth in local district championships, but in the Jarrow, Hebburn and Felling area there was one outstanding athlete called John Trainor, who won the Northern Counties Boys cross country title. Gradually I found myself finishing closer to him in local races.

One night, when I was about fourteen or fifteen, a chap from Jarrow Athletic Club called at our house and spoke to my Dad to see if I would join them. Fortunately, as I look back, I was out, otherwise I probably would have joined them and I'd never be where I am today, because that club did not have a system to bring their youngsters through then.

About the same time, I ran against John Trainor again and finished a close second to him, and after the race the coach from Gateshead Harriers came up to me. It was Stan Long, who in later years was to be so important in my development as an athlete, but at that time, when he asked me to join Gateshead, I said no. To be honest, I wasn't terribly interested. I still preferred soccer to running because at least in soccer you were running after something.

I was still persuaded to run in a race between the local district schools team and Gateshead Harriers, and I remember seeing all these big lads jogging round in tracksuits with 'Gateshead Harriers' on their backs. They looked very impressive, but actually the club was not really all that strong at that time. Stan was building up a good junior section, with runners like John Trainor and John Caine, but the seniors were next to useless. Stan, and John Trainor, were still on at me to join Gateshead Harriers, and still I declined. It was not for another year, in fact, that I finally agreed to join.

Until then, I had been playing soccer on Saturday mornings and running cross country races in the afternoon, but naturally my results were not always as good as they could be. I knew that soccer was taking something out of me, but there was one particular day when I did not play in the morning and then found I ran so much better in the afternoon that I decided that from then on it would be just running for me. For I had also realised that I was getting more satisfaction out of athletics, where you stand or fall on your own efforts, than as a member of a football team.

Although I was doing reasonably well at cross country races, despite constantly being runner-up to John Trainor, my track distance was 440 yards, which is more or less a sprint all the way. In 1963 I began the season by running just under 60 seconds for the distance, but gradually chipped away at my time until at the Durham Schools track and field championships at Houghton in June I ran 54.8 seconds, my best time. I didn't win, because another quarter-miler named Bruce Adams was also in the race, and he was really good. But I was selected, along with Adams, to attend my first major athletics meeting, the English Schools championships, which that year were being organised by Essex Schools at Chelmsford.

It was a good performance and, looking back at the results, I see that he beat into fifth place a young lad from Luton whom I was to race quite frequently ten years later – Tony Simmons. But then I was still thinking of myself as a quarter-miler, even though I had made a reasonable debut at 880 yards, and had brushed with officialdom for the first time.

The race had been the Tyneside Grammar Schools 880 yards, and I had set a record time of 2:09 in winning at my first attempt over the distance. But I was disqualified for being shouted at by a friend from the inside of the track, which is technically construed as 'assistance'. But my reaction then was the same as it would be now. I was not worried about it, because I knew that I had won the race and whoever they gave the prize to, I was still the fastest runner in the field.

The English Schools meeting at Chelmsford was, incidentally, the first and last time that I competed in the track and field championships and even that, fourth place in a heat, was hardly memorable. But the saddest thing about the English Schools championships is that year after year the most outstanding natural talent in the country is assembled after having to qualify through local, district and county trials, which is the nearest approach we have to the Eastern European method of 'screening' all their youngsters for potential medallists of the future. Then somehow in this country so many of them are lost to the sport. The athletes who win English Schools titles, and then go on to achieve international honours as seniors in later years, are very much in the minority, and a potential international athlete seems more likely to be found among the 'also rans'. Perhaps too much success early on can spoil the athlete's determination. Like a hungry fighter, he has to have a little chip on his shoulder to want to keep going out training in all weathers.

At that time there did not seem too much danger of finding myself swamped with success. As we moved into the 1963–64 cross country season, John Trainor was still winning everything in sight, and if he wasn't there, then I was beaten to the line by a tall Darlington lad named Max Coleby, who was destined, like me, to become a Gateshead Harrier, and eventually run internationally.

John Trainor was ill, and missed the 1964 Durham Schools cross country championship, but Max beat me, and we were all three selected to run in the English Schools cross country championships at Leicester in March. The race there was won by Tony Simmons, with Max twenty-ninth and John, still recovering from his illness, forty-fourth. Nothing much can be said about my own sparkling sixty-fourth place, except that it helped Durham Schools to take fourth place in the team race. Yorkshire won it, while Warwickshire had a newcomer called Ian Stewart in their second-placed team, with Ian finishing forty-seventh. So in that race I was easily beaten by two runners who were also destined to give me a hard time in later years, Tony and Ian. What a humiliation!

Then I had my first taste of injury, which meant that for three months during spring of 1964 I could not run at all. By the time the Durham Schools championships came round in June, I was able to run again but my lack of training was a real handicap, and I finished only eighth in the 880 yards, so there was no English Schools appearance for me that year. Or indeed again, because my studies took precedence over my athletics and, apart from winning the mile at the school sports in 4 minutes 54 seconds, I did not race at all in the summer of 1965. I had taken my GCE 'O' levels a year early, and did the same with my 'A' levels, which meant that I had a year from the autumn of 1965 to the autumn of 1966 before I went up to university. It turned out to be my best year of running so far, because with the pressures of GCE work behind me, and the university work not yet upon me, I had a freewheeling twelve months in which I could concentrate a little more on running.

I also took a job in the research and development department of a local detergent manufacturers, because I was studying chemistry. My task was to put together ingredients to make a particular brand of cleaning powder. It seemed the right thing to be doing because I thought I might eventually make a career in a laboratory, but this experience put me off commerce and industry. I didn't like it at all. It was so boring. The cleaning powder I was making was supposed to be light green, but eventually I didn't care whether it was light green, dark green, or sky blue with pink spots. It was a good cleaner though, and we did a special demonstration to the company's salesmen to show how effective was a new 'secret' ingredient.

I went with another chap down to Harrogate, my first-ever experience of staying in a big hotel with all expenses paid, for the demonstration. We got dressed up in white coats, with white caps and goggles, and we had two big white boards on a stand. We sprayed these with a mixture of soot and fat, and then we had to clean them to show how good our product was. My mate used it to clean his board, and I was supposed to be using a rival powder, so obviously he had to win. I made sure I had more soot and more fat on my board, and I didn't press so hard when I tried to clean it. I even smudged it. My mate, meanwhile, had to cut effortlessly through the dirt with one swift wipe, which was easier for him because he was using piping hot water and mine was stone cold! Unfortunately our ploy was discovered when one of the salesmen leaned forward and asked, 'Why is that bucket steaming, and that one not?'

In fact, our powder *was* better, and when we did controlled chemical tests we could prove it was better, but you just could not *see* the difference, so we had tried to exaggerate it. That was our one and only sales demonstration. We did not get invited to the next one, for some reason.

But it was still a good year for me, for quite apart from the breathing space between school and university it provided, my running was beginning to go well. I had joined Gateshead Harriers, but John Trainor was still my bogeyman, and another useful lad had appeared on the scene – Brooks Mileson from Sunderland. By the autumn of 1965, they were both beating me. Then in January 1966 I won a three miles cross country race at North Shields, the Sherman Cup, beating John Trainor into third place in the Youths event by over 20 seconds, and I began to realise that the training was paying off.

It was my best race to date, and my pleasure was heightened when one of the lads from Gateshead Harriers told me that he had heard John Anderson, a local star from Saltwell Harriers who had run for Great Britain, say, 'That young Foster's a good 'un'.

But at the Northern championships the following month I had a setback, finishing only thirty-first in a race won by Brooks Mileson, while Trainor got his revenge on me, finishing fifteenth. The race was held at Huddersfield on a terrible day, with ankle-deep snow at the start, which soon churned into a clinging quagmire of slush and mud as the race progressed, and a bitter east wind which seemed to blow right through us. In the senior nine miles championship, a quarter of the field dropped out, and it was just the kind of day I hate.

*The Sherman Cup race, January 1966. That's me, sixth from the
right in the dark vest and shorts.*

The English National championships that season were held at Graves Park,
Sheffield, on March 5th, and I had a far more inspired run then, finishing tenth
out of 432 runners, because the ground was much firmer, suiting my style. Brooks
Mileson added the National Youths title to his Northern victory, but there was a
lot of controversy over whether Tony Simmons would have won if he had not been
misdirected and lost about thirty yards while in the lead. He finished only four
seconds behind Mileson, in second place. I beat John Trainor, who was thirty-
sixth, but an indication of the strength (or rather the weakness) of Gateshead
Harriers then was that we had to wait for 251st and 324th places before we had
our scoring team home, and we finished twenty-ninth in the team race.

I was, of course, delighted with my own run, and a week later travelled down to
Leicester for the Youths Inter-Counties championships. This time Tony Simmons
turned the tables on Brooks Mileson, winning by fourteen seconds. I finished
nearly a minute down in twentieth place which, after my National run, seemed a
bit disappointing at the time. In retrospect though it was probably consistent with
my new-found form.

In the summer I began to concentrate more on the mile, since my cross country
successes convinced me that I had perhaps more strength than speed. I had a lot
of local races that year, and gradually my times came down, from 4:26 to 4:24 and

then 4:15.8 in a race at Gateshead. I even managed to beat Brooks Mileson in the Northumberland and Durham county junior mile championship, setting a record of 4:19.4. Afterwards Mileson stormed off the track, calling me a 'bum', and I was upset by his poor sportsmanship. In later years I realised that some athletes like to get defeat out of their system in this way, but I was glad at the time that two local internationals, Jim Alder and John Hillen, came to my aid and put Mileson in his place.

As things were going well, I decided to enter the AAA Junior championships at Hurlingham Park in August, and my first-ever trip to London was not by train or plane, but in the cab of a fish lorry which made the trip every night from the fish-quay at North Shields down to Billingsgate Fish Market. We left North Shields at 7 pm, and I was drinking tea in Billingsgate at 3.30 the following morning. It may not have been the best preparation for competition, but it was a chance to race the leading youngsters in the country. I just hoped I would not smell of fish when I was racing!

I do not know whether it was the journey, or simply that I was overawed in the company, but I did not get through my heat, finishing fifth in 4:25. The final was won by Andrew Herrity of Small Heath Harriers, near Birmingham, who covered the last 880 yards in 2:01 for a time of 4:13.4. I see from the results that Ian Stewart was sixth in that race, and Tony Simmons eighth, and that sort of hindsight again makes me feel sad. Not for Ian or Tony, who have done all right for themselves, but for the others who were better than them (and me) and had so much natural talent, yet unlike Ian or Tony or myself were never to have the enjoyment and excitement of competing in something like the Olympic Games. Young athletes like Brooks Mileson and Andrew Herrity were, to the rest of us down the field, like superstars when they won their national titles, yet neither of them were destined ever to reach full international status as seniors.

And there have been plenty of others, runners whom I would have given my right arm to emulate in those early days, but who just drifted away from the sport for one reason or another. Perhaps some of them just did not like athletics, or the training, or found their careers more important. Fair enough. But I wonder how many of them would have stayed in athletics with just the right encouragement, or word of advice here and there? Since the British Amateur Athletic Board has established its Junior Commission to look after the most promising youngsters, things have improved. Yet from time to time I still wonder 'whatever happened to so-and-so?'

In 1966, though, it would not be much longer before people were in danger of thinking the same thing about me.

Three

In October 1966 I began studying at the University of Sussex in Brighton, and went through a period which, although distinguished mainly for its lack of sporting success, was still, I am sure, a contributory element in my appreciation of what was to happen in later years. Sussex had been one of six universities offering a place, but from the time I went to Brighton for an interview I fell in love with the area. The university is situated on the outskirts of the town, at Falmer, with beautiful parkland surroundings, and my immediate thought was that if I went there I would be able to live on the seafront and train on the beach. Little did I know that there was no sand on the beach, only pebbles! All the beaches I'd ever seen up north had miles of sand, and I had never heard of one that did not. So when I arrived in Brighton to begin my course I found that all my fantasies of striding across golden sands, mile after idyllic mile, were no more than that, and I was considerably disappointed. In fact, if I'd known that there was no sand, I might not even have gone to Sussex.

The night before I left Hebburn, we had a little farewell party with my Mum and Dad, and my younger brother Frank, to whom I had always been very close, and my sisters Kathleen, Margaret and baby Anna. My other younger brother, Peter, was away at a religious college then, and perhaps the fact that he went there at twelve years of age has since made him the most independent of any of us. For we are a close family who were used to always doing things together, partly because our house was of a size for it to be a necessity.

I knew I would find it a bit of a wrench, as the eldest child, to leave the fold, and as I waited for the bus to take me to Newcastle next morning, I could not help wondering what this new life would hold in store.

I humped two massive suitcases, full of books and all my worldly possessions, on and off the bus and through the station, and when the train finally jerked into life, and we pulled out of Newcastle, across the River Tyne towards London, a mixed feeling of anticipation and loneliness swept over me.

I did fancy going south, I must admit, and the prospect of being so far away from home for the first time did not worry me too much. If you go ten miles, you might as well go 300. But I did find it difficult at first, coming from a big family and moving into a single room with virtually just a desk and a bed. I was one of a dozen new students who spent their first year in a guest house near the Palace Pier. It was called Braeside, in Upper Rock Gardens, a sort of 'hot and cold water in all rooms' place, but for that first year it was a home from home.

At the university I suppose I felt a little bit inferior at first, because I was from a working-class area, and there were so many other people from public schools. Sussex was popular, a sort of 'in' university at the time, for those who decided not to go to Oxford or Cambridge, and my first temptation when I got there was to try to talk like them, changing my accent. I soon gave that up when I realised how ridiculous it was, but settling in was a bit of an ordeal initially. I found it difficult to identify with people whose fathers had two or three cars, but strangely the lad I got on really well with was a chap called Graham Wick, whose father was actually managing director of a big company. Graham had a Cortina GT to drive round in at university, and we were great mates, although we were miles apart on the social level. On every level really, except that we did the same chemistry course, and shared a flat for three years. He is now European Marketing Director of a big Japanese company.

In the first week at university I joined the cross country club, and won their trial race, so through athletics I immediately got to know a wider circle of people other than just those on my course. I quickly got into the routine of training again, even despite the deprivation of my precious sand, and I often ran the four miles from our flat to the university or back. At other times I would go in Graham's car, but I was so disorganised that I occasionally ended up with all my everyday clothes in one place, and all my running gear somewhere else. Sometimes I'd run to university in a tracksuit, and realise when I got there that I only had another tracksuit to change into, so I'd have to run all the way back again. Stanmer Park, near the university, was an excellent place to train, and I began to work out some regular routes. I ran a few times for the university team that autumn, but injured my foot and couldn't run for most of December.

By February I was still not very fit, but ran for the first time in the British Universities six miles cross country championship at Parliament Hill Fields in North London. The race was won by Roger Robinson of Cambridge University, and I was an inglorious 163rd. The heavy mud and my own lethargy did not help, but my injured foot gave me a lot of trouble after the halfway point, and in fact I could not run for ten days afterwards. I hated the course, and vowed I would never ever race there again. Fortunately, I later changed my mind, because ten years later it was the scene of one of my best-ever races.

Competitively, 1967 was a year to forget for me. One injury after another, first to my foot, then to my hip, kept me stopping and starting, and although I had some hard spells of training I did not get the rewards I expected. At Easter, at home in Gateshead, I ran a hundred miles in training one week, including forty-four miles in two days with John Trainor, and I was only just nineteen at the time. Before the winter the most I had ever run was about fifty miles in a week, and the increase seemed to be having a detrimental effect on me. I was beginning to feel constantly tired and sometimes it was a real effort to get out and train. I usually managed it, but when you knew that on a bad night in Brighton the wind was going to be whipping off the Channel, blowing rain through your tracksuit, and that you had the alternative of going out and running, finishing soaked, battered and exhausted, or staying in a warm armchair reading or studying, it was often a difficult decision. Fortunately, I was never that keen on reading or studying.

My training mileages that year were high, and my performances poor. I was often training twice a day, for a total of seventy or eighty miles a week, yet my diary records some terrible races: 'Dropped back after one mile, dropped out after one lap'; 'terrible time, bad run'; 'felt tired from start, very poor throughout, bad run'. In theory, all the extra training should have been making me run faster. Instead, it seemed to be having the opposite effect.

It was a mystery to me. If I missed a couple of days' training, then I seemed to run reasonably well again, but if I trained for a week, I ran badly. When I came home to Gateshead I never used to tell anyone about my results. I kept them a secret, because I was ashamed. I had gone down to university with a reasonable reputation, and they thought – and I hoped – that I was going to thrive on the diet of study and training. But it had all gone wrong. You didn't have to be very good to be the best runner at Sussex University, and I wasn't even that. In fact, I must have been one of the worst runners in Britain.

At the time I assumed that perhaps I was not after all cut out to be a cross country runner, and that I should aim to be a track runner instead. Chris Carter, who then held the UK 800 metres record, lived in Brighton so I did a couple of sessions with him, and in April I ran against him in a mile race at the local Withdean Stadium. We went through the first lap in 62 seconds, then he went on to win in 4:07, and I faded to finish in 4:37. I can smile about it now, but I did not smile then, because the previous year I had run 4:13 for the mile. It really was a blue period, when I was scaling the heights of mediocrity. That summer I ran 9:45 for two miles, compared to 9:20 the year before, and that was about it for the season. I still nursed my hopes, though.

At Whitsun I went to White City Stadium in West London, then the home of all the big athletics meetings, to watch the Inter-Counties Championships. My Gateshead clubmate Lindsay Dunn was representing Northumberland and Durham in the one mile, and I went specially to see him run, but I remember thinking as I went into the stadium and saw all the crowds there: 'What I'd give to be one of the star athletes here'. It might seem strange now, but even though I was only running 4:37 for the mile myself then, I always thought I would be.

Time and again, though, I felt like packing up when things were going wrong, when my legs just didn't seem to belong to my body any more. But somewhere inside there was a little voice saying 'you're going to be good, you're going to be good', and the only person who believed it was me. And even I doubted what I was telling myself from time to time. But I kept thinking about doing well and, above all, winning. I had some photographs on the wall of my bedroom at home. Some of them were, naturally, of runners, like Jim Ryun, Kip Keino and Dick Taylor. But I also had photographs of two men in space helmets. One was the pioneering Soviet astronaut Yuri Gagarin, and the other was a face nobody knew, the second man in space. And there was a photo of Mount Everest, the highest mountain in the world, together with a photo of the second highest mountain in the world, whose name no one knows. And under the photographs it said in big letters 'NOBODY REMEMBERS WHO IS SECOND'.

While I was at university, even when things were going badly, I'd still be training religiously. Once I remember travelling back from Newcastle to Brighton by train, a nine-hour journey, getting into my room, dumping my case on the bed, and going straight out on a seven-mile run round Brighton Racecourse, which is a hell of a place to train, especially as I had to run a mile uphill to get there.

Still I was getting worse. When I started my second year at Sussex, I finished only second in the university trial, which I had won the year before, so once again things did not look too exciting. I must have been really miserable in those days, reading through my old training diaries, but I kept bobbing back. 'Finished 21st in match against Bristol University', 'Portsmouth relay, terrible time', and so on, were the sort of entries I find in my diary.

I went home for Christmas that year and managed to avoid any races, so the lads at the Harriers still did not really know how badly I was running. I remember we, the new breed of university students, used to go to the club, and someone asked me, 'Well, when are you going to race?' But I just would not race, and nor would I tell them why. Someone said sarcastically: 'Oh, yes, he's saving himself for the Olympics again.' They were bad times.

Then the Olympic Year of 1968 began, and looking at my 1968 training diary there is one immediate improvement over the closing months of my 1967 diary. It's much tidier, because I got a new pen for Christmas! But that is the only difference. I missed the British Universities cross country championships in February, thank goodness, so I was not able to sink below my 163rd place of the previous year. Instead I spent the afternoon doing repetition runs up a hill at Telscombe Village, near Brighton – once more planning for the future which still seemed an eternity away, and dreaming about winning races. Later in February I ran in the traditional Imperial College relay in Hyde Park, and covered my stage in 16:40. The record was about 13:20, which gives you an idea of my standard then, and I felt really tired, with sore aching legs. Next day, in a real trough of depression, I actually took a day off training, feeling completely fed up, but the next day I was back into it again with a morning session of twenty uphill runs, and an evening seven miles run around Saltdean. Running is something on which you just get hooked. If you don't train, you suffer from withdrawal symptoms, and your day feels incomplete without having run at least once.

In my second year at Sussex, four of us had moved into a flat at Saltdean. There were two Rhodesians, Philip Pascall and Adrian Gargett, plus Graham Wick, and myself. I learned a lot about politics, because Philip and Adrian were on completely opposite wings, and with a managing director's son, and my working class background, we were a really good mixture. We used to have some healthy debates both in the flat, where we took it in turns to cook, and in a pub at nearby Rottingdean, where we used to go most evenings. With the university four miles away, you had to make your own entertainment most of the time.

Philip Pascall provided the entertainment one night when all the lights went out. I had wandered along the corridor of our flat shouting at the various bedroom doors to see if anyone had got any coins for the electric meter, which had run out. Pascall, who had gone to bed early, apparently took particular exception to being woken up, so he came rushing out of his door in a rotten temper, and threw me headlong down the passage and into the glass front door, which smashed into smithereens.

As he was six feet six inches tall, I took this to be his way of telling me that No, he had not got any coins for the meter. Anyway, he went back to bed, and I had to be driven to the hospital to have eight stitches in my hand; I've still got the scar today. When he got up next morning, Pascall just acted as if nothing had happened,

26

so the following year, when we moved to a different flat, which was three storeys up, we did not take him along with us. None of us really fancied the flight.

Two or three times a term I'd go home, hitch-hiking or by bus or train, sometimes not getting back till 2 or 3 o'clock in the morning. I never told my Mum or Dad I was coming back, I just used to arrive, which was probably not the best of surprises to spring in the early hours.

Although running was making me miserable because it was going so badly, getting a degree was still the most important thing to me, because that was why I was at Brighton in the first place. Running was important too, of course, although I could not see why at the time because I was no good at it. I wasn't getting anywhere. I was going backwards. But I had to keep going, as I knew that if I wasn't running well when I came home in the holidays all the lads at the club would take the mickey out of me. So it seemed to be a vicious circle.

I hardly had any races in the summer of 1968, apart from a few 800 metres, when I ran 2:08 on a good day and 2:15 on a bad day, and in the holidays I went home and got a job with John Trainor working on a building site. We had to carry doors on our backs up sixteen storeys, and before or after work, or in the lunch break, we would go out and run an easy seven or eight miles. The job was so boring that we used to have competitions to see who could carry the doors the furthest without stopping. It was good strength training anyway, and it served its purpose of passing the time away.

It was about this time, as the leading athletes of the world were putting the final touches to their preparations for the Mexico City Olympic Games, that I reached the turning point. It was not a new-found inspiration, because I had never really been short of that, nor of the determination to get out and train hard and often. It was something much more physical and basic.

I had been describing my symptoms to another runner at university, Dave O'Neill, who studied these things. I told him how I always felt tired and lethargic, sometimes ill or dizzy, and that if I rested there was a marginal improvement.

'It sounds to me as if you are anaemic,' he said. 'Why don't you start taking a course of iron pills?'

I was, of course, ready to try almost anything that might help my running, but with not much more hope than my previous 'remedies' had provided. Harder training, more often, with a different emphasis, had produced only a negative effect. But Dave told me the iron tablets I should get, and I went to the chemist and bought some.

Success in distance running is very much dependent on how quickly the blood can transport oxygen to the muscles, and if iron is deficient in the blood, it cannot do its job properly. The blood may be only half strength, and that is like trying to drive a car on watered-down petrol. It is also what had happened to me in the past two years. Normally, a balanced diet gives the body the iron it needs, but a student living away from home for the first time is by no means guaranteed to be consuming a balanced diet. Junk food, quick and easy to buy, or whip up, is more likely to be on the menu. My own staple diet at the time was cheese and yoghurt, although for a really big occasion I used to produce my speciality: pork chops (because you could grill them), peas (because you only had to boil them for five minutes), and rice (because you didn't have to peel the potatoes), followed by fruit yoghurt. It was laziness, I suppose, which got me into this routine, partly because the food was quick and easy to prepare, and partly because there was very little washing up to do afterwards. But it was not exactly the most nourishing diet imaginable.

So gradually I was getting run down by harder and harder training, and the wrong food. By taking iron tablets, I was able to restore my blood to normal; what had happened was that I had been inadvertently trying to run in the equivalent of a pair of heavy boots. As soon as I took them off, I felt I was flying. Suddenly the whole mystery was solved, and I could hardly wait to get back and have a go at the 1968–69 cross country season. The memories of people at university who said, 'look at him going out training every day, and getting hammered when he races' echoed round my ears, and I found myself looking forward to races again instead of waiting with dread to see what latest disaster could befall me.

My first race was a relay at Parliament Hill, where I ran second leg for the University in a time of 8:35, compared to the day's fastest of 7:52, which was a little bit more respectable than I had been doing. I could feel such a great improvement in my running, it was like a dream coming true. I was able to write comments in my diary like '20 times 150 yards – felt as if they were too fast', and 'finished quite strongly, good run'.

My training was getting better, and my racing was improving too. We watched the Olympic Games on an old television we bought in Brighton for five bob, and a few weeks later I was racing against one of the British team, Mike Tagg, in the Southern Universities championships at Bristol. I had dropped out of this race after one lap the previous year, but this time I felt quite good, and eventually finished fourth. Tagg, who was thirteenth in the Olympic 10,000 metres at Mexico, won the race.

I actually won a race on our own Sussex University course in 29:56, whereas the previous year the same race had taken me 33 minutes. So I was improving hand over fist.

With fellow members of the
University of Sussex cross country
team at Falmer, 1969.

Then it was time to go home again for the Christmas holidays, and a couple of local races. The first was on Boxing Day, a six miles road race, known as the Congers race, and I started off fast and kept with the leaders, John Hillen and Bill Robinson, all the way. I can still see the officials in the pilot car looking back at us and saying, 'Who's that with Hillen and Robinson?', because I'd been a non-racing scrubber for the past two years, and they simply didn't know me. I finished the race very tired but well pleased with third place behind John and Bill. Then a fortnight later I ran at North Shields in the Sherman Cup six miles cross country race, on the day before my twenty-first birthday. Bill Robinson won this time, from Jim Alder of Morpeth, who was the reigning Commonwealth marathon champion. But my placing must have embarrassed the Northumberland and Durham team selectors because they had left me out of their side for the Inter-Counties championships the following week, presumably thinking that my Boxing Day run had been just a fluke. Now several of their selections had finished behind me again, but it was too late to change the county team. I had not even been nominated as a reserve. The real irony, though, was that the scene of the Inter-Counties championships that year was to be – Brighton Racecourse! Just a jog away from our flat, in fact.

The Inter-Counties race itself saw the breakthrough of Trevor Wright, the long-striding Yorkshireman who surprised everyone by winning the seven-and-a-half miles race by nearly half a minute from Mike Tagg. Jim Alder was Northumberland and Durham's first man home, in twentieth place, and their team finished fifth, with the last scorer down at 110th. I watched the race with interest, and afterwards burned up some of my frustration at not being in the event by running a very hard seven miles round the course. But in fact I probably was not as upset as I might have been over the omission, because I knew that I was running well and that there would be other days to prove it.

I was also to have another good reason for being glad that I was missed out of the team. As I had reached my twenty-first birthday the previous Sunday, we had planned a party at our flat after the race. I had intended asking the Northumberland and Durham team to it, but partly because I wasn't in the team anyway and partly because most of them wanted to get back on Saturday night, that plan never happened. Which was just as well, because it was that night I met my wife, Sue, and if we had had a roomful of runners we would have spent the whole time talking about athletics!

Actually, to say that I met Sue that evening is not quite correct, because I had known her since my first year. She had started at Sussex the same time as I did, but she was studying economics, and some of the boys from my flat knew some of the girls from her flat, which is how she was at the party that night. But it was the first time we had ever sat talking together, rather than in a group. We danced a bit, and from that evening we started going out together. So you could say that the Northumberland and Durham selectors did me a big favour by leaving me out of their team. Perhaps they knew something I didn't?

The following week I ran in an inter-varsity race at Parliament Hill, but nearly missed the start and had to run in the wrong shoes. I went off much too fast, and was almost walking when a bunch came past me, before I got going properly. I felt quite good then, and knew that I had a good race in me, but this one was poorly judged. I finished thirteenth, but it gave me some encouragement for the next week, when the British Universities championships were being held at Sheffield, with a huge entry from all over the country.

Now remember that in my first year I had finished 163rd in this race. In my second year I had not even bothered to go, but instead spent the afternoon training in Sussex. But now, in my final year at Sussex University, I felt I could produce a reasonable performance, something that I could be remembered by rather than all my terrible performances in my two years of abject misery.

Imagine my chagrin then when I discovered that Sussex had only been entered in the 'B' championship, instead of the main race. It was true that our team was not a tremendously strong one, but I desperately wanted to be running against the best students in the country. I went to the Sussex University Sports Headquarters and told them my feelings, and they agreed to get on to the British Universities Sports Federation office in London and request a transfer of entry. But the general secretary of the BUSF, Pat Besford, turned this down flat, and said we had to stick to our original entry. So I had to resort to hatching a little plan of my own.

I travelled up to Sheffield with four others, and just before the start of the 'B' race, which was held first, I disappeared quietly in Graves Park. And while that event was being held, I was going diligently through the events' programme, and found the highest competitor's number in the 'A' race – 482. So on the back of the number I had been given for the 'B' race, I made my own – 483 – with a ball point pen. Then I pinned it on my chest and lined up for the 'A' race. I thought that if they had around 400 athletes running, they were hardly likely to spot me amongst them until it was all over. It was not a very nice day, 1st February, and there was a light covering of snow on the ground and a cold wind blowing across the Park. The race was over four laps of one-and-three-quarters miles each, and at the end of the first lap the holder, Frank Briscoe of Leeds, was trying to break away, but a large group, including me, was holding on to him.

By the halfway mark, a group of four had broken away, and I couldn't keep up with them, but I felt I was running well all the way round and finally crossed the line in a kind of phantom ninth place. At the end of big cross country races, as you go over the line, you are given a metal disc with your position on it, and your team manager then hands all the discs from his athletes back to the officials in one envelope to assist with team scoring. So there I was clutching this little piece of cold metal with a figure 9 on it and wondering 'What the hell should I do now?'

I was, of course, delighted with my run, which I felt justified my action and that I should have been in the 'A' race, but now sooner or later someone was going to find out. My resulting instant decision that discretion was the better part of valour was assisted by the knowledge that there was a birthday party planned in Brighton that night which Sue would be attending, so I made a rush for the next train south, with the disc in my pocket.

I don't know what happened after I left, but I did hear that the results took an extra one-and-a-half hours to work out because some mystery man had finished ninth, and no one could find him, or knew where he was. In fact, he was sitting in a train, going to a party in Brighton.

On the following Monday I send an apologetic letter to the BUSF, explaining that I was the mystery man, returning their disc, and saying that I hoped I had not caused too much inconvenience. But I had known I was running well, and I wondered whether they would consider me for the British Universities team to compete against the English Cross Country Union (ECCU) and the Combined Services the following month. To be honest, I did not think they would, but unless they knew who the 'mystery runner' was, they certainly couldn't pick me. If they did not, then at least I had still made some progress – I had beaten some runners who had actually had their names in the newspapers.

My next race was the Imperial College road relay in Hyde Park a fortnight later, and my lap time of 13:53 was the eighth fastest of the day. It was also a considerable improvement on my 16:40 when I had last run in it two years earlier, and it helped Sussex University to finish eighth out of eighty-five teams, which was quite good for us. At this time I had also begun training in Brighton with a young man named David Bedford, who had started a course at the local College of Education. Dave, of course, had already been making a name for himself as a prodigous runner, and we ran together two or three times a week. Our flat was only a hundred yards from his hall of residence, and he often came round scrounging food.

Dave had already done very well at national level, although he was still only nineteen, including eleventh place in that Inter-Counties race I had watched at Brighton, and the fact that I could run with him comfortably in training, and stay close to him in local races, all added to my growing confidence. I needed boosts like this because there was always a fear that one day I would wake up and find it had all been a dream, and be back to my scrubber standard again.

We actually formed a club called the Falmer Striders, so that Dave, who wasn't eligible for the University team, could run with us in races, and in early March we won the Bognor College road relay. I managed to knock 20 seconds off the lap record, covering the one-and-a-third miles in 5:47, and Dave anchored the team to victory.

A few days later there was a cross country match between Sussex University and the Essex Police at Chelmsford, and Sue came along to watch. Her interest was more than just seeing me run, though. Her father was Deputy Chief Constable of Essex at the time, and not only did I get to meet him for the first time, but he also acted as starter for the race. Fortunately I was able to make the right sort of impression. I took the lead from the start, and managed to win by three minutes. It seemed to be quite a reasonable way of getting my feet under the table! So life was changing radically that winter. I was in my final year at Sussex, I was running well, and I had started going out with the girl I was eventually to marry. And there was still one more plus to come.

I received a letter saying that I had been selected for the British Universities team to face the ECCU and Combined Services at Fareham on March 15th. So all that subterfuge to get into the right race at Sheffield had been worth while, and at least if not forgotten by the BUSF, seemed to be temporarily forgiven. I must have written about six letters home to my Mum and Dad, saying that I was going to run for the British Universities team, and they still say now that even in my first two years at Sussex I at least trained as though I was a good runner. It was all I used to think about and talk about then. But now I actually had an embroidered Union Jack badge to wear.

The match was an annual one, with each of the three teams determined to field their strongest possible squads, and I knew all of the runners by name, even if none of them knew mine. There were nine runners in each team, and I was listed as ninth in the universities team, my position in the championships. I felt a bit like a lamb going to slaughter, convinced I was going to finish last in that standard of company, with internationals like Gerry North, Mike Beevor and Gerry Stevens in the ECCU team.

But Adrian Gargett, my Rhodesian flatmate, said he would drive me to the race in style. He had an old van, and put a mattress in the back of it so that I could lie down as he drove to Fareham and not use up any nervous energy worrying about his driving, or at least not be able to see his driving. We picked up Sue, and off we went to Fareham, with me lying in the back like His Regal Majesty, off to run for the British Universities. Unknown to me until afterwards, Adrian had even painted 'Sussex University Cross Country Team' on the side of his van as an extra effect, but he got into trouble with the Sussex authorities about that because he had not asked official permission.

The course, at HMS Dryad, was a muddy one which did not look as though it would suit me at all, and I was ready for the field to run right away from me, despite my grand entrance. We set off, and after two miles I was still there, right up with the leaders. I couldn't really believe the situation, because runners like North and Stevens were men I had seen on television, running at White City, and who even got their photographs in *Athletics Weekly*. And here I was keeping up with them. It did not seem possible.

So I did a quite illogical thing. Heaven knows why, because I was terrified, but I took the lead and adopted an expression of confidence. At least it was supposed to look like that. Somehow I managed to open a small gap, and I just kept running

*I missed the graduation ceremony, so I borrowed Sue's gown to
pose for this picture, taken behind the Brighton flat in June 1969.*

harder and harder, almost oblivious as to whether I would even finish the race.
As I reached the end of the first lap I came past Sue and Adrian and they were
shouting themselves hoarse because I was leading. They were excited, and that
excitement transmitted itself to me, and kept me going, pulling further ahead. It
was a tremendous feeling.

Towards the end of the six miles race I started to slow, and the last mile seemed
like ten. With 600 yards left, Gerry North, a former national cross country
champion, was catching me and everyone thought I had misjudged the race, and
that he would sweep past to win. But I pulled out one last desperate effort, skating
around on the mud as in one of those bad dreams when you are running but cannot
get away from a pursuer, and managed to hold on to an eleven seconds lead as I
crossed the line. I actually danced across the line, and began jumping up and down
with Sue and Adrian, while everyone else stood around saying, 'Who the hell's

that who won the race?' I didn't care. It is always nice to go into a race and surprise people – unfortunately it doesn't happen much these days!

The amount of satisfaction I got out of that race was huge. Since then many of my apparently more important races have paled into insignificance compared to that. It was only a muddy old field in Hampshire, and later I was to run on Tartan tracks all over the world, win medals in major Games, and set world records, and yet that domestic cross country race was the one which gave me the greatest pleasure. After being a scrubber for two years, having been trodden down, depressed and ridiculed, I had managed to come through six months of good running by finally winning a race of significance.

I knew from that day that I really was going to be a good runner, and that was what my whole life had been about – becoming a good runner. We went back to Brighton that night, had a meal and a few beers and next day the result was in the paper. Brendan Foster's name actually in a newspaper! That had not happened for a long time, and even then it had only been the local paper when I had won a junior race, and they never make the headlines. On Monday I even got a headline in the *Daily Telegraph*. Under the heading 'Foster surprises Gerry North', athletics correspondent James Coote wrote:

> 'Brendan Foster, 21, of Sussex University, an "unknown" in the athletics world until Saturday, was the surprise winner for the British Universities in their triangular cross country fixture against Combined Services and the English Cross Country Union at HMS Dryad, near Portsmouth.
>
> 'Over a slippery, muddy course on which runners had difficulty keeping their feet, Foster, from Newcastle, a chemistry student in his final year, recorded 30 min 45 secs for the six miles, beating by eleven seconds Gerry North, the experienced international.'

At university people began stopping me and shaking hands, and I had my photo in the local paper. I felt like a star overnight, and I quite liked it, I must admit. But at Sussex University, where they did not have a great deal of sporting success, you were a star if you even won a tiddlywinks match, so it was best to try to keep a sense of proportion. It had been a good race to win, a breakthrough for me personally, but the world had not actually stopped turning.

I just said that this was the race which gave me the greatest pleasure, but that is not strictly true. It is not really the *race* at all, which is rarely a pleasure. It is the struggle to get there and knowing what you have had to do to reach a certain level of fitness, overcoming the downs and the depressions when everything seems to be going wrong. That is what actually contributes to the pleasure after a good race, and to surmount the problems was a personal victory for me.

I don't suppose I was in any way different from thousands of other young students when I first went to university. I missed home quite a bit, because we were such a close family, and in common with everyone else I had the pressures of having to work and the pressures of not really knowing anybody. Basically, I'm quite shy although I've had to try to overcome that simply by being thrust into circumstances where you have to get on with people to survive. And when I first went to Brighton I had the added pressure of not running well, which meant a lot to me.

But by the spring of 1969, getting towards the final months at Sussex University, I felt there was finally light at the end of the tunnel. Sue and I did our final exams together in May, and on the last day we went with a group of students to watch the horse racing at Brighton Racecourse. The father of one of the girls owned a racehorse, and we backed it at 20–1. It won its race, so we all collected a packet, and just to add to my sporting celebrations that night, Newcastle United won the Fairs Cup. The next day, our exams finished, I spent all my money taking Sue out for a meal in an expensive restaurant in Brighton, so we left the town with happy memories. It had not exactly been three solid years of rollicking fun, but it ended nicely. And neither of us has been back since.

Four

Getting to the top in athletics, or indeed anything, is like negotiating a series of stepping stones, and my next target was to become an international. My victory at Fareham, over a number of good runners, had convinced me that I could aspire to that level, but first I would have to improve my best track times. In cross country races, times do not mean anything, because every course varies in distance, terrain, and difficulty. But in the summer season, when the sport switches to the standard 400 metres track, comparative times are among the most important aspects of the sport. An athlete living in Penzance can judge how well he is running compared to a rival in Aberdeen on the track.

The memories of the day I could not run a mile faster than 4:37 were slow to clear, and in the summer of 1969 I made a conscious effort to improve my track times at different distances, which any runner carries round like a mental hand of cards, ready to put down on the table for comparison with any other runner he meets.

I ran in the British Universities track championships at Motspur Park in June, setting a personal best for 800 metres of 1:53 in my heat, and in the final three hours later I led up to the 600 metres mark, before Andy Carter went past me to win in 1:51.5. I finished third in 1:52.6, my fastest, and I even got my picture in *Athletics Weekly* for the first time. Actually, it was a picture of Andy Carter breaking the tape, and it looks as though his right hand is punching me in the mouth, but at least you could see my number clearly. And my legs came out well.

Several weeks later I won the 1500 metres at the Gateshead Games in 3:48.4, which is equivalent to around 4:07 for the mile, and in July ran 4:05.6 for the full distance to win an invitation race at Hartlepool. That could have been even faster, but it was a blustery night, and after a pacemaker had taken us to the half distance in 2:00.3, I decided to have a go in front myself. The rest of the field bunched up behind me, and the pace inevitably slowed as I took the full gust of the wind. I managed to get away, though, and Mike Baxter of Leeds took second place in 4:06.8, with one of the untouchables of my youth, Brooks Mileson, third in 4:08.3.

These successes boosted my confidence no end. I ran a two miles race at Jarrow a few days later and just outsprinted Ernie Pomfret of Houghton, who had run for Britain in the 1964 Olympic steeplechase. We both clocked 8:48.8, after I had made up twenty yards in the last 220. The bell for the last lap had been rung a lap too soon, and we all had to make two finishing efforts, which is a very hard way to run a race. Even one is sometimes too much.

I realised that I had now run fast enough times to be able to enter the AAA National Championships at White City, an event I had previously only watched on television, and furthermore I was unbeaten in the north-east that summer. I decided to go for the 1500 metres, but two weeks before the event I got a poisoned toe, which needed penicillin treatments, and the result was that I was a bit under par when I ran in the heats on the Friday night. Unfortunately, I was drawn in the fastest heat, which was won by Ireland's Frank Murphy, the eventual winner of the title in a championship record. I finished seventh in the heat in a disappointing 3:51, and I was not even the leading runner from the north-east because Ronnie Bell of Morpeth and Davey Wright of Jarrow were both ahead of me.

So my first and last visit to the historic White City was not that memorable. I recalled having read an athletics novel as a youngster about a northern runner who went down to race at White City, got beaten, and as he was leaving the stadium with his bag he turned round and thought romantically to himself 'I'll be back to fill the stadium one day!' I would like to have done the same thing, having run on the same circuit as such great names as Sydney Wooderson, Jack Lovelock, Gordon Pirie, Emil Zatopek, Vladimir Kuts and Roger Bannister. But I am afraid I thought it was a terrible track. I had got hammered in my heat, and quite honestly I was glad to see the back of it!

A fortnight later I ran in Middlesbrough and recorded my best time of 3:47.1, which would have won three of the four heats at the AAA championships, but it is never any use looking back like that. I had made as much impact in my first AAA Championships appearance as a marshmallow hitting a brick wall.

But while the running was, on the whole, going well that summer I was also mulling over what to do in my career. I had left Sussex University with a B.Sc (Hons) degree, but with no clear course ahead of me. I had thought about teaching, however, and I finally made up my mind that this really was for me. I wanted to teach PE as well as chemistry, and I applied for a place at Loughborough College, which was generally reckoned to be the top PE college in the country. I thought that if you were a reasonable runner, it must help your chances of getting in, because the College prided itself on its athletics team. The annual match between Loughborough and the Amateur Athletic Association was one of the leading domestic fixtures of the season.

So I went for an interview, in which I thought I did all right, followed by a practical, which I had been dreading. It is no good being just a theorist. You have to be able to actually perform the sports you are teaching, so you have to go into a gymnasium and carry out a number of activities while the examiner watches and marks you. I had to dribble and kick a football, and throw a basketball into the net, which was all right. But then came the gymnastics tests, and I nearly broke my neck. I had to stand on my hands, and I couldn't. I had to climb up a rope, and I couldn't. Then I had to jump over a box. Well, I could just about jump, but I couldn't do the proper vault. It was awful, a terribly embarrassing joke. When I tried the handstand, I ended up in a crumpled heap on the floor, looking up at the examiner and imagining him thinking what a nerve I had applying to come to such a great PE college and not even being able to do a handstand.

So Loughborough decided it could do without me, which was very disappointing at the time. But I suppose that my athletics achievements up to then, a third place in the British Universities 800 metres, were scarcely earth-shattering. You had to be a really good athlete to get in. And able to do a handstand, even though a teacher is rarely required to do one.

A couple of weeks later I tried Carnegie College at Leeds. Again I went for the interview, which seemed all right, and then into the torture chamber for the practical. Again the football and basketball were okay, but when we came to the gymnastics I admitted to the examiner: 'Look, I can't do this, I'm sorry.'

'Well, just have a go,' he said.

So once more I did my impression of a jellyfish climbing up a rope, and then doing a handstand. Or, rather, not doing a handstand. If he was generous, the examiner probably gave me about two out of ten, including one for knowing my name. My prospects looked hopeless again. People are often surprised that I cannot do things like gymnastics. Yet, when you come to think about it, there is no real reason why I should be able to climb a rope, which needs strong arm and shoulder muscles, when I am a distance runner, using primarily leg muscles. In the same way, you would not expect Geoff Capes to run a marathon, or Ian Thompson to putt the shot. When people ask me why I don't enter 'Superstars' I usually avoid giving a truthful answer.

In any case, I assumed that my attempt to enter Carnegie College as a student would go the same way as that at Loughborough. But to my surprise, I was accepted, to start in September 1969. I could not help thinking that the 4:05 mile I had run a week or so previously had caused the College to turn a blind eye to my gymnastic ineptitude.

So that autumn I went to Leeds to begin what was to turn out to be a great year. I moved into a flat, and a good mate from Gateshead, Lindsay Dunn, later joined me there. Lindsay was already working for an insurance company in Leeds, and to me he had always been one of the big Gateshead stars when I was a junior. He had run 4.06 for a mile, and together we quickly built up our training to about a hundred miles a week. Mind you, I thought that was a ridiculously high level for a miler like myself to be doing, and Lindsay and I had many arguments about it. But he persuaded me that the strength, added to my natural speed, would produce good results.

It certainly did for him, and he was racing well at that time, but I wasn't racing much at all, so I still had my doubts. Through September, October and November we piled up the training miles, and every night I'd be out plodding round the roads in the dark, wondering how it would affect my racing. I used to take part in the occasional event for the college on a Wednesday afternoon, but I never eased up in training for it, and in fact used to run on Wednesday morning and evening as well, so I couldn't tell what my best form was. Sometimes I'd win the races, sometimes not, but it did not really matter.

My first significant event of the winter was to be the National PE Colleges five miles cross country championship at Twickenham, when I would be competing against athletes like international steeplechaser John Bicourt, and the unbeaten Malcolm Absolom, who were the college circuit stars then. I had not run a race all winter, just this high volume of training, and when I travelled down for the event I was quite worried as to how I would fare.

In fact, I found the benefit of the increased mileage quite considerable, and took an early lead. I won the race by 15 seconds from Bicourt, with Absolom suffering his first defeat of the season in third place. It was clear that Lindsay was right, and when I got back I found he had written a song to celebrate the event, and stuck it on my door. It was supposed to be sung to the tune of the Beatles tune 'Yesterday', and part of it went:

> *Big Bren won.*
> *He didn't even put the pressure on.*
> *He just went 'bye-bye Malcolm Absolom'*
> *On Saturday at Twickenham.*

My year at Leeds was a most enjoyable year. When we were not actually running, Lindsay and I used to talk about running all the time, just like we do now. He has been a hell of an influence on me, for running is Lindsay's life, and he is as keen now as ever, even after eighteen years of competing.

In Leeds we had begun training with a local runner named Mike Baxter, who was destined to make the Commonwealth Games team the following year, and that also helped me a great deal. For one thing it gave me confidence knowing that I, as a 1500 metres/one mile runner, could do the same training as an international 5000 metres man like Mike.

I did not study a great deal that year. I was supposed to be doing chemistry and PE, but I knew the chemistry from university, so it was really just how to teach it that was the fresh part. A lot of the time I read athletics magazines, trained, and travelled up and down between Leeds and Chelmsford, where Sue lived. She was back at home, and working in London, at that time.

Early in 1970 I finished thirty-second in the Inter-Counties cross country championships at Derby, my first appearance in the race, and one with which I was quite pleased. But the summer was more important, and I kept up a hard training regime, often two or three sessions a day, with Lindsay or Mike Baxter. In July the Commonwealth Games were being held in Edinburgh, and in September the World Student Games were to be in Turin. I would not say that I was confident of being in either, but I was determined to have a go, and see how close I could come.

To get into the England team for the Commonwealth Games, I realised that I would have to establish myself as a candidate early in the season, because the England Trials were being held at Leicester in June, and they were by invitation only. As I was still virtually unknown at the beginning of the summer season, I had to show some good form, and the best – perhaps the only – race in which I could catch the selectors' eyes might be the Inter-Counties championships at Leicester in May. The only problem was that there was another candidate for the Northumberland and Durham team, Maurice Benn, who was living and racing in London at that time. Maurice had run for Britain at the Mexico Olympics, his best times were faster than mine, and he was more experienced. It seemed highly possible that he would be picked as the Northumberland and Durham representative in the mile at the Inter-Counties event, and with only one athlete allowed for each county, that seriously worried me. I needed to run in the Inter-Counties if I was to run in the Commonwealth Games trials. I could hardly expect Maurice to come up to the north to race me, because he was in the stronger position as it stood. So if the mountain would not go to Mohammed . . .

41

I managed to find out that Maurice was running in a special mile race, organised by the British Milers' Club (BMC), at West London Stadium on May 10th. I asked if I could run too, and was invited on the understanding that I paid my own way. I was just about broke, but I went to see the bank manager who agreed to lend me twenty pounds for my return fare to London, and went down the day before the race to stay with Sue's family at Chelmsford.

At West London Stadium I had a word with Maurice before the race, and we agreed to share the pace. It was a grey, damp afternoon, the track was still cinder then, and it was a really uninspiring setting, with Wormwood Scrubs Prison in the background. For me, though, the race was worth the time, trouble and money, because I went past Maurice with 220 yards left to win in 4:06. He clocked 4:11, and on the basis of that I was selected for the Inter-Counties – another stepping stone towards the Commonwealth Games.

Although the race was held on a Sunday afternoon, in the middle of a local women's club championships with only a few dozen spectators, virtually the entire band of Fleet Street athletics correspondents were, rather incongruously, standing together in the middle of the arena. Not, I hasten to add, to watch our race, but because the women's mile a few minutes later, also organised by the BMC, was to feature the debut at the distance of Lillian Board. Only eight months before Lillian had won two gold medals for Britain in the 1969 European championships at Athens, and she was very much the star personality of British athletics at that time. She brought a glamour and vivaciousness to a sport which virtually lives by its personalities, and everything she did was big news.

She was the reason why all the national correspondents had gathered at this unlikely meeting. Lillian finished third in her race in 4 minutes 55.7 seconds, although she improved that to 4 minutes 44.6 seconds in Rome a week later. But what no one knew then, and could never have guessed on that grey afternoon, was that Lillian, only twenty-one, was only a month away from the end of her athletics career, and only a few months away from her tragically early death from cancer at Christmas 1970. It is something like that which can shake you out of your own little world; if it sometimes seems a catastrophe to miss out on a team or a record or a medal, you can at least be grateful that you can still run.

The Inter-Counties championships were also at Leicester in late May, and after winning my heat in 4:08.2, I lined up with the European 1500 metres champion John Whetton and the others for the final. It started off very slowly, so I went ahead after 100 yards and pushed the pace along for the first lap before moving out to let someone else have a go. But there were no takers, so I pushed it again until just beyond the halfway mark, where Frank Briscoe made a break, but I stayed with the leaders, and with 330 yards left I went back into the lead. That was a foolish move, because there is always a strong wind down the back straight at Leicester, and I sheltered the others from it by leading at that point, so that as we swung into the home straight, where the wind was suddenly behind us, Whetton and Peter Stewart went past for first and second places. Norman Morrison was given third place, which I thought I actually got, but we had both run 4:06, and I felt sure that I had done enough to be invited to the Commonwealth Games trials.

A day or so later the names of the athletes for the trials were announced. Mine was not among them. But Maurice Benn, whom I had beaten by five seconds at West London, and Paul Dennis, who was last in the Inter-Counties mile, were both included.

So Lindsay rang the AAA, and said he was my coach. He told them that I ought to be in the trials, and that if I was, I would make the team. Wilf Paish, the national coach for the north, also stuck up for me. Fortunately, the 1500 metres trial field was already getting thinner because one of the twelve named, Ricky Wilde, had decided to retire; the Stewart brothers, Ian and Peter, both announced their intention of running for Scotland rather than England; Jim Douglas had fractured his leg; and Chris Mason, studying in the USA, was unable to get back to England for the race. Eventually, only eight – including me – ran in the trial, with seven finishing. But I wonder where I would have been left if all twelve original selections had accepted their invitations?

The trials were held the following week, on a warm, muggy afternoon. There were no heats, just a straight final, and I felt very much the raw youngster, ready to have a go. The Inter-Counties mile had been my only other big race, but that was nowhere near as important as this. The first lap was quite nippy, around 60 seconds, but by the 800 metres mark I had moved into the lead, and pushed the pace on the third lap, helped by Maurice Benn. I led past the 1200 metres in 2:58.6, but John Whetton, the master of the sprint finish, gave me a nudge to let me know he was still there coming into the home straight, and then breezed away to win in 3:41.5. I was second in 3:42.8, an improvement of over four seconds on my previous best, and John Kirkbride from Cumberland was third.

I travelled back to Leeds after the race on a cloud. It was clear that I was going to be in the team for the Commonwealth Games, and when I got back to the flat, Lindsay, who had watched the race on TV, had pinned another notice on the door: 'Next stop – Edinburgh!' As Robbie Brightwell had given me an Adidas tracksuit and a new pair of shoes that day, I really felt I'd arrived.

That night I hardly slept a wink in my excitement, tossing and turning, and re-running the race over and over in my mind. Although the team had not even been announced, I was in no doubt that I had made it. At last I would be an international, and inevitably my memory flashed back to the miserable days in Brighton. Next morning Lindsay and I went out and ran eighteen miles, talking non-stop about the Commonwealth Games, and it must have been the easiest eighteen miles I have ever run.

Being at a sports-orientated college like Carnegie added to the pleasure when my name finally appeared in the newspapers as one of England's 1500 metres selections, because at such a place any sporting success is inevitably given a great deal of attention, and I must admit that it was a real ego-tickler to have so many enthusiastic people congratulating me!

By now I had just one more race to run before the Commonwealth Games, a two miles at the Sward meeting at Crystal Palace in early July, less than a fortnight before the Games opened. I could have had another 1500 metres, because I was selected for the Great Britain team to meet East Germany at the White City only a few days before the Commonwealth Games, but I did not want to have a race so close to Edinburgh. It would have been my first full British, as opposed to English, international, and I expect I'm the only athlete to have turned down his first international, but I wanted to concentrate on the Games.

The two miles was not too much of a worry, because I'd only run the distance once before, and knowing the class of runner I was up against, including the Olympic 1500 metres champion Kip Keino of Kenya, whom I would be running against in Edinburgh, I did not expect to do very well.

There were several British runners from the 1968 Olympics, including 5000 metres men Allan Rushmer and Alan Blinston, who were used to the longer distances, but one of my real incentives for going down to London was simply to be able to collect my Commonwealth Games kit – the blazer, tracksuit, raincoat, sunglasses and all the other equipment – with which all team members are supplied. It was just like Christmas.

When I arrived at Crystal Palace I remember seeing Allan Rushmer, who said, 'You must have a great chance today. You'll beat me,' and I thought, 'Hell, no, you're the great Allan Rushmer, bronze medallist in the last Commonwealth Games.' It was only later that I learned he was like that, he did not have a great deal of confidence in himself, but it is a common reaction among athletes just before competition, whatever their level. Self-doubt can be worst among some outstanding competitors, and it can either spur them to greater things, or else wreck their performance if they let it get on top of them. Whoever you are, or whatever you have done in the past, the time comes before a race when you begin to doubt yourself, and you have to try to contain that sort of thought, know that

44

I did better than I expected in the 1970 Sward two miles at Crystal Palace, and finished second to one of my heroes, Kip Keino of Kenya. (Tony Duffy).

it is going to cross your mind, handle it, and then step on the track with real confidence. Herb Elliott, the former Olympic 1500 metres champion from Australia, used to say that it was the last ten minutes before a race that decided who was going to win, and if you could maintain your confidence up to that point, and then go on the track and do something about it, then you would probably win.

Keino did not look as though he could ever be worried, though. His long, elegant, raking stride was barely stretched as the field went past the first mile in 4:19. Then on the sixth lap he suddenly went steaming away, covering the circuit in under 62 seconds. My only reaction was to go with him, and I moved up to his shoulder, only vaguely aware that the rest of the field had dropped back. We went through one-and-a-half miles in 6 minutes 25.8 seconds, with me struggling to stay close to him, and on the seventh lap, which he completed in another 61.8 seconds, I just had to let him move away.

As the bell sounded, he was some 25 yards ahead of me, but I decided that I must have one more go at closing that gap. I dug down hard, and managed to close it to about 15 yards at the finish, but I am sure that Keino was satisfied to simply win the race. His time was 8:29.0, while mine was 8:30.8, which missed Dick Taylor's UK National record by just over half a second. But more pleasing to me was the news that I had covered the last mile in under 4:12, and the last three-quarters of a mile in 3:04.8. Once more it showed the benefit of my high mileage during the winter, which had given me the strength to run the last three laps of a two miles race at the same pace as I had been doing for one mile in the previous season.

Such proof of progress could scarcely have come at a better time. For soon it was time to travel up to Scotland's capital, where already sportsmen and women from over forty countries had begun to gather for the 1970 Commonwealth Games.

These Games are known as the Friendly Games, because there is not the same high tension as at Olympic and European championships, but the standard in most events is just as good. The Athletes Village at Edinburgh was at the Pollock Halls of Residence, normally used by university students, and therefore a ready-made 'village' in itself, not too far from the city centre. It was around here that I used to walk, lapping up the unique atmosphere of a major Games like the novice I was, looking at people from different countries, swapping badges, and all that kind of thing.

Some of my friends had thought I might be disappointed that this Common-wealth Games was being held 'only' in Edinburgh, two hours away from Newcastle, whereas the previous Games had been held in Kingston, Jamaica, and the next Games would be in Christchurch, New Zealand. But even if my selection did not

lead to worldwide travel on this occasion, it was still to show me a new aspect of the sport, and it also meant that my family could come to Edinburgh to watch me run, as well as teachers from my old school, friends and neighbours. Sue came up too, and she stayed near the Village with the wife of another Gateshead Harriers runner, John Caine, who had qualified for the England team at 10,000 metres.

When we marched in for the Opening Ceremony at the new Meadowbank Stadium, I remember thinking, 'I wish I was one of those blokes who stood a chance of getting a medal in the Games,' because the atmosphere generated by the crowd was so strong that you felt you wanted to do well for them. Although, of course, it was the Scots they really wanted to see doing well, and the success of the Games was probably assured on the second day of the athletics competition when the little Glasgow dental technician, Lachie Stewart, scored a surprising and emotion-raising victory for Scotland in the 10,000 metres.

It was a cold, windy and wet afternoon, and nationalism apart, everyone's sentimental favourite was the great Australian runner Ron Clarke, whose last major Games this was. Clarke had set nineteen world records in his career, been one of the most consistent runners ever, but had always failed to get a gold medal. He had silver and bronze medals, plus his records, but no gold, and at thirty-two this was to be his final chance.

When three runners were together on the last lap – Clarke, Stewart and England's Dick Taylor – it was really a time for mixed emotions, but eventually Stewart was the man with the sprint, and won by about 15 yards from Clarke, with Taylor third, and my clubmate John Caine also running well for fifth place. It was good to see John running so well in a big Games because I had trained with him quite a lot, and learned a great deal from him.

Earlier in the afternoon I had run my heat of the 1500 metres, where the rivals I had been drawn against included Keino and the unpredictable Scot, Ian McCafferty. There were three heats, with the first four in each qualifying for the final, but Keino almost danced it. He stayed last for 300 metres, then went ahead to pass 400 metres in 59.9 seconds, and 800 metres in 1:58.3, with me some five metres down. The third lap of the race is always the hardest, but he actually increased the pace with a 57.9 circuit (2:56.2 at the bell), opening his lead to 15 metres, and then almost floated the last lap to win in 3:40.4. I was second in 3:43.8, and McCafferty, after a typical last-minute panic, only just made it from fifth to third in the closing metres of the race. He had, it transpired, lost his spiked shoes before the event, and Keino had sportingly lent him his own. Qualifiers in the other heats included John Whetton, Peter Stewart and a certain little-known New Zealander called Dick Quax.

The final was four days later, on Wednesday, July 22nd, and those days can seem very long when you are waiting for a race. I was still learning all this, and I must have put on pounds between heat and final because I was always in the Village canteen drinking Coca-Cola and eating whatever was available – which was a lot. With 2000 competitors from forty-two countries at the Games, all trying to keep up their strength, the catering had to suit everybody and be available all the time. In this situation the temptation to pop along and get something to eat or drink, not because you are necessarily hungry or thirsty, but simply bored, is a very real one.

I had a single room at the Village, which is a luxury you do not often get at big championship meetings, but I remember that David Hemery, then the reigning Olympic 400 metres hurdles champion and world record holder, was just down the corridor. He came along specifically to wish me luck in my race one day, which I thought was really tremendous. I did not think he even knew who I was, as a new boy in the team, and there he was a real, live Olympic champion. I had a lot of respect for him anyway, but that incident sticks in my mind, and from his example

I always try to wish good luck to newcomers to the team now. I feel it is some sort of responsibility which the older athletes ought to assume. The genuineness of his concern for others was never better illustrated than when he crossed the finishing line in his own 110 metres hurdles final at Edinburgh to retain his Commonwealth title. Instead of a great display of elation he immediately expressed concern for Alan Pascoe, the potential silver medallist, who had injured his foot in the race and had to drop out before the last hurdle.

That day was also David's twenty-sixth birthday, and the stadium band later interrupted their normal diet of national anthems to play 'Happy Birthday', with which the crowd serenaded him.

The whole of the atmosphere surrounding the Games was an exciting one, and I still found it very difficult to consider myself a part of it. I went around for some of the time with Dick Taylor and Allan Rushmer, who were well travelled and experienced and seemed to know most people in distance running. They went to see Ron Clarke, and I went with them, and while it would be nice to say that I had a long conversation with him, I actually just sat in a corner and listened to them talking, lapping it all up.

By the day of the 1500 metres final I was very nervous, and felt terrible when I was warming up. It was sunny but windy, and as we lined up for the start at the beginning of the back straight, I had John Whetton and Ian McCafferty on my inside and the rest of the twelve-man field on the outside.

When we passed 150 metres, Keino was right at the back, but edged forward so that at 300 metres he had moved to second place, just behind Quax and just in front of me. At 400 metres (57.6) he went ahead, putting in a stinging second lap of 57.4, and only Quax went with him. I knew I should go too, and had intended to, but when the break came I just could not match the pace. At the bell (1100 metres) Keino and Quax were some 40 metres ahead of the rest of us, and while these tactics had worked for Keino in previous major Games, simply daring the opposition to stay with his pacemaking, Quax was the revelation. I certainly did not think he would be able to stay with Keino for as long as he did, and even as they pressed on down the back straight he was still on Keino's shoulder. As we passed the bell, Stewart, McCafferty and Whetton were ahead of me, fighting for third place, but when we came into the home straight for the last time I managed to get through them, and held off Whetton, who tried to come back past me on the outside. Peter Stewart, urged on by the Scottish crowd, came at me hard on the inside and we both crossed the finishing line together. Fortunately, I just remembered to dip my chest at the line, and it was that action which decided that I was third and Stewart fourth, although we shared the same time of 3:40.6. I could

Keino and Dick Quax leave the rest of us behind in the Commonwealth Games 1500 metres at Edinburgh, while I try to hold off Whetton and Stewart. (Press Association).

scarcely believe it – I had won a medal in my first-ever Games, and in a time two seconds faster than I had ever run before. Sue says now that of all my big races, that Commonwealth bronze in Edinburgh was the most exciting, simply because it was so unexpected.

She had been sitting in the stands at the bottom bend, and straight after the race I rushed over there, waving like a madman, as if I had won the race, and as she came down to meet me I threw my arms around her. I was simply bubbling over with the thrill of doing so well, and you would have thought that no one had ever won a bronze medal before!

Keino was a supreme champion, setting a UK all-comers' record of 3:36.6, but he only managed to get away from the dogged Quax in the final 200 metres. The New Zealander took the silver medal in 3:38.1, his best-ever time, and afterwards

50

he and I swapped vests. People began predicting great things for Dick on the basis of that run but in fact because of continuing misfortune it was to be another six years before he was to figure prominently in a major Games again, although in between he did run some fast times.

What no one, except Kip Keino and a handful of officials, knew before the race in Edinburgh that afternoon was that Kip's life had been threatened three times in the forty-eight hours leading up to the final. The threats – two by letter, and one by a telephone call – warned that if he ran he would be shot by a rifleman using a telescopic sight from a building overlooking the stadium. Looking back and knowing now that nothing happened can perhaps lessen the impact of those threats. But just imagine what tension he must have been under before the race, having to step out into the crowded stadium and remain on public view for all that time. Yet afterwards he even jogged a lap of honour, waving to the crowd, and his participation in the Games was by no means over. I had finished, but he still had the 5000 metres to run.

Later the three of us – Kip, Dick and I – had the honour to receive our medals from Her Majesty the Queen, who had rearranged the timing of her visit to the athletics competition at the Games so that she could see the 1500 metres.

The Games ended the following Saturday, July 25th, with another memorable Scottish triumph. This time Kip Keino had to settle for the bronze medal in the 5000 metres, as two Scottish runners, Ian Stewart and Ian McCafferty, took first and second places.

Stewart, no relation to the 10,000 metres winner, unleashed a searing final lap of 55.4 seconds to win in a European record time of 13:22.8, with McCafferty only 0.6 seconds behind him. For the Scots, who had staged the Games so well, there could hardly have been a greater climax, even though I kid Ian Stewart that he is about as Scottish as me – and I live nearer to Scotland than him!

It had been an exciting fortnight for me too, and I felt I could really call myself an international athlete now. But I did not realise just how much physical and mental effort goes into competing in such an event until I got home from Edinburgh. I got back on Sunday afternoon, felt so tired that I went straight to bed – and woke up on Tuesday morning. I had slept right through Monday as though it did not exist. That was an indication of how much energy is used just living in such an atmosphere, and it was a valuable lesson for the future.

Five

With the Commonwealth Games over, I suppose that would have been a good point to end the 1970 season, on a high note. But Britain is in a unique position in international athletics. We not only take part in Commonwealth events, but also the tougher European programme, and there, just a week after the end of the Commonwealth Games, when everyone was relaxed and happy and free of tension, loomed a big obstacle. The semi-final of the European Cup was due to take place in Zurich, and Britain had to field a team. The same day, there was a 'B' team match against France in Cwmbran, and at first I was selected to compete at Cwmbran. But I was also warned to stand by for the European Cup, because Ian Stewart was being asked to run in the 1500 metres and there was a chance he would turn it down.

He did. Ian, quite rightly, argued that he could not hope to bring himself to another mental peak so soon after his Commonwealth triumph, and said he was 'unavailable' for Zurich. I was feeling pretty unavailable myself at the time, as I seemed to have brought some kind of bug back from Edinburgh, but finally I agreed to run in Zurich, which was, after all, my British international debut.

The European Cup is a different sort of meeting from the major Games, with only one athlete per country competing in each event, and points being scored for their placing. In that respect it is a little like the television programme 'It's a Knockout'. Times, particularly in the longer races, tend to be unimportant because tactics play a much greater part. Only two of the six participating countries would qualify for the final, and as the Soviet Union would almost certainly be one of them, Britain was really chasing second place.

But we never got near it. Unlike the other five nations, virtually the whole British team was suffering from a reaction after Edinburgh, and the great heat and humidity in Zurich was oppressive. Poor Lachie Stewart, the hero of the 10,000 metres at Meadowbank, could only finish a tailed-off fifth out of six in a time nearly two minutes slower than his gold-medal winning performance. Pole vaulter Mike Bull, also a newly-crowned Commonwealth champion, failed to clear any height in his event and scored no points at all.

I did not really know what to expect in my 1500 metres, but before the race I felt no nerves at all, which was rather worrying because, whatever anyone may say, you have got to be nervous if you are really going to run well. We almost shuffled off when the gun fired, and the first lap took nearly 68 seconds, as we all tried to avoid falling over each other's feet. But despite the sluggish pace, I felt rough, and when the Soviet runner Zhelobovskiy decided to speed it up on the second lap I got dropped for a while. The pace got faster still on the third lap when Jean Wadoux of France, who the previous week had set a European record of 3:34.0 (equivalent to less than 3:52 for a mile), took the lead. I managed to struggle back into contact, and on the last lap moved into third place, where I stayed to the finish. My time of 3:48.6 meant nothing, but Wadoux covered the last 800 metres in around 1:52, and was scarcely stretched.

It was not a very happy weekend for Britain. The French surprisingly tied with the Soviet Union on points, 97 each, to qualify for the European final, while we were third, nearly 30 points behind, and only just held off Spain, which was hardly considered a world strength in athletics.

Yet that position was by no means a true reflection of British athletics, but simply the predicament of having a foot in both Commonwealth and European camps. In later years, the European Cup was to provide some great moments for British athletics, but in 1970 it was a fairly downhearted team which flew back to Heathrow Airport next day. Apart from one man. Javelin throwers do not get a great deal of publicity, but Dave Travis had been our only winner in the two days, and in doing so he had beaten the Olympic champion Janis Lusis of the Soviet Union with a British record throw of 273 feet 9 inches.

The following week the AAA championships were being held at White City, but I decided to give them a miss, and just get some training done for the World Student Games, which were in Turin in early September. I had been selected for the 1500 metres, but I was beginning to feel a little jaded from the long season. Then in the middle of August I had to have some time off training because of shin soreness, which did not increase my confidence before we left for Italy.

I qualified for the final reasonably comfortably, finishing third in my heat in 3:45.0, but in the final next day I wished I had not. I felt nervous before the race, but they were the wrong sort of nerves, and I had very little confidence. The pace

*A race to forget. The World Student Games in Turin, as the lanky Arese
waits to pounce, and I run wide to begin my move to the back!*
(Fionnbar Callanan).

was extremely slow, but instead of taking it up and making it faster, as I should
have done, I languished at the back. When the big sprint came on the final lap, I
had little answer and gave up in the last 250 metres, just jogging down the finishing
straight. I was tenth and last in 3:59.7, and angry with myself for giving up.
'Ridiculous' is what I wrote in my training diary. The gold medal was won, to the
delight of the staunchly partisan Italian crowd, by Franco Arese of Italy, and my
teammate John Kirkbride took the silver medal. I took nothing except a rest.

For that was what I obviously needed now. The hard work had started twelve
months before, when I moved to Leeds, and started piling in the training miles,
and I had forced myself to be strong and fast for that BMC mile against Maurice
Benn in early May. From that race everything went on in a chain reaction, one
race leading to another, until here in Turin my batteries had almost run down.

But before I began a three-week rest, I made some notes for the future, based on what I had observed and learned in my first international year. These were some of the things I wrote:

1. Must train to sprint at the end e.g. 330s, 220s in 28.
2. Must run 800m races until I can get well under 1:50. (*I'm still waiting!*)
3. More speed work is essential.
4. Try to run like Keino.
5. Elliott-type sessions.
6. Weights.
7. Swimming.
8. Suppleness.
9. Downhill sprints for leg speed.
10. Hill work.
11. Speed work in winter?

My rest from running also coincided with the start of my first teaching job, which was at my old school, St Joseph's, in Hebburn. There were about 700 pupils when I began there in September 1970, including some who must have been there during my final years, although I did not know them. I did know some of the teachers, though, and it seemed strange to be sitting in the staff room with them as a colleague, rather than sitting in a classroom as a pupil. But I got on well with them all, and some of the teachers had even been up to Edinburgh to see me run in the Commonwealth Games.

There were two pupils I did know, though. They were my sisters, Margaret and Kathleen. I taught Margaret chemistry in the sixth form, and I couldn't have been too bad because she got her GCE 'A' level in the subject and is now a teacher herself in Yorkshire. But having two sisters among my pupils did not lead to too many problems. It could have been as embarrassing for them as for me. I could not resist pulling Kathleen's leg one day, though, when it turned out that I was going to be her form master. I went round the class on the first day, asking each pupil his or her name, until I came to her.

'Name, please.'

'Kathleen Foster.'

Pause.

'Pardon?'

'Kathleen Foster!'

'Oh?'

The class was in stitches, but of course, she was furious when we got home that night.

'What did you want to go and ask me that in front of all the class?' she said. 'You know my name!'

In fact, it was quite useful having Kathleen and Margaret at the school, because I used to run to and from St Joseph's, and they would take my clothes in to school and home again afterwards. Or else they would carry a pile of exercise books home for me to mark in the evening, and then carry them back to school next day. So they had their uses!

I was to teach at St Joseph's for only four years, although when I started I had planned on a long teaching career. And being at a local school where sport was considered quite important meant that I could spot the outstanding young runners and channel them through to Gateshead Harriers. Other teachers who were members of the club, like John Caine and John Trainor, did the same thing, and if more school-club links were established like this, I am sure we would lose far fewer promising athletes when they leave school. If they can be involved in a club while they are still at school, then the link is ready made. Many kids never bother to get in touch with their local club when they leave school.

I took quite an interest in how the St Joseph's athletics and cross country teams were faring, but it was very difficult to get deeply involved and still try to train myself. Standing and watching other people run can be physically more tiring than running yourself.

In class, though, I rarely let athletics become a subject of discussion. When I was at St Joseph's, I was a school teacher first, and an athlete second. Only when I went through the gates at 4 pm each night, and started running home, did I become an athlete again. Often I would walk into a classroom when I had run in a big race the day before, and there would be a sort of buzz among the pupils, as though they wanted me to talk about it, but I never did. I could be quite strict when I wanted to.

Sometimes St Joseph's did, I suppose, get a little local reflected glory from a race I was in, but as my athletics career had got under way at the school, it was only fair. Towards the end of my time at the school, though, things did get a little bit intrusive. Camera crews would turn up at the school, or there would be telephone calls for me which meant leaving a class on their own. And, most important, I was often away for days or weeks at a time on international trips. On television a race in, say, Germany may take up only a few minutes, but if I am travelling with a team it often means flying out on a Friday, and back on a Monday. So that is two days of the week gone, even supposing that I do not have to travel

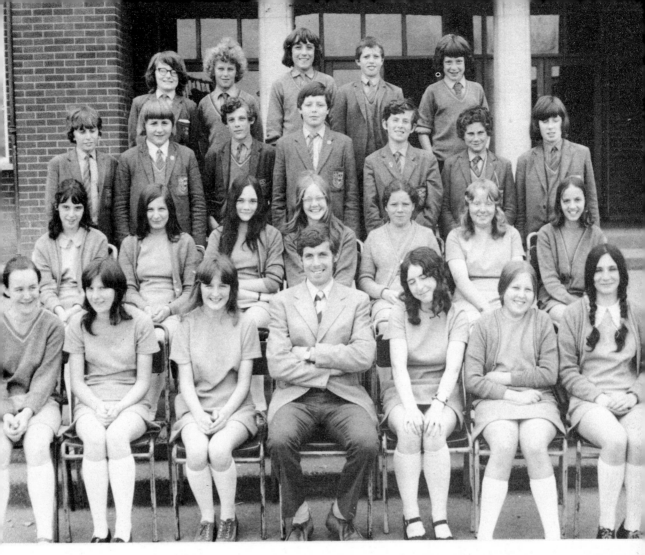

This rough looking lot was my form at St Joseph's, with my sister Kathleen third from the right in the row behind me. At least I think that's what she said her name was?

down on Thursday night to meet the team for an early departure on Friday. It also meant that a colleague had to stand in for me and take my classes while I was away, and some of them often used to say to me: 'Off abroad again? You're always away! What a great life.' And although they did not mean it to sound sarcastic, they did have a valid point. We were all teachers together, but they were having to do more than their fair share in the school, because I was doing less than mine.

The problem of time off work to compete for Great Britain has always been a particular hobby horse of mine, and in 1977 I even prepared a special report on the subject at the request of the Minister for Sport, Denis Howell. My argument was that it is now so difficult to reach top levels in international amateur sport and hold down a responsible job at the same time. In athletics, I have to train two or three times a day, and it is difficult to fit it all in, but if I was a pole vaulter I am sure it would be much harder. I can go running at 8 o'clock in the morning in mid-winter, but who in their right mind would try to pole vault at that time?

Now I work in a local government department, I know that some of our employees are in the Territorial Army, and they get an automatic two weeks leave every year for that. But when I (or David Jenkins, when he was working in Gateshead) wanted time off to compete for Britain, the application had to go before committees for approval. Fortunately, Gateshead is very sports-minded, and there has never been any trouble, but I often hear about other athletes who cannot get time off, or else have to lose their pay for every day they are away. If being in the Territorial Army entitles you to two weeks off work, then should not representing Great Britain in the Olympic Games carry a similar automatic dispensation?

But I enjoyed my time at St Joseph's a great deal, and although suffering, as I did, leg injuries during that first autumn term which hindered my training build-up, it did at least give me a chance to concentrate on my new teaching career. And, for the first time in my life, I actually had a little bit of money in my pocket; my student days were finally over.

It was shin soreness that caused the problem that winter, but it was finally cleared up by a local physiotherapist called Norman Anderson, and he has got me out of a few tight corners since then, I can tell you. I used to go and see him in Newcastle every night after school for some weeks, and I'd be sitting on the bus, completely miserable, because normally I would be running home. He would treat me, and then in the evening I was limited by Norman to going out and running only about four miles at the most.

By Christmas it had just about disappeared and I got my first good week's training since the summer, and then agreed to run in the Inter-Counties cross country championships in mid-January. It was a silly thing to do really, because I had no winter background to speak of at all, yet there I was lining up and wondering how on earth I would ever get round. I went straight up with the leaders, throwing caution to the wind, and somehow stayed reasonably close to the front, eventually finishing eighteenth out of over 300. It was ridiculous, because I was just not fit enough to finish eighteenth, ahead of a lot of runners who had been training all winter, and yet there I was. I suppose it was that race which showed me what an important part the mental aspect plays in successful racing, for I was able to overcome a definite physical lack in that instance.

58

In March I was invited to some track meetings in Trinidad and Barbados, and although I had not done anything like the amount or type of training I would normally prefer before track races, the trip was really too good to turn down. What happens in such cases is that the organising body or federation sends an official invitation to the athletics federation of the country whose athletes they are inviting. In the United Kingdom, that is the British Amateur Athletic Board. Sometimes the invitations are for specifically named athletes, and sometimes just for a 5000 metres runner and a pole vaulter, for instance. The leading international athletes get far more invitations from all over the world than they could ever hope to accept, of course, but for someone like myself the prospect of an all-expenses paid trip to the West Indies was perhaps going to be a once-in-a-lifetime opportunity. On overseas trips like this, everything is paid for by the meeting organisers, including air travel, hotel and meals, and being invited to such meetings is one of the perks of reaching international level in athletics. So it was in Trinidad that I ran my first-ever 5000 metres, finishing second in 14:36, about half a minute down on Kip Keino, on a bumpy old grass track. Next day, in red-hot temperatures, I finished third in a 1500 metres behind Keino and the American John Mason, and a week later ran in a mile, again finishing third behind Keino and Mason, but much closer. My time of 4:04.0 was a great improvement too, and that encouraged me before the last race of the trip, a 1500 metres in Barbados.

Keino and Mason had gone home, so I did not have too much opposition in the race, which was to be held on a brand new all-weather track. The atmosphere there was absolutely tremendous, with a crowd of 10,000 packing the stadium, thousands more locked out, and a fence round the track to keep the spectators from spilling onto it. The crowd were banging tin cans and singing and everyone seemed very happy, especially as the meeting was held around midnight. It was too hot to have it earlier.

The only problem was that the track had been designed by a local architect, who had obviously got rather confused in his plans. Whereas standard running tracks are usually 400 metres in circumference, or occasionally 440 yards, which is about the same distance, he had produced a track that was 440 *metres* – about 45 yards too long! As part of the work to adjust it to the correct distance, the inside lane had been dug up on the bends, and on the two straights the inside lane was covered with old shale and chippings. We were told to run in the second lane throughout the race, and as we set off I went into the lead. Then about halfway down the back straight, about five local runners came past me on the inside lane, ploughing their way across this shale and muck. So I speeded up a little, and went past them, but on the next straight the same thing happened – they all came past on the crunchy bit. I eventually got away from them and won in 3:44.0, which was a Barbados all-comers record, but although my lap times added up, and although I was capable of running that time then, I've never been quite sure about it.

A week later I achieved a small personal ambition when I broke four minutes for the mile for the first time. It was in the Inter-Counties championships at Leicester and I finished third in 3:58.5, behind Walter Wilkinson (3:56.6) and Peter Stewart, but although it was nice to get under what had once been regarded as an 'impossible' barrier, I had previously run the equivalent times at 1500 metres, which is about 120 yards shorter, and a time of around 3:41 for that is generally accepted as being 'worth' four minutes for the full mile.

My main concern was to get selection for the British team to compete in the European championships at Helsinki that summer, and the following week I was again racing a mile. This time it was the traditional Emsley Carr Mile, being held that year at Edinburgh as part of the British International Games.

With seven sub-four-minute milers in the field, everyone had been expecting a super fast race, but the strong winds which blew across Meadowbank Stadium put paid to that. I just could not get mentally into the race, and although I went into the lead with just two laps remaining, the wind nearly stopped me dead in my tracks. The others were content to shelter behind me, which was good tactics for them in the conditions, and I eventually ended up fourth, behind Peter Stewart, John Kirkbride and Walter Wilkinson. Stewart's time of 4:00.4 included a last lap in 56 seconds, while my time was 4:01.8, and I was annoyed with myself that I had not really driven the last 30 yards harder.

The outstanding running of the meeting, though, came from Dave Bedford, who powered through the winds in the 5000 metres to set a European record of 13:22.2, making his own pace and winning by nearly 20 seconds. It was an astonishing run, and only the world record holder, Ron Clarke, had ever run faster. Bedford reckoned that the wind had probably cost him the opportunity of breaking Clarke's mark of 13:16.6, and he was perhaps right.

Then I had a 1500 metres race in Milan, against Franco Arese and the American Marty Liquori. Or rather I was against them until the last 350 metres, when they breezed off to stage a tremendous sprint finish which Liquori narrowly won in 3:36.0. I finished fourth in 3:39.4, and was quite pleased with that because it was a personal best.

Early in July Britain had a match against France at Portsmouth and I really should have won the 1500 metres there. I made the early pace, passing 400 metres in 57.2 seconds, but the whole field was still together coming into the final bend and I was last. I managed to work my way up to second before the finish, and I was running well that day, but I misjudged it, and the race was won by Jean-Pierre Dufresne in 3:40.6, while I ran the same time in second place.

But once again the star of the meeting was Bedford. Having set a European 5000 metres record in the wind at Meadowbank, he found the weather still against him at Portsmouth. The AAA 10,000 metres championship was being held in conjunction with the match, and selection for Helsinki in this event depended on that race. Unfortunately, it was a scorching hot afternoon when the field set off and, the track being dry, the crumbly cinder surface soon cut up.

It did not stop him, though. After breaking away with a second lap of 59 seconds, he set off on a tremendous solo run. His time of 27 minutes 47 seconds was another European record and once again he had missed breaking one of Ron Clarke's world records by just a handful of seconds, to become the second fastest man of all time. Where Clarke had set his records on cool Scandinavian evenings, Bedford had to overcome the extremes of British weather, and in doing so I think he may later have regretted leaving several of his finest runs behind him that early in the season in relatively unimportant races.

More significantly, his brilliance was bringing more and more pressure on him to win both events at the European championships, and indeed some people were foolishly not even asking *whether* he could win in Helsinki, but simply by how much he would break the world records there. At that time he was king, and what happened to him later was a lesson from which a lot of British athletes were to learn, myself included.

I had established myself as one of the candidates for European championship selection at 1500 metres, and by finishing third in the AAA Championship race a fortnight later, behind the New Zealander Tony Polhill and Peter Stewart, I made sure of my place on the trip to Helsinki.

For Dave Bedford, though, there was a sudden halt to his successful season, as he dropped out of the 5000 metres with cramp after 3000 metres, and a performance like that just before a major Games is the last thing you want. The days before a big race are always days full of self-doubt, when you need constant reassurance that everything is going well and to resist the temptation to overtrain because of anxiety.

With the European championships approaching I found my own preparation rudely interrupted by a leg injury, the first time I had ever had such a problem before a big race. Usually in the week or so leading up to a big event I run a certain series of training sessions, and from that I can tell I am going well. In August 1971, though, I could only jog four miles in the morning and five in the evening for a fortnight before the European, and I was terrified of what would happen when I came to race. Ted Chappell, one of the outstanding physiotherapists in athletics, was treating the injury, and he insisted that I did no stretching or fast running at all. 'Just jog very easily on it,' he told me, and I found that very tough to handle. But I had a lot of faith in Ted, and it proved justified.

Going to a meeting in Finland always seems like returning to the home of the sport, because of the Finns' great tradition among distance runners like Paavo Nurmi and Hannes Kohlemainen. There is a statue of Nurmi outside the Helsinki Stadium, which was the scene of the 1952 Olympic Games where Nurmi made a moving reappearance as the torch-bearer at the Opening Ceremony. But in post-war years the Finns, to their enormous regret, had very little athletics success, and as the 1971 European championships began in the historic stadium most of the eternally enthusiastic and knowledgeable Finnish spectators had come out of a sheer love for the sport rather than in great hope that Finland would do very well.

Yet on the opening night of the championships we saw one of the greatest races of all time, the 10,000 metres final, which put Finland back on top of the distance running pile. Dave Bedford, whose confidence must have taken a severe knock after his AAA championships disaster, was responsible for a fast race, and led up to the bell, where six athletes still had a chance. Then with 300 metres to go two men – Jurgen Haase of East Germany, and Juha Vaatainen of Finland – burst away together and sprinted side by side to the tape, where the mutton-chop whiskered Vaatainen just won from Haase, the defending champion, by little more than a stride.

The memory of the noise in the stadium, and the rockets exploding in the purple night sky before the race was even over, still evokes the tingle of excitement at just witnessing a race like that. It was to mean more to Finland than just one victory (or two, because later in the week Vaatainen was to become a double hero when he won the 5000 metres gold medal as well); at Helsinki in 1971 the revival in Finnish distance running was ignited, as I was to know only too well in both the following Olympics.

Juha Vaatainen is one of the most interesting and controversial figures in athletics I have ever met, and a story not generally known about him is that he wanted to run the marathon as well as the 5000 and 10,000 metres in those European championships, but claimed that the Finnish selectors would not let him. So on the morning of the marathon, the final day of the championships, he went out and ran about twenty-one miles of the course at seven o'clock, and timed himself. The time, he told me, was 'much faster' than the speed at which the eventual winner ran, and ever since then Vaatainen has maintained that the Finnish selectors prevented him gaining his true immortality in athletics history.

Bedford finished sixth in that epic 10,000 metres, and looking back now, coldly, I suppose it was clear that he did not have a chance against a man like Vaatainen, a former sprinter who covered the last lap in under 54 seconds. Vaatainen had also been able to prepare solely for that race, and made only a couple of low-key competitive appearances beforehand, whereas Bedford had already taken on the burden of being favourite by his European records.

At the time I was not very objective about it all, and I really believed Dave was going to win, partly because he was running so well early on, and partly because he kept telling everyone he was going to win. I believed him. But I also learned a lot from him simply by observing his situation, watching how he reacted to what happened, and weighing it all up. There were several times when I thought that he was wrong in his preparations for the race, but then he was Dave Bedford so I felt sure he knew what he was doing. As it turned out, he didn't.

My own race, the 1500 metres, was not due to get under way until the Friday, four days after the championships opened. All this time I was unable to run faster than a jog and I was very worried about not getting through my heat. What I really needed was a good pipe opener to blow the dust out of my lungs in the heats and give my breathing a chance. So I led my heat and made it a fast one, easing only when I knew I was safely through to the final on Sunday.

Traditionally, the European 1500 metres final always seemed to be a slow race with a very fast finish, and I knew that if it was like that here I would have no chance. But on the day of the race I bumped into the Italian, Franco Arese, coming out of breakfast in the Athletes Village at Otaniemi. We had raced each other several times before, and I got on well with him.

'Good luck, Franco,' I said. 'You can win the gold medal today.'

'Perhaps, but I am very worried in case the race is one of *tactique*,' he confided, meaning that he did not want to risk a slow-run tactical race, even though he had a tremendous finish.

'I think you can win anyway,' I told him.

'No – I can only win if it is a fast race, not *tactique*,' he answered.

'Well, if it's *tactique* then I've got no chance either,' I said, and I reminded him how I had been left for dead in Turin the previous year, when he won the World Student Games 1500 metres title.

'Then let us make sure it is not a slow race, Brendan,' he said, with a twinkle in his eye. He wanted me to share the pacemaking with him, and because I knew such a plan could help us both, I agreed.

If that seems an unusual alliance, I had already asked John Kirkbride, who was also in the final, if he would assist with such a plan, but he declined. I could understand why because John's best tactics were to follow the pace and use his terrific kick in the last 200 metres.

As we lined up for the final on a damp, miserably grey afternoon there were, I thought, a lot of people who should not have been there – last lap sprinters, who had got through in slow heats, while some good runners like Peter Stewart and the Irishman Frank Murphy (silver medallist in 1969 in the same event) had been eliminated. I had made up my mind that I would do all I could in the final to make it a race for the best runners and not the best sprinters.

Arese, a tall wiry man with a black goatee beard, dashed straight into the lead at the start, and pulled the twelve-man field around in a swift 57.1 seconds for the first 400 metres. Then it was my turn, and I led through the 800 metres in 1:58.7,

As his part of our pact, Arese leads at the bell in the 1971 European 1500m final in Helsinki, with Kirkbride between us and Pekka Vasala fourth.
(Tony Duffy).

until Arese took it up again with a 59.2 seconds third lap. At the bell he led fractionally from Kirkbride, me, and Pekka Vasala of Finland, with the rest close up behind us.

From the bunch Poland's Henryk Szordykowski moved up to second place, and for a few moments I was out of the medals. Kirkbride had edged past me, but as we came into the finishing straight for the last time I tried to dig for every last ounce of effort and about 30 metres from the line I went past John and into third place. Arese won in a championship record of 3:38.4, with Szordykowski taking the silver medal in 3:38.7, while I had got the second bronze medal of my career and in my best-ever time of 3:39.2, a fifth of a second outside the British record. John Kirkbride was fourth in 3:39.5, his best 1500 metres time, and his decision to run his own race almost brought him a medal. Almost.

As Franco Arese and I embraced each other on the track, both delighted that our plan had worked the way we wanted it to, I took a special pleasure in realising that it was the first medal I had actually *planned* to get. At the Commonwealth Games, it virtually just happened, for it was a race in which I had apparently no chance. But there is a unique satisfaction in knowing that you have raced well, using your mind and body together in a competitive situation, and coming out on top.

When I came back to Britain after the championships I was due to run in a two miles event at the Edinburgh Highland Games, which looked like being a fairly hard, but uneventful run. How wrong I was. Meadowbank Stadium was packed with 16,000 spectators, who had been glued to their television sets during the European championships and wanted to see some live athletics now. And of course they particularly wanted to welcome back David Jenkins, who lived in Edinburgh and who, at only nineteen, had won Britain's only gold medal in Helsinki, at 400 metres. He won both the 100 and 200 metres here.

Then we lined up for the two miles, and among the competitors was Ian Stewart, who had missed most of the 1971 season through injury, but was now making his way back to full fitness. I expected him to give me a hard time, because this was the arena where the year before he had won the Commonwealth 5000 metres title and he was a big favourite with the local crowd.

At the gun, however, two Belgian runners took the lead. The Highland Games was incorporating a Scotland v Belgium match, so we let them go, thinking they would come back to us in due course. One of them, Emiel Puttemans, had finished sixth in the Helsinki 5000 metres, but I was still more concerned about Ian Stewart.

The other Belgian, Andre Boonen, led through the opening laps in 61.4 seconds and 2:02.0 before dropping out at two-and-a-half laps and leaving Puttemans some

20 yards clear of the field. The long-striding Puttemans, a gardener from Louvain, was urged on by a noisy group of Belgian sailors, who came from a destroyer anchored in the River Forth, but the rest of us did not expect him to keep going at such a fast pace as he passed the mile point in around 4:07.

As the bell sounded for the last lap it was clear that we had underestimated him. He was still going well, and although Stewart and I were locked together, it was obvious we were fighting for second place. Puttemans was away, and I still look on that race as the only time, apart from the Montreal Olympic 10,000 metres final, that I have been dropped before the final lap. I used to go with the leaders and get beaten on the last lap often enough, but that time I could not have gone with the surprising Puttemans, who to this day remains an enigma. He can run world records, but he has yet to win a major championship race.

And this was his first world record. He crossed the line in 8:17.8 to knock 1.8 seconds off Ron Clarke's existing mark, while in second place Ian and I were having a furious sprint battle. I managed to hold him off by 0.2 seconds, in 8:24.8, my first UK record.

I had one more race that season, which was disastrous. It was a 1500 metres for Britain against West Germany at Crystal Palace, and John Kirkbride and I were up against Harald Norpoth, who had taken the bronze medal in the Helsinki 5000 metres and had a very fast finish. By this stage of the season, I knew my training was only half-hearted because the big challenge was behind me, and my run that day was also only half-hearted. These days I would have packed up before the international match, but then I ran. Mel Watman described the race in *Athletics Weekly* as follows:

> 'If Brendan Foster and John Kirkbride had any thoughts before the race that Harald Norpoth's legendary kick was not so potent these days they were much the wiser and sadder afterwards. They played into his hands by allowing the race to be conducted at a dawdle, and Norpoth's 54.4 last lap (with most of the running put in over the final 200) taught them quite a lesson.'

I finished third in a poor time, noted in my training diary that I was 'not racing at all', and decided to have two-weeks rest. The next season would be the most important yet because 1972 was an Olympic year. I recalled how, at the time of the previous Olympics in 1968, I had been a student in Brighton, struggling to make my university cross country team, and watching the Olympic events on my old five-bob telly. I would not be watching the Munich Olympics on TV if I could help it. I wanted to be there, racing on the track.

Another of my races memorable chiefly for its mediocrity. I lead Kirkbride in the 1500m against West Germany at Crystal Palace in 1971, but (partially hidden) Norpoth was just biding his time. (Tony Duffy).

Six

With the prospect of running in the Olympic Games at stake, there was an added incentive to train hard in the winter of 1971–2, and by January my weekly mileage was around a hundred. I ran few cross country races, not taking them too seriously, as a mental break from the sheer repetitiveness of the high mileage, and I never cease to admire those athletes who train at those levels all year round without hope of ever doing anything more than running well at club level. They never really have a light at the end of the tunnel, and yet they turn out week after week, year after year, just for the pleasure of running. When I have finished my international career, that is what I would like to do – just to be able to run every week, not caring where I come in the race. Somehow, though, I do not think my pride will allow that.

But there was one event back in that winter where every one of a thousand athletes, from scrubber to international, shared an experience which none of us would like to repeat. The race was the English National cross country championship, held at Sutton Coldfield on March 4th, 1972, and runners everywhere still talk of that race in awed tones, like old soldiers recalling a battle long ago.

What happened was that after the race began, with three circuits of Sutton Park to be run, the weather conditions deteriorated badly. The temperature suddenly plummeted, rain turned first to sleet and then to snow, and an icy wind gusted across the open parkland. Visibility was reduced to a few yards in the driving snow, conditions underfoot became treacherous to say the least, and here were a thousand blokes in vests and shorts trying to decide a national championship.

I have run in bad conditions many times, and cross country runners expect it in an English winter. But the conditions that day were unprecedented. As we ran we got colder and colder, instead of the other way round; our limbs were gripped by an icy numbness with muscles almost refusing to work; and all the time there was this constant battering of sleet, hailstones, the lot.

It was like a battle scene in a film, as all around me I could see runners slipping and falling on the mud and snow, and it seemed that those who stood up the longest would finish the highest in the race. I felt I was running quite well, even though every deep breath sent another blast of freezing air down inside me. I managed to keep my feet, until with about 600 yards to go I fell at a stream, and three other runners passed me as I tried to scramble up. It turned out that the fall cost me a place in England's team for the International championships a fortnight later, but at the time I did not give a damn whether I was in the team, out of the team, or on the way home. I just wanted to finish and get the hell out of Sutton Coldfield as fast as possible.

The freak conditions caused a few surprises in the results too. Although one of the favourites, Malcolm Thomas, the big, strong Welsh champion from Thames Valley Harriers, overcame the weather to win, the almost featherweight Trevor Wright, who had been well up with the leaders early on, dropped to twenty-third in the last few hundred yards when his limbs completely seized up. In second place finished, amazingly, our own Bill Robinson from Gateshead Harriers, who had never been placed higher than twenty-third in the National, and was only sixteenth in the Northern championship a few weeks before. Bill is a big lad, which probably helped him through the ordeal, but whilst all around him finished in a state of collapse, he managed to strut around like a prize peacock, and I'm sure his feet did not touch the ground for a fortnight afterwards.

I staggered across the line in fourteenth place, my best-ever position but it didn't mean a thing at that moment. Sue came rushing over with my tracksuit and started rubbing my arms and legs to try to get some life back into them, and I was really feeling sorry for myself, freezing cold, wet, and shaking. Then John Trainor and Lindsay Dunn came in, and suddenly from victim I became the doctor, rubbing their legs as we shared a communal misery. What made it worse was that the changing rooms, for some inexplicable reason, were one-and-a-half miles away from the finish, and the muddy paths and roads back looked like Napoleon's Retreat from Moscow, as cars, bicycles and hundreds of people on foot fought their way back through the wind and sleet.

Athletes who had run world-class marathons and put their bodies on the rack of hard daily training without concern, were crying with the misery of the situation, and the few small tents and marquees that had been erected at the finish for officials and Press soon became casualty clearing stations, with athletes propped up against the canvas walls, still groggy and only semi-conscious. Some were taken to hospital, while the luckier ones wandered around trying to find their wives, tracksuits, or teammates.

Of course, the ones who finished first were the most fortunate because they were out in it for the least time. The solid clubmen, scoring for their teams, were facing that weather for up to half an hour longer, and it must have been a terrific temptation at the end of the second lap, going past the tents, to drop out instead of heading out for a third circuit of the treacherous parkland. But the National means so much that it was a temptation to which few of them responded. It was a credit to their determination that no less than 887 athletes finished in that race and, as was suggested in *Athletics Weekly* afterwards, every single one deserved a medal that day. It really is something now to be able to say, 'I was at Sutton Coldfield in '72!', and everyone you meet who was there has his own story of the day to tell.

Alas, the day was not without its tragedy, and one of the race officials, who had been out in the worst of the weather controlling the finishing funnels, died from a heart attack on his way home afterwards, which must surely have been brought on by his ordeal. But it served to remind all runners just how much they owe to the officials who are prepared to give up their own time to see that cross country events go on, whatever the weather.

The irony of the day's events was that the team selected from the race to represent England in the International championships, which were held that year in Cambridge, found themselves faced with a glorious warm spring day for the International a fortnight later. It says a lot for the versatility of the team that they were still able to win the team championship there despite the complete contrast in conditions. I was a reserve, but of the non-travelling variety, so I missed out on the chance of an all-expenses paid trip to Cambridge, and did a couple of training sessions at home instead.

In May I had the opportunity to try out training at high altitude in St Moritz when the British Board sent a party of middle distance runners there to test the facilities which they intended to use just before the Munich Olympics. Not everyone adapts successfully to altitude training, and I think the idea was that the national coaches should find out then, rather than on the eve of the Olympics, who would be better staying at sea-level.

The theory of using altitude training really arose from the 1968 Olympic Games, which were held at the 7000 feet high Mexico City. Because the air at that height is considerably thinner, and contains less oxygen, it is much more difficult to train or race over the longer distances and the performances in the endurance events at the Mexico Games were well below the usual sea-level standards.

But athletes who had stayed at altitude for a period of some weeks found that when they returned to sea-level their blood had automatically produced extra red cells to cope with the lack of oxygen, and these remained in the blood for a week or ten days afterwards, giving a kind of 'super-charged' effect, even if it was only temporary.

So, by deliberately going to altitude for training before a major Games, an endurance event athlete could produce at will this extra supply of red blood cells to help him in a competition at sea-level, and still break no rules by doing so. The difficulty was in judging how long you needed to return to sea-level before your race. If you came down too soon, the effects wore off; if you came down too late, you did not have enough time to reacclimatise properly. And as everyone's 'best' time for coming down seemed to be different, it was a tricky business to judge.

As so many other countries seemed to be indulging in the practice, it was felt that Britain ought to consider it too. On this occasion we went there for three or four days, and for me it was a first experience of altitude. Perhaps those of us who had not been before had heard too much about its effects, because as soon as we got out of our coach at St Moritz we were all sniffing around trying to spot the difference.

It would be ideal if you could go to altitude without knowing you were there because apart from being a little tired, there did not seem to me to be a noticeable difference, unless you deliberately thought to yourself, 'Oh, yes, I'm at altitude. I mustn't walk up those stairs too quickly or I'll be exhausted.' But then I always managed to adapt well to altitude training, while some others did not. More than one potential medallist in Britain's Olympic team that year was to wish afterwards that they had stayed at home before the Games and not dabbled with altitude. Like everything else, it is horses for courses. First, though, we had to get into the team.

Each country is allowed to send up to three athletes for each event at the Olympic Games, provided they have reached the qualifying standard set for the event, and Britain has so much talent in the middle and long distance events that it is almost as hard to get into the team as it is to run in the Olympics. As the summer approached it was clear that any of half a dozen or more British athletes, including Peter Stewart, Jim Douglas and John Kirkbride, as well as myself, could make it. Someone was going to be left behind.

I started my track racing late, as usual, and was pleased to be able to finish second in the Emsley Carr Mile at Crystal Palace on June 10th. Peter Stewart won the race in a UK record of 3:55.3, while I ran 3:55.9, easily my best, after leading the middle two laps as hard as I could. There seemed little point in running slowly with a sprint finish, because we were supposed to be aiming for the Olympic

Games, not the Toytown Sports. We reached the bell in 2:58.5, which a journalist was quick to point out afterwards was 15 seconds faster than the same point in the Inter-Counties race a few weeks earlier. I told him the athletes should have been taken off the track on the second lap, a comment which was later widely quoted and didn't endear me to certain other athletes. I think they knew I was right, though.

A few days later I turned the tables on Peter Stewart in the GB v Poland match at Meadowbank, where I won the 1500 metres, and in early July I headed off to Scandinavia for a couple of races. In the first I was outsprinted in a 1500 metres race at Oslo by the Dane, Gerd Larsen, and then two days later I went to Stockholm for a mile with Peter Stewart, and among our opponents was a tall, lean Finn called Pekka Vasala, who had finished ninth in the European championships the previous season.

It was quite a good race, with Stewart, Vasala and myself coming down the extra long home straight at the stadium on the last lap together. I just got the

I beat Vasala and Peter Stewart over a mile in Stockholm early in 1972, but I wrongly thought the crowd was slow-handclapping us. (Press Association).

narrowest of verdicts from Vasala, and we were both given a time of 3:57.2, with Stewart just 0.2 seconds behind us. But my immediate reaction was that I never wanted to go back to Stockholm again because all through the race the crowd had been slow-handclapping, even on the last lap. I was disgusted, because it had been a close race to watch, in a reasonable time, and it really annoyed me that they should treat us that way.

Only when I finally did go back to Stockholm two years later did I discover that they had not been slow-handclapping us at all. The Swedish crowd was simply clapping in time to the runners' feet, as their way of participating in the race, and so I had been upset quite needlessly!

It was only just over a week to the AAA Championships at Crystal Palace, and the time seemed to drag by. In that Olympic year the championships took on an extra meaning, because the team for Munich was due to be announced on the Monday following the championships, and I found myself worrying about other runners, and what they were doing, rather than about my own preparations. As usual, we were not clear as to whether the selectors would simply take the first three finishers in the AAA championships, or else review the whole season. The essential thing was to get in that first three, anyway, just as a precaution.

I got through my heat comfortably, behind a Birmingham University student named Ray Smedley, who had been running well recently. But my mind was not totally on athletics that weekend, as it probably should have been.

Sue and I had been making quiet plans for an autumn wedding and we had been on the lookout for a house. We thought we had the problem solved, and on that Friday night we had to make a single phone call to confirm that all was well. When we phoned, we found the deal was off. No reason. We had obviously been 'gazumped' – someone must have made a late offer, higher than we could afford. So suddenly we were back to square one, with no house, and we were in a hell of a state that night. I also slept in a room that looked out on to the main street and I didn't really get a decent night's sleep.

It could be just a coincidence, and I might have run badly anyway, but next day the AAA 1500 metres final was a disaster for me. I found myself at the back of the field at the halfway stage and in a moment of blind panic I went right up to the front and took the lead. With 200 metres left I found myself flagging, and three runners went past me on the outside. In the straight I had nothing left. Of all the days to run like that, this had to be it.

Peter Stewart won in a UK record of 3:38.2, with the surprising Ray Smedley also under the record in second place at 3:38.5 and John Kirkbride equalling it in third place with 3:38.7. I was fourth in 3:39.3, and my fate hung in the balance.

Leading the 1972 AAA 1500m final from Peter Stewart (33) and Ray Smedley,
who surprised us not only by his running but also his unpronounceable vest.
(Mark Shearman).

Was I out of the team, or would they take the whole season into account? If they did not, it would not be fair, because this was my first off-day of the year.

The team was being selected on the following day, Sunday, and I went for an easy run of about nine miles, wondering what was being said at the meeting down in London. Whatever it was, I would have to hold on for another twenty-four hours because the team was not being announced until Monday lunchtime. In that time I went over the situation in my mind, time and again. Sometimes I felt sure they would leave me out; at others I could see that they had to put me in. It was a frustrating time, because I couldn't *do* anything except wait.

On Monday I went for another easy run in the morning, thinking that it would not be long before I knew – yes or no. In fact, no decision had been made after all. When the team was finally announced, sixty-seven athletes had been chosen, but I was not one of them. Neither, though, was John Kirkbride, who finished ahead of me in the AAA race. Instead the selectors had picked, quite rightly, Peter Stewart, who had a good season, and also Ray Smedley, who must have won his place purely on the one race, and left one place open.

What was to happen was that Kirkbride and I would be the British representatives at 1500 metres in Helsinki later that month, where we had a match against Finland and Spain, and whoever finished ahead would get the place. It was a daunting challenge, not only physically, but mentally too, but at least I had another chance. It was not as good as being selected, but it was better than someone else being selected.

That night I went out and did a really hard training session, including running one mile twice, then 600 metres three times, and two 100 metres sprints – all flat out. The next night I went back to the track and ran three flat-out 800 metres, and finished absolutely exhausted and being sick by the side of the track. I poured everything into my training that week, quantity and quality. I had worked so hard in the previous winter to try to get to Munich that I owed it to myself to have one last all-out go at making the team. If I missed out, there was nothing else that season worth bothering about.

John Kirkbride, who came from Cumberland, and I were good mates, and we even sat next to each other in the plane flying out to Helsinki. But it didn't make any difference, because we both knew the situation. Mentally, it was a real ordeal as we knew that one of us would be going to the Olympics, and one of us would not.

In the race Kirk went into the lead at the gun and led us round the first 400 metres in 63.6 seconds, a rather gentle pace, and at that point I went ahead and picked it up. The second lap was a 58.1 and the third 58.9, and from the inside of the track I heard one of the British team calling out to me 'Kirk's dropped'. He had drifted around 40 metres down, and eventually finished fifth.

Pekka Vasala, whom I had beaten in the Stockholm mile, was the better of the Finns, and he sat on my shoulder until at the final bend he came past me. The crowd, of course, went wild, but I would not have cared if ten Finns had come past me at that moment as long as John Kirkbride did not. As Vasala crossed the line and waved to the crowd, I felt like doing the same thing, and the smile on my face afterwards must have looked very strange to the Finns who did not understand why I should be so pleased at being beaten.

I felt sorry for John, who was disappointed not only in losing out but with, for him, such a poor run, and I thought that Britain could be leaving a potential Olympic finallist behind. That night we went out into Helsinki for a meal together, and had a good evening, forgetting the tensions of the previous week.

For although some athletes will tell you that they have to 'hate' their rivals to win, it really is not true. Our sport is concerned with challenge, and one man racing another, but once the race is over there is nothing you can change. You just carry on being normal human beings. He was not John Kirkbride, the Monster from Outer Space; he was another young chap, like myself, and he and I were the only two people who really knew what we had been going through in the past ten days. The officials who had set up our 'trial' could certainly not have imagined it. The matter had been resolved, and at last I could tell myself that I really was going to run in the Olympic Games.

Yet there was still one more twist of fate. Several weeks later, Peter Stewart, who during the summer had broken the UK records at both 1500 metres and one mile, withdrew from the Olympic team because of a persistent back injury which had not cleared up. His unselfishness in withdrawing from the team because he was not fully fit really made a mark on me, because it must have needed a lot of courage to do it, when he could so easily have gone along 'for the ride'. But neither Peter, nor his brother Ian, are the type of athletes who go anywhere for the ride, and so a fortnight after having been in the depths of despair at his failure, John Kirkbride was added to the Munich team. All the strain and tension had been in vain. We were both going, after all. We had shared a room in Helsinki as rivals, and later were able to share a room in Munich as teammates.

Seven

Before going to Munich, I had one more race, which was an 800 metres at Crystal Palace. There were only four runners, and I was the only non-specialist at the distance, which rather put a damper on things before we even started. However, my time of 1:51.1 was a personal best, which showed I was running well, and I managed to finish just outside the first three!

Then on August 9th, I travelled with a group of our other distance men to St Moritz, where we were to undergo another period of acclimatisation at high altitude immediately before the Games. I coped with the altitude quite well, but although St Moritz may be a marvellous place when the snow is on the ground, with all the jet-setters and royalty gathering in the Alpine town for the winter sports and high-flying social life, in August it is pretty dull, like an English seaside town in the winter.

There was not a lot to do, and sitting around waiting for your red blood cells to multiply is not the most fascinating of pastimes. I shared a room with Ian Stewart, and I learned a lot from talking to him in that time, watching him, and even just listening to him. We trained together twice a day in St Moritz, but some of the others used to go up to heights of 8000 or 10,000 feet. Ian and I would just go up with them in the cable car and watch, while we sat and drank tea and ate chocolate. At that height we felt we must be getting fitter simply by breathing the even thinner air!

It was while we were in St Moritz that a new chapter in the Dave Bedford saga blew up, and was for a time to knock every other story off the front pages of the newspapers back in England. Dave had been disappointed at the way things turned out for him in 1971, and had trained even harder in the winter, determined to win a gold medal in Munich. Things had been going well for him early in the season, and at the AAA championships, while I was having such a hard time in the 1500 metres, he put on a scintillating display. On the Friday night he won the 5000 metres in 13:17.2, breaking his own European record by five seconds and missing the world record by only 0.6 seconds. Then, less than twenty hours later, he returned to win the 10,000 metres in 27:52.8, another super-fast time on a very hot afternoon, and one which won him the race by no less than 46 seconds.

But in an Olympic year, everyone wants to put a gold medal round your neck much too soon, as I was to find out myself four years later. A lot of journalists who can barely tell a pole vault pit from a steeplechase barrier suddenly become athletics 'experts' when an Olympic Games approaches, and many of them seemed to think that Dave only had to turn up at the Olympic stadium, trot round the track, and the gold medal would be his. Once again Dave found himself under a lot of pressure through running so well before a major championship, and he did not exactly help matters by telling everyone that he was going to win the gold medal. An athlete may *think* that, but he does himself no favours by spreading the word around.

Dave was up in St Moritz with us, and did some of his training with Ian and myself, and then the pair of them decided to travel to Stockholm for a two miles race. That proved a mistake, at least for Dave. In Stockholm they came up against a Finnish runner named Lasse Viren, who was still not very well known although he had impressed many people in Helsinki a couple of weeks before when he set a Finnish 5000 metre record of 13:19.0, in the match against Britain. This time Viren really demolished the field after Dave had led early in the race, and knocked nearly four seconds off the world record, with 8:14.0. Ian finished fourth in 8:22.0, breaking my UK record, while Dave faded to sixth in 8:28.2, a hundred metres behind Viren. Both British boys therefore suffered a knock to their confidence, and Dave was talking after the race about pulling out of the Olympics altogether after such a 'terrible' run, even though it was his personal best for the distance.

He also had other things on his mind. The International Olympic Committee was meeting in Munich to discuss whether he was eligible for the Games, after a newspaper series featuring him had been widely advertised, and in St Moritz he had upset several members of the British team by taking pot shots with an air rifle, one of which only just missed the British 10,000 metres runner, Lachie Stewart.

On top of all this he was having persistent stomach trouble which was affecting his training, and a medical officer suggested that he was showing the symptoms of a man on the edge of a slight nervous breakdown. In the end the IOC decided that he had no case to answer, so he was cleared, and while he was in Stockholm several British athletes broke into his room at St Moritz and dismantled the air rifle, so that caused no further trouble.

But the uncertainty of this most talented athlete, whose mind was in a turmoil at the time, came to a head on the rough cinder track at St Moritz a few days later. I was warming up to do a session of eight 300 metres runs flat out when Dave came up to me, and asked what I was doing. I told him, and he asked if he could join in, so I reluctantly agreed.

As Dave went to get his spiked shoes on, I had a word with the British coach, Harry Wilson, who was watching.

'Don't let Dave do this session,' I said, 'because I'm running well, and there is no way he is going to stay with me. It won't help him.'

But Dave wanted to do the session, so we set off. The runs were quite fast, I was moving well, and Dave was having trouble holding on, as I suspected. As I was a 1500 metres runner, and he was primarily a 10,000 metres runner, there was no reason to suppose that he would be able to match my speed, and yet after his defeat in Stockholm he was obviously keen to try to sharpen up his speedwork.

After the fifth run, Dave suddenly stopped and I found that I was doing the rest on my own. Dave put his tracksuit on, and went back to the hotel. And that was the last we were to see of him for some time. That night he returned to London in search of treatment for his stomach ailment and, above all, for some peace. Every newspaper had journalists in St Moritz just to keep an eye on what he would be getting up to next, especially after the air rifle incident, and the place must have been getting a little claustrophobic for him.

Distance runners get on well with each other, despite what you may sometimes read, because we are all in the same boat. We see each other at races week after week, month after month, season after season, and I am sure that one of the skills of being a successful international athlete is simply becoming very good at wasting time. You tend to have a lot of it to kill, hanging around, waiting for a race. By August 30th, the day we were finally to travel to Munich, we would have been in St Moritz for three long weeks, and we were not even to have the honour of marching in at the Opening Ceremony, because the Games would have opened a few days before. We watched the colourful ceremony on television, because to enjoy the maximum benefit of the altitude training we had to stay there for as long as possible, while allowing time to reacclimatise on our return to sea-level.

Some of the athletes had already gone to Munich, because they were competing earlier, but the 1500 metres was scheduled for the last three days of the Games and were eventually moved on a day as a result of the tragic Israeli massacre in the Games Village. At one time it looked as though the Games would be stopped, as politics and sport became bloodily intermingled, but I think the decision to carry on with the Games was the right one because it showed the power of sport.

While I was in St Moritz, Sue telephoned to say that she had found a house for us in Gateshead and had put a deposit on it. I can remember saying, 'Oh, smashing, thanks very much' or something equally inane. But when you are in a situation as we were in St Moritz, just sitting around waiting to run, and surrounded by other people who are just sitting around waiting to run, the real world becomes very distant and unreal. In fact, knowing that Sue and I now had a house to move into when we got married was a great relief, even if I did not show it in the best way at the time.

In Munich the pressure on Dave Bedford increased, especially after he looked as if he was back to his best in his 10,000 metres heat. He ran over the line with Emiel Puttemans, in first place, as both of them broke the Olympic record by over half a minute. In the final, though, it was the same story as in Helsinki. Dave tried everything he knew to burn off his rivals with a fierce pace from the front, but a group of them just latched on to him and at the 6000 metres point they began to pull away. Lasse Viren of Finland, who had fallen earlier in the race, timed his effort perfectly and broke up the leading group with a long run for home to win in a world record of 27:38.4. Bedford finished sixth, but he was not disgraced.

The Olympic Stadium, with its unique roof which looked like a series of vast spiders' webs, was an awe inspiring place, where the noise seemed to echo round and round, and waiting to come out onto the track from the competitors' tunnel was rather like the Christians must have felt in Ancient Rome before being led out to the lions.

I was reasonably satisfied with my own preparations, and six days before my 1500 metres heat I ran a session of eight 400 metres with 90 seconds rest, with an average of 56.8 seconds, my best-ever for the session.

There were to be seven heats, with the first four from each plus the two fastest losers, to go through to the semi-finals next day. I was fairly relaxed before my heat, because I knew I need run just reasonably to get through, even though I had the American Dave Wottle (with his trademark of the peaked cap), who had earlier won the 800 metres, in my heat. In the end, four of us – Thomas Wessinghage of West Germany, Wottle, Jean-Pierre Dufresne of France and myself – crossed the line together with just a stride between us, all safely through.

There were casualties in other heats, though, the most notable being Jim Ryun of the USA, the world record holder for the event. He had been drawn in the same heat as the reigning Olympic champion, Kip Keino, because the American authorities had submitted his best time for the season as 3:52.8, without adding

80

that it was for a mile, not 1500 metres (for which it would have been about 3:35). The seeding computer, not being an athletics fan, had obviously not heard of Ryun. That need not have mattered, though, except that he collided with a Ghanaian runner, fell over, and by the time he got to his feet it was too late to catch the field, and he was eliminated, despite running the last lap in under 55 seconds. His time was 3:51.5, including the fall, so I daresay the computer would have turned round and said 'Told you so!'.

Ray Smedley got through his heat safely, but the other British runner, John Kirkbride, was run out of it. John could hardly have been in the best frame of mind in his preparation, not really knowing whether he was coming or going, as first he was out of the team, and then a fortnight later, in.

The semi-finals were next day, and divided into three heats, with the first three in each, plus the fastest loser, to qualify for the final. I was very nervous warming up this time, because I had several people who had beaten me earlier in the season in my heat, including Vasala of Finland, and Larsen of Denmark, plus the European champion Franco Arese and the strong New Zealand 'dark horse' Rod Dixon. We did have one advantage in that being the last semi-final and knowing that the first two had been won outside 3:41, we could try to ensure that the fastest loser came from our heat if the pace was quick enough.

So Arese and I made a plan, as we had in Helsinki a year before, to share the pace. Franco led round the first circuit in 57.7 seconds, then I took over, leading through 800 metres in 1:59 and the bell in 2:58.4, at which point I was swallowed up by the field. But I found the strength to come back around the final bend and down the home straight until I was in a qualifying position, and then eased back a little in the last 20 metres to finish third. Rod Dixon and Pekka Vasala crossed the line together in 3:37.9, while my time of 3:38.2 equalled Peter Stewart's UK record. I was happy with the run, because I had felt quite comfortable, almost coasting in at the end, but then I remembered that I had to do it all again the next day.

Warming up for any race is a nerve-wracking business, but warming up for an Olympic final must be the tensest situation in which an athlete can find himself. There was a big warm-up area outside the stadium, across a road, and you reached the stadium by an underground tunnel system, where you were checked for your number, the spikes in your shoes, and so on, and then checked again.

In a way, it was quite amusing, because there were all of the other 1500 metres finalists warming up, looking grim, and with a coach and a physiotherapist accompanying each one, or so it seemed. All I had was steeplechaser Andy Holden to carry my bag!

At the gun, I went straight into the lead, not because I had any particular plan

82

There was no holding Pekka Vasala in Munich, as he wins the Olympic 1500m title from Kip Keino, Rod Dixon and Mike Boit. I was nearly caught napping for fifth place by Mignon (59). (Tony Duffy).

to push the pace, but because I wanted to be able to see clearly when Kip Keino made his break, as I was sure he would, so that I could try to follow. We went round the first 400 metres in 61.4 seconds, and all the time I was waiting, waiting for him to come, but he did not. I was still ahead approaching 800 metres, with my head down and afraid to look up, because it was such an important event.

My legs felt stiff and tired from two fast races in two days, but I was ready for Keino to come. Just before the 800 metres mark, he came. He began driving hard, covering the next 300 metres in 42 seconds, with Vasala and Dixon right behind him, and myself grimly trying to hold on in fifth place. At the bell there was still a bunch of us together, elbows digging into each other, desperately trying to stay in contact with Keino, but the man in charge was really Pekka Vasala, who was showing very little sign of strain, despite the fact that we were now rocketing along, and making up for the slow start.

Down the back straight of the final lap I could see Keino and Vasala pulling away from me, and as the leaders came into the finishing straight, Vasala got up onto his toes and sprinted past Keino. In the stands, of course, the Finnish fans were going mad, because they had already seen Lasse Viren win his second gold medal of the Games, the 5000 metres, earlier in the afternoon, and now here was Vasala winning Finland's third. Between them, they had won the three classic middle distance track events of the Olympics – the 1500, the 5000 and the 10,000 metres.

Keino, who could not answer Vasala's challenge, took the silver medal in the 1500 metres, and Rod Dixon of New Zealand, who like myself only just made his country's Olympic team, was a surprise third. It was not the last I was to see of Mr Dixon either.

For myself, fifth place was pleasing enough, even though I made the inexcusable schoolboy mistake of easing up before the finishing line, and nearly got caught by the fast-finishing Herman Mignon of Belgium. But I had done all I could, including my fastest-ever 800 metres – 1:51 – in the last two laps of the race. Yet Vasala ran the last 800 metres in 1:48.8, and that sort of speed was just beyond me even in a scratch 800 metres, let alone at the end of a 1500 metres. Although I did not consider it at the time, I am convinced that I was running the wrong event in 1972, and that I should have been in the 5000 metres, where Ian Stewart took the bronze medal behind Viren.

Still, I now at least had some Olympic experience. I no longer felt a novice, and I was sure of one thing. That would not be my last Olympic Games. I would be back in 1976.

Eight

It was good to be able to relax for a while when I got home, for the tensions of the actual Olympic competition, the most important in athletics, was magnified by the intense security surrounding the Olympic Village. After the tragic end to the Israeli affair, everyone was naturally on tenterhooks, and our peace of mind was hardly helped by the sick jokers who put round rumours that bombs had been planted under certain team quarters in the Village and were due to go off on the final night of the Games. Not only was this in very poor taste, in view of the already heavy loss of life, but a lot of young competitors, particularly the girls, were extremely and genuinely frightened by the rumours.

Everywhere you went in Munich you were watched by police and armed guards, and you almost needed your identity card to clean your teeth. It was extremely sad that international sport, supposedly fostering goodwill, had come to this, but I suppose that the sheer size and international importance of the Olympic Games has made it a tempting platform for any political group wishing maximum publicity.

Personally, I would like to see the Olympics awarded to a country rather than a specific city. At present, I feel the Games are too large, with too many sports, and everything unnecessarily concentrated in one place. If a nation held them, then the sports could be spread out around different centres, possibly cutting down the cost, by using existing facilities, and also reducing the temptation for various groups to use the Games as a political stage. For the 1984 Olympics only one city, Los Angeles, has applied, and yet if a country could put in for them then perhaps Britain would have done so (with the athletics, naturally, to be staged at Gateshead!).

When we flew back to London it was an immense relief. I had been away nearly five weeks, three of them in St Moritz, before going straight to Munich, so it was marvellous to be reunited with my family again. My mother had been terrified, as she always is when she watches me run, and was probably as nervous as me before the 1500 metres final. In fact I think she was half hoping that I wouldn't get through to the final so that she would not have to watch it.

I had no more races after the Olympic final that summer. I just stopped running for a month, and relaxed a little. Everyone seemed very pleased with my Munich performances, and there were letters and phone calls and newspapers calling round. I felt for a while as if I had won the gold medal, instead of finishing fifth, especially when I was presented with a big cake at school decorated with the words 'Well done, Brendan', and when Hebburn Council presented me with a silver salver.

But I had one more important Saturday fixture coming up. On October 28th 1972 Sue and I were married at St Peter's Church, Low Fell. It was a quiet wedding, because we did not want much of a fuss made, and there were about thirty guests – my family, Sue's family, and a few close friends from Gateshead Harriers. Sue had done all the organising while I was away, and it all went like clockwork.

There were so few problems that even though it was an 11 o'clock wedding, I still had time for a six-mile training run beforehand. But, looking at my training diary, I see that I missed out training next day. I wonder why on earth that was?

We went to Edinburgh for a short honeymoon. Very short, in fact, because we could not afford more than a day there, and we came back skint on the Monday. The local evening newspaper, meanwhile, ran a story that day saying, 'Secret wedding of Brendan Foster. Has he gone to Edinburgh, Majorca or Scandinavia for his honeymoon?' In fact, I bought a copy of the paper at the corner shop in Gateshead and sat at home with Sue that Monday night, wondering with all the other readers whether we had gone to Majorca for our honeymoon.

We started our married life with a few chairs borrowed from an aunt, and I did a bit of painting during the week I had been given off school. That is probably the last time I did any painting. But it was a pleasant house in Wells Gardens, Low Fell, on the outskirts of Gateshead, and we were to live there for five years.

In that time I came to realise even more just what a great source of strength Sue is to me, because without her support I could never hope to go on putting my head on the competitive block. You cannot take on the world by yourself, because if you get absolutely hammered, and everyone is saying 'Foster's useless', and nobody wants to know you, then you have got to have somewhere to go to regain your composure and determination. Thankfully, I suppose I am a fairly reliable runner, and not given to quitting or being content with second place, so Sue knows that at the end of the day I will have done the best I can.

Sue was a good all-round sports girl herself when she was at school in Essex, playing hockey, swimming and high jumping, but like so many others she unfortunately gave it all up when she went to university, where we met. Now, though, after a few years of relative inactivity, she has taken up jogging and yoga, and I know that she would like to play squash and badminton too if she had a husband who was more inclined that way. The trouble is, I simply cannot risk getting injured in sports which demand muscular exertion of such a different type from running.

I feel sad about this, but Sue is not the sort of girl to let herself become an athletics widow. We often combine our holidays with my concentrated training periods, and while I am pounding out the miles in Spain or South Africa, Sue is quite happily engrossed in a book. She is a keen reader, and has always been good at occupying herself. Since our son, Paul, was born that has not needed a great deal of effort either.

She still insists on washing my running kit every day, because although I am not all that concerned about whether my tracksuit has been freshly laundered before I go out training, Sue tends to be. On Sunday mornings she manages to cope quite easily with hordes of Gateshead Harriers descending on our house, where some of us meet for a 'ritual' twenty miles road run every week, and she supplies endless cups of tea for everyone while still cooking our Sunday lunch and looking after Paul.

The one area where Sue is not happy is in the spotlight, and she has often turned down requests from women's magazines to interview her. We also have a rule not to let the media into our house, because so much of our life now is in a kind of public arena that we like to have somewhere to go for privacy. We feel the inside of our house is private to us, and the friends we choose to invite in.

Sue says she can always tell when I'm ready for a big race, but although I don't think I'm particularly awkward around race time, she is probably right. In fact, I know I *do* get irritable, but when she says she can tell, it makes me worse! She understands, though, very clearly what I go through in the tense build-up to an important event, and this understanding in itself is a great strength and reassurance to me.

She shares my disappointments and my successes, but above all she keeps my feet on the ground, because to her I am not 'Brendan Foster, the Olympic Athlete'. I am simply her husband, and although that is easy to say, I imagine it can be a problem in show business or top-class sport if a wife starts to believe that her husband is anything more than a husband.

Although she is a southerner, Sue did not need to adjust to living in the north-east when we married, because she had already done so for over a year. She had moved up to Gateshead to live in a flat in Low Fell, and worked as a commercial assistant in a local office, while I had been living at my parents' home in Hebburn. Now we were facing a new life together, and it was also time to have a re-think about my future as an athlete. Was I in the wrong event?

My experience in Munich, where I had found myself running my fastest-ever 800 metres at the end of the 1500 metres and still being dropped by Vasala and Keino, had left its mark on me though. I wondered how I could ever hope to match that sort of speed, because my best 800 metres was 1:51, and shortly before the Games Vasala, for instance, had run 1:44.5. I had a long talk with Stan Long and Lindsay Dunn that winter, and we all agreed that my cross country and road performances indicated that I could handle a longer distance on the track. So the decision was made: from now on I was going to be a 5000 metres runner.

This did not mean that I woke up next morning with an extra head, or turned green overnight. The winter training was virtually the same, with two or three runs a day, totalling around a hundred miles a week. The regularity of the training is as important as the volume. That year we spent Christmas with Sue's parents at Clacton, and on Christmas morning I was out doing a hard session of 1000 metres runs, with a seven-mile steady run in the evening. It is not the sacrifice you might think, either, because running becomes such a part of you that to miss a day's training, even if it is Christmas Day, leaves you feeling as if you have not bothered to clean your teeth that day. It is second nature, and it has to be, because there are plenty of days when you feel tired or rough, and would gladly find an excuse to miss training. But once you do that, it can become a habit, and the whole of your background training programme is undermined by the blank days.

In January 1973 I had the chance to run on an indoor track for the first time when I was invited to take part in some US indoor meetings. Ian Stewart came with me, and at the first meeting, in Washington, he set a European indoor two miles record of 8:28.4. I finished third in the mile in 4:01.9, being outkicked on the last lap by the Americans Bob Wheeler and Juris Luzins, but the time was very satisfactory for me as I had done no proper speedwork and it was only the middle of January.

The next night we were in New York, where I won the two miles in 8:38.6, while Ian was second in the mile (4:05.3). My feet were sore with blisters after only half a mile, because running indoors was a new experience. There is a terrific atmosphere at an American indoor meeting, rather like a circus. There is no concept of laps, because with eleven to the mile they are just too short to think of as a specific distance, so you just run until they tell you to stop.

88

Those were, it transpired, the only two indoor races I have run. The following Friday we were due to race in Philadelphia, so we travelled there on the Sunday, and then spent two days trying to get in some proper training. If we wanted to run on an indoor track we had to travel right across the city to Villanova University and we got a bit sick of this. No one from the meeting seemed to be around to show us where to go, or take any interest in us at all. There was no hospitality, we had to pay towards our own meals, and the meeting organisers generally did not seem to care that we were even around town.

By Wednesday we were thoroughly fed up with this, and decided we were going home. The only problem was that, like all British athletes travelling overseas,

Some of my best competitive runs have been around Sutton Park, Sutton Coldfield, scene of the annual AAA national road relay.

whether in a party of one or one hundred, we had a team manager with us, appointed by the British Amateur Athletic Board. He insisted that we stayed; we insisted that we left. Finally, after a few well chosen words from Ian, who always speaks his mind whatever the subject, the team manager came round to our way of thinking, and we left for the airport.

Only when we had gone safely through the check-in desk did we phone the meeting organisers and tell them that we were leaving, in case they tried to stop us, but they did not. In fact, they had shown so little interest in us that I doubt whether they even knew we had arrived until we left.

Now technically the team manager was right. We had agreed to run in the meeting. But meeting organisers also have a certain obligation to look after their athletes, and this was simply not happening. So we went home.

The National cross country championships that year were at Parliament Hill Fields, Hampstead, and a complete contrast to the blizzard at Sutton Coldfield in 1972. The course was dry, the day had a pleasant touch of early spring, and the team race turned out to be the closest for many years. In cross country events such as this, the finishing positions of each club's first six finishers are added together so that the team with the lowest total wins. In this sort of race, with nearly 1200 runners, you have to get as many of your club runners 'packed' together in the low-scoring high positions.

We had Bill Robinson in sixth place, proving that his run the previous year had not been a fluke, and then I was twelfth. John Caine was thirty-fourth and Charlie Spedding thirty-sixth, so we had two-thirds of our scoring team home before anyone else. Then came an agonising gap, as other clubs saw their fourth, fifth, and even sixth men finish to complete their team. Our two big rival clubs were Bolton and Tipton, and Bolton's final man was 103rd, Tipton's 104th, and then our last two came in – Lindsay Dunn (105th) and John Trainor (106th). With nearly 200 clubs being represented in the race, it was amazing that the Big Three should all finish their teams so close together, and when the scores were added up it was found that Gateshead Harriers had won by just six points!

The journey home on the train that night was one of great celebration, as we were running up and down the corridor, filling the coveted Frank Wynne Cup, awarded to the winning team, with beer. It was the finest form of celebration, because if you are going to celebrate in athletics, you might as well do it with the people with whom you train and compete most of the time.

In my case, that meant the lads of Gateshead Harriers. From being a small club not so many years before, here we were the National cross country champions, and the companionship and mutual respect built up over many thousands of

90

It was a proud moment for coach Stan Long (wearing glasses) when Gateshead Harriers first won the National cross country team title in 1973. (Ron Linstead).

shared training miles in that time had paid dividends. We had achieved something *together*, which in an individualist's sport like athletics is very rare.

Celebrating a success with the Great Britain team is never anywhere near as meaningful. If Geoff Capes throws the shot more than 70 feet, then that is great for Geoff, but it is not relevant to how fast I run the 5000 metres. Some of the athletes in the British athletics team you never see from one year's end to the next. But at Gateshead we had sweated and gasped, often on cold, wet winter nights when anyone in their right mind would surely be in front of a warm fire instead of running themselves to exhaustion over a hilly ten miles.

Gateshead went on to win the National cross country title again in 1975, 1976 and 1977, but that first time still lives as a memorable day. My own twelfth place in the race meant that once more I was non-travelling reserve for the International Cross Country Championships, but I did get a run abroad several weeks later, in Italy. The race was the unique Five Mills event at Vittoria Olona, near Milan, which is an experience in itself, and that year produced one of my best-ever cross country performances. The race starts in a stadium packed with 20,000 people, and the whole course is so swamped with spectators that when you are running you cannot even see where it is, because they are standing on it. But as you run towards them, around the one-mile circuit which comprises each lap, they move back, like the Red Sea parting, and the course appears, marked out by human bodies.

You go across some fields, then alongside the smelliest river you have ever known in your life, jumping over holes in the canal bank, and then run into the mills themselves. You have to enter through someone's backyard and into their back kitchen, then up about six steps on to the mill, which is next to the kitchen because the flour used to come straight into it from the mill.

Then you go across a bridge, where wheels are turning and water is being thrown all over the place, and get barked at by yelping dogs, while trying to keep your feet on the slippery cobblestones. The course goes through a chicken yard, where all the chickens fly up in the air, and then you go back into the stadium for a lap of the track before heading out again for the next circuit. There are five laps in all, and everyone has run there over the years, including Abebe Bikila, Ron Clarke, Billy Mills, Mamo Wolde, and even the former Olympic 400 metres hurdle champion, John Akii-Bua of Uganda, who was last when he ran.

I shared the lead in the early stages with Frank Shorter, who six months before had won the Olympic marathon title in Munich, and after a great battle he got away from me over the final 800 metres. But we were well ahead of a good international field, including Finland's Olympic steeplechase bronze medallist Tapio Kantanen, and Dave Bedford, who had won the National cross country title several weeks earlier.

I knew I was running well, and my training mileage had been good. In the week after the National, for instance, I had reached 123 miles, which was a lot for me. The question, though, was how best to treat the summer season, which would be a difficult one. Although it was only March 1973, I was already thinking about the 1974 Commonwealth Games, which were to be held the following January, and

In the 1973 Five Mills cross country race near Milan I followed Frank Shorter along the banks of the smelliest river in which I've ever tried to avoid falling.

the trials for which were to be staged in September. It was no good coming out with a blaze of good early season track times if I was not able to continue it until the trials.

In the middle of April I wrote in my training diary: 'As things stand at the moment, I must aim for the Commonwealth trials 5000 or 1500 metres. This means that I must be at a peak on September 29th. After that, if selected, I will build up again for January. Looking at last year, I ran my first serious race thirteen weeks before the Olympics. If I use the same principle, then I can start racing seriously on July 1st. Before this date I must only run 400 and 800 metres.'

So on July 1st I had my first serious race of the year, a mile at South Shields, which I won in 3:59.2. The build-up to it had not been without problems: a nasty hamstring injury in May cost me quite a bit of training, but I felt that I was getting back into good shape. Then a fortnight later I ran my official debut at 5000 metres in the AAA Championships at Crystal Palace. Although I had run that 14:36 in Trinidad two years before, I felt I could perhaps trim a second or two off that now, and went down to London on the Friday reasonably confident.

Dave Bedford had offered to put me up overnight at his flat, an offer I gladly accepted. Like myself, Dave had suffered some injury problems, and was making his first major appearance of the season in the 10,000 metres at the AAA championships on the Friday evening. He was holder of the title, but his training had been only a fraction of his normal load in recent months. Only he knew that in the past month his form had picked up considerably, and at the South Shields meeting he had won the two miles in 8:35.0, nearly 20 seconds ahead of the next man. Only he knew that he was going for a very, very fast time, because on this occasion he said nothing beforehand, and just got on with the running. The change in his fortunes was quickly apparent.

He broke away at the half distance, reached in 13:39.4, and with only the relatively small crowd which attends the Friday evening of the meeting to cheer him on, he finished in a new world record time of 27:30.8, knocking 7.6 seconds off the time Lasse Viren had set when winning in Munich. Dave had not forgotten Munich, either, and one of his first actions after hearing the time was to jog over to the main stand and stick a couple of fingers up in the direction of the press box, as his answer to some of the things that had been written about him after his Munich disappointment.

That night he was walking on air, completely unable to sleep, and ended up going for a walk on Hampstead Heath in the early hours of the morning. When you train for year after year with an achievement like that as one of your targets, you simply cannot just pack up your bags straight afterwards and say, 'Well, that's

1973: My 5000 metres debut in the AAA Championships at Crystal Palace. (Wilf Wardle).

that then'. You need time to unwind. But he did everything he could to help me because he knew I was competing next day, and although he had real cause for celebration that night he treated me well.

In fact, he was competing next day too, and I was to challenge him for his title in the 5000 metres. I knew he would be in no condition for a fast run, though, because even world record holders need to sleep, and that is what he was unable to do that night.

In the race I felt comfortable for the first eight laps, before hitting the front and opening up a gap on the rest. The last 2000 metres took 5:13.6, which was ten seconds faster than the first, and the last lap was 60.4 seconds. I was told afterwards that my time, 13:23.8, was the fastest-ever 'debut' by anyone in the 5000 metres, which was encouraging, especially as I beat Ian Stewart by some seven seconds. 'Typical bloody Crystal Palace run,' groaned Ian afterwards and, as I told a group of journalists afterwards who wanted to know if my switch was permanent, 'You can't consider yourself a 5000 metres runner after one or two races'. But I was quietly pleased that it had seemed so comparatively easy, and that Stan, Lindsay and I had made the right decision. I did have a new event.

The following week I took a group of boys from the school on a hiking trip to the Lake District, and then a week later Sue and I went with my mate and regular training partner, Wilf Wardle, and his wife for a week's holiday in a Northumberland cottage. Wilf and I got some great training done, well over a hundred miles in the week, and I had turned down selection for Britain's European Cup semi-final team who were to compete in Oslo that week.

In mid-August I ran a 1500 metres at the Edinburgh Highland Games, and managed to get tripped and bruised at the first bend, and had to limp almost the first 200 metres. Rod Dixon and John Kirkbride had a little too much for me that day, and I finished third in 3:42.0, but as I was still doing a very high bulk mileage, I was not too worried. A couple of days later, though, a sore hip developed and this was a little bit more worrying, because I had planned to have two races in three days the following weekend: a 1500 metres for Britain in the match against Hungary at Crystal Palace on the Saturday, and an invitation two miles during the same meeting on the Monday, which was August Bank Holiday.

Norman Anderson, my physio in Newcastle, treated it with ultra-sonics, and diagnosed that it was a muscle stretched over the hip bone which was causing the trouble, probably brought about by the running on uneven surfaces in Northumberland. 'All it will do is hurt,' he said, 'it shouldn't get any worse.'

So that was a load off my mind, because after the 1500 metres, in which I dead-heated with Frank Clement in 3:38.5, my leg was so sore I could hardly walk. If

On the way to my first AAA 5000m title, as Dave Black and Ian Stewart try to close the gap in the 1973 championships. (Mark Shearman).

Norman hadn't talked to me as he did, I certainly would not have run the two miles, because I would have been afraid of aggravating the injury. I have got a lot to thank him for, because that weekend was probably the turning point in my international career.

The two miles was to be more than just another race. Stan Long, Lindsay Dunn and I had sat down over a couple of pints in the pub a week before and decided that it was a good opportunity to go for the world record. The current record stood to Lasse Viren at 8:14.0, set just before the Munich Olympics in that race at Stockholm which had Dave Bedford worrying about his Munich preparation.

We set a target of 8:12 – two separate miles in 4:06 – but the problem was going to be finding a pacemaker who could take me through that first mile fast enough

Is it? Isn't it? It was some time before I found I really had broken the world two miles record at Crystal Palace in August 1973. (Ed Lacey).

for me to have a chance of the record. A lot of our 1500 metres specialists were asked but none was willing, which was a bit disappointing to me as I felt I had contributed to some of their fast times by leading in the past.

Eventually Andy Holden, a steeplechase specialist, was the man who took us through the first lap in 60.8 seconds, and although I kidded him about it at the time and said he only did it because he likes to be seen on TV, he laid a valuable foundation for a fast time. Then Tony Simmons took over and we went past the half-mile in 2:01.4 and the three-quarter mile in 3:03.9, but midway through the fourth lap I could tell he was flagging and I had to make a quick decision whether to pick it up myself, even though there was still more than half the distance to run. There was really no choice. I wanted that record. At the end of the first mile, reached within schedule at 4:05.4, I could sense that I was well clear of the field.

In the sixth and seventh laps the fast early tempo caught up with me, and having to run alone they were both outside 63 seconds, as against the average of around 61.7 seconds. I needed to break the world record. The crowd in the main stand were tremendous, and lifted me mentally each time I came into the home straight. If you feel that someone else wants you to succeed, it makes you that much more determined when your legs and body are crying out for a rest.

98

But at that time the back straight at Crystal Palace did not have its own stand, as it does today. It was just an open emptiness, and it was like running into a vacuum every time I left the comforting noise of the main stand. It was also here that I felt the pain more intensely, particularly in my head, but now as I approached the bell for the last lap I knew I had to raise the pace for just one more circuit, as I had done so many times in mile and 1500 metres races.

My mind shut off the noise of the crowd momentarily as I approached the start of the last lap. I had to hear what the timekeeper called out this time, so I knew how close I was. I had come this far, I had to try to finish the job.

'Seven-thirteen, seven-fourteen . . .' and I was past him. One more lap in under 60 seconds, something I had done so many times in training and racing, and a world record would be mine. But I was not starting fresh. I had the fatigue and heaviness of seven hard laps piled up in my body, and the green grass on the infield looked like an inviting place to lay a weary body.

As I set off on that last lap, I was cursing to myself, because I knew it was going to hurt. Once more into the vacuum, and then a final rally in the home straight, trying to find an extra surge of energy which would take me round that circuit in under a minute. And then I was through the tape, and it was too late to worry. I looked briefly back down the home straight and there was no one else in sight. I have never liked running purely against the clock, I prefer a racing situation, but if I had relied on that, I would still be coming round the final bend.

Had I or hadn't I broken the record? No one seemed to know. Then finally the announcement: 'First, number four, Brendan Foster of Gateshead Harriers in 8 minutes 14.2 seconds . . .'. I had missed it, by a watch's tick, a mere fifth of a second. It was a United Kingdom national record, knocking nearly eight seconds off Ian Stewart's time, and it was ten seconds faster than I had ever run for the distance, but it was not a world record, and it was difficult not to be disappointed at coming so close.

After the prize presentation, I went up to the Press Box at the back of the main stand at Crystal Palace, and told the assembled journalists of my talk over a couple of pints with Stan and Lindsay, and how we had hoped for 8:12. They were annoyed on my behalf that no pacemaker had been added to the field, but really there was no one to blame for my missing the record, I felt, other than myself. I had slowed down to outside 63 seconds for two laps, and for that lack of concentration I felt that I probably did not deserve the record.

It must have been at least half an hour after the race that I was suddenly given a piece of stunning news. Mel Watman, the editor of *Athletics Weekly*, came in to the room and said, 'I've got some good news, Brendan. You've broken the record.'

I didn't understand what he meant, until he explained that the judges had studied the photo-finish picture at the request of Arthur Gold, the secretary of the British Amateur Athletic Board, and the time recorder on that clearly showed that I crossed the line in 8 minutes 13.68 seconds. Three official timekeepers had originally taken my run as 8:14.2, 8:14.2 and 8:13.8. But there is always a fractional delay in human timekeeping, as the brain sends the message to the thumb to press the button, and the introduction of automatic electrical timekeeping was becoming more widespread. I was certainly glad it was in use that day, because although my time had to be rounded up to the nearest fifth of a second – 8:13.8 in this case – it still meant I was inside Lasse Viren's record.

I did not sleep much that night, and it took a few more days to finally sink in. But as I travelled back on the train to Newcastle next day, I was able to savour the feeling of being a world record holder. There was only one irritating snag about it. Although it was the fastest outdoor performance, and was accepted as a world record by the International Amateur Athletic Federation after they had been sent a copy of the photo-finish, I had to recall that it was not the absolute fastest two miles of all time. Emiel Puttemans of Belgium had clocked 8:13.2 on an indoor track earlier that year, which was probably more difficult with its tight bends. So my world record had a little shadow over it, and I thought how nice it would be to set one that no one could dispute with photo-finishes or indoor performances.

There was one more chapter to the story of my run, though. Several years later the IAAF, which ratifies world records and awards special plaques to the athletes concerned, decided in their gradual switch towards metric events only, to discontinue a two miles world record list. So although one day soon someone will certainly run outdoors faster than my 8:13.8, at least I managed to have the last official word on the event.

Less than a fortnight later, I was due to have my second serious 5000 metres race. I had been picked to run the event for Britain in the European Cup final, which that year was taking place at Meadowbank Stadium, Edinburgh. It was a race I approached with some trepidation because it included the Olympic champion, Lasse Viren, representing Finland, and the man known as the 'running skeleton', Harald Norpoth of West Germany, the bronze medallist at the 1971 European championships. Norpoth had won all three of the previous European Cup final 5000 metres, and possessed one of the fastest finishes in international racing, as John Kirkbride and I had found out when he breezed past us, in that 1500 metres at Crystal Palace two years earlier. This was to be Norpoth's fiftieth and last international appearance for his country, and so naturally he wanted it to be a winning one.

MONDAY... AUGUST 27th.... CRYSTAL PALACE
2 MILE WORLD RECORD ..... 8 min. 13.8 secs.

To.... A
'REET CANNY LAD'

Ye'ave dun the
Geordies prood.....

well
done
Brendan!

From J.D. and all club members of
GATESHEAD HARRIERS ATHLETIC CLUB

*A unique message of
congratulations from
the lads at the club.*

It was a formidable field, and my confidence was not improved by suffering a severe stomach upset in the ten days before the race. Every time I went out for a run I had to dive for the nearest bushes after a few miles, and it did not seem to be getting better, even though I had some tablets to combat it.

The European Cup final was quite a memorable one for Britain, because on the opening day, Saturday, Frank Clement won the 1500 metres by leading most of the way, and on Sunday, with the weather at its worst, there was a string of British successes. Alan Pascoe won the 400 metres hurdles in his first season at the event; Andy Carter beat the Soviet Olympic silver medallist Yevgeniy Arzhanov to win the 800 metres; and, most surprising of all, Chris Monk held off a strong sprint field to win the 200 metres. Perhaps it was being used to the miserable weather, and having to train so often in it, which helped the British athletes, or perhaps it was just an inspired day. But, great though that was, it put a lot of pressure on me as I warmed up in the biting wind with everyone saying, 'Your turn next, Brendan.'

I do not like making excuses before a race, because so many people do it as a sort of psychological crutch on which to lean if things do not go as well as they hope. So I said nothing, but I felt far from comfortable as the six of us lined up for the race, with the rain-soaked track covered in puddles, and those of the 12,000 crowd who were in the open huddling under umbrellas, soggy newspapers and programmes.

At the gun we hardly moved, and the first 200 metres was covered in 40 seconds, which is terribly slow. But with points counting for so much in this competition, times meant nothing, and I had half expected a very slow race with a fast finish. Lasse Viren moved into the lead to pass the 400 metres mark in 75.2 seconds, but he looked heavy, even overweight, and had not been running well enough since Munich to suggest that he was in anything like his Olympic form.

So around and around the track we went, scarcely more than jogging, although with my stomach rumbling and protesting I would have been quite happy to walk if the others had wanted to. The crowd began to get a little irritated, and some booing and slow handclapping broke out, except in one part, where a whole party of 300 Hebburn kids and teachers from St Joseph's School were sitting. (Afterwards I was asked if the booing worried me, and I replied that I knew they weren't booing me, because I had brought half of the crowd with me!)

The race was being played just as I wanted it, because if the others had done their homework properly they would have realised that the best way to dispose of me, a novice at the event, would be push it hard all the way. Instead, we almost had time for a committee meeting on the way round.

I did not want the race to go to the other extreme, however, because I knew that Norpoth was very rarely beaten in a fast last lap at the end of a slow race. So as we approached the 3000 metres mark, I took a quick look up at the stands and then charged into the next lap as hard as I could. Momentarily the others hesitated, or perhaps they were asleep, but three of them – Mikhail Zhelobovskiy of the USSR, Norpoth, and a little-known East German named Manfred Kuschmann, followed me.

The next 400 metres was just a shade outside 60 seconds, and it was too much for Viren, who dropped back, out of contention. His post-Munich celebrations had left him short of training and, as I had suspected, he would not be a factor. Not that he was too worried, I'm sure. Unlike the rest of us, he at least had two Olympic titles safe in his pocket.

I kept the pace boiling, but at the bell Kuschmann and Norpoth both went past me, sprinting hard. It was slightly worrying to see them going as fast as that, but by attempting such a long run for home they would be slightly susceptible in the closing stages. I tried to keep my head, and on the back straight gradually pulled back the emaciated figure of Norpoth, and around the final bend closed up on the dark blue vest of Kuschmann. As we came into the home straight I knew the race

1973: Wilf Wardle's view of the European Cup Final. (Wilf Wardle).

was mine, because the German was wilting, and I launched one last sprint past him. It was a great relief to have maintained the tradition of Britain's success that afternoon by winning, and helping the team to finish fourth overall. It was an even greater relief to get round without disgracing myself on the track, and the first journalist to talk to me after the race had to do so with a toilet door between us.

The stomach complaint is something from which I have suffered on a number of occasions, and the doctor tells me that I have got a nervous and very active stomach, and that my eating habits are not always sensible. I eat very quickly, and I like fizzy drinks, and the combination of the two causes a bit of a flutter in the stomach. But if that coincides with a time when I am nervous – in the days leading up to a big race – then my stomach is working quickly, and a chain reaction sets in. The bowel starts working, everything I eat goes almost straight through me, and when I realise that I've got a bad stomach that makes me more nervous, makes it work faster, and so on, in a vicious circle, until I can hear my stomach whirring like a demented washing machine. I can escape if I avoid eating too quickly, or

Victory over Kuschmann and Norpoth – and my stomach – in the 1973 European Cup final at Edinburgh. (Mark Shearman).

taking cold fizzy drinks, and I now have some tablets of a type used by spacemen when they are sitting in their rockets waiting to blast off to the moon.

But then it was a real problem, and when I tried to resume training after the European Cup 5000 metres, it returned and I had to bring a premature halt to the season. This meant missing the Great Britain v Sweden international, which was no great loss, and the Coca-Cola invitation meeting one mile, where I was looking forward to racing against the Kenyan, Ben Jipcho, whom I knew would be one of the toughest rivals at the Commonwealth Games in Christchurch. It also meant having to miss the England Commonwealth Games trials, due to be held at Crystal Palace at the end of September, but I felt that I had shown during the summer that I could cope with the longer distances, and when the England team was announced at the beginning of October I was named for both the 1500 and 5000 metres. The Games were due to begin in Christchurch, New Zealand, in January, so there were three months to prepare.

Nine

The problem facing British athletes in the winter of 1973/74 was that they had to reach a peak of fitness at the coldest, bleakest time of the year for the Commonwealth Games in New Zealand. Basically, a distance runner does his bulk of stamina work in the winter, running high mileages and cross country races, and then in the summer switches to faster, shorter running, including plenty of speedwork and sprinting to enable him to be at his sharpest for track races. Not since the 1956 Melbourne Olympics had British athletes had this task to tackle, when the Games were held in November and December. Now, with the team selected some three months in advance, we all had to plan our own ways of reaching top form in January.

I had a mental boost in late October when the British Athletics Writers Association voted me their UK Male Athlete of the Year for 1973, and it was good to pop down to London for the presentation dinner and compare notes with some of the other New Zealand-bound athletes to see how they were making out. But meanwhile I was piling in a very high mileage, between 120–130 miles a week, week after week. The side effect of this was that I was feeling very tired at school, and it was all a bit of a strain, both physically and mentally. Training for international distance running is more than just popping down to the nearest running track for a few sprints, it is almost a full-time effort, and I was usually training three times a day, seven days a week, and still teaching at St Joseph's. Apart from the many hours occupied by the running, you also really need time for the body to recover between sessions, to build up the muscle fibres you have been breaking down, and this was simply not happening with me.

I managed to avoid any major injury, which was fortunate because I had to mix in some speed work in very cold weather, when the muscles are most liable to tearing. At the beginning of December I tested my form by taking part in a five miles cross country race at Vanves, near Paris, and finished second to Emiel Puttemans of Belgium. The difference between us seemed to be that he was running over the ground while I was running off it, and he won by 17 seconds. It was clear that I needed more fast work, because my mileage had left me strong but slow, and I had done only three track sessions in the past two months.

The difficulties of trying to run fast in an English winter are typified by a session I did on December 15th. I ran 400 metres eight times with a rest of 90 seconds in between, at an average of 60.2 seconds for each one, which was quite reasonable. But I had to do it in driving snow, a strong wind, running in the fourth lane because the inside of the cinder track was so messy, and wearing a full tracksuit and tights.

It would have been impossible to continue trying to run faster in such conditions, and as part of my preparations for Christchurch, Sue and I had decided to spend a fortnight in Spain over Christmas and the New Year. We left Newcastle on Christmas Eve at 10.30 am, but after a delay in our connecting flight at London finally arrived at Malaga after 10 o'clock that night. Still, it was good to be in a warm climate at last, and on the morning of Christmas Day I went for a ten miles run in the hills and along the coast road. On the way, and purely by chance, I bumped into Juha Vaatainen, the reigning European 5000 and 10,000 metres champion from Finland, who was running the other way, but joined me for the last three miles.

Vaatainen, who had been so dominant at the 1971 European championships in Helsinki, had not had much success since, mainly through injury. We had Christmas lunch with him, and he was a great help in giving me tips about how much training to do when travelling. He was a bit of a globe-trotter himself, and was in Spain to avoid the bitter Finnish winter, which was considerably worse even than in England, and was preparing to defend his European titles in Rome the following September.

In fact, he never made it to the European championships, because he was later injured again, which was not all that surprising to me in view of the training he was doing. 'Further and faster' was his motto, and he was running around thirty miles a day, with amazing sessions like running a hard 1000 metres *twenty* times on the track. On long road runs he was almost sprinting along, and although I was beginning to run really well then, I had great difficulty in keeping up with him. I found his company and advice most helpful, but I was glad he was not competing at Christchurch!

On New Year's Eve I did my best-ever set of repetition 800 metres runs (six, in an average of 2:01.8), and on January 2nd one of my best-ever sets of repetition 400 metres (ten, in an average of 58.16 seconds). The warm sunshine and ideal training conditions made a complete contrast to the driving Tyneside snow of a couple of weeks before, and my legs were very stiff after each track session, simply through not having been used to such speed recently.

My enthusiasm was high, because I knew I was running well, and when we were delayed on our return journey to Newcastle I even ran the thirteen miles from Newcastle Airport to my parents' home in Hebburn, while Sue went ahead with the luggage in a taxi. Then I went out for another eight miles from home later on.

The England team flew to New Zealand on January 10th, via Bahrain, Singapore and Melbourne – an exhausting twenty-eight hours of travelling. Because it was a charter flight shared with part of the Scottish team, everyone was quite relaxed (except for shot putter Geoff Capes, who hates flying and spent a lot of time up front making sure the pilot was awake), and there were bodies lying all over the seats and gangways, trying to sleep.

The distance runners, of course, were glad of any opportunity to stretch their legs and a group of us had planned to do a five-mile run while the aircraft was refuelling at Bahrain. However, the airport police would not allow us out of the 'In transit' lounge, so we decided to run round there! It could not have been more than 125 yards to the lap, as we jogged round and round for half an hour in between the seats, along a short corridor, through the bar, and round the back of the duty-free shop. You can imagine the looks we got from the Arabs.

It did not take too long to get used to the time change in Christchurch, and I had over a fortnight to prepare for the heats of the 5000 metres. The Games could scarcely have got off to a better start for New Zealand, as the little-rated Kiwi Dick Tayler won the 10,000 metres on the opening day, to the delight of the crowd at Queen Elizabeth II Stadium. Just like Lachie Stewart winning in Edinburgh, his last lap sprint caught the imagination of the host country and the success of the Games was assured.

Once more, too, Dave Bedford finished out of the medals after doing a lot of the early leading. Dave had been training in New Zealand for two months before the Games and felt he could break his own world record, but he got involved in a battle of elbows with several Kenyan runners and allowed it to destroy his concentration, which is fatal. Instead it was England's Dave Black who rose to the occasion, finishing second to Dick Tayler just 15 metres down in 27:48.6 seconds. The pattern was set, for the warm New Zealand weather was going to help the athletes to a series of performances in the middle distance events unequalled anywhere outside the Olympic Games.

The press unfortunately built up Bedford's battle of elbows, and predicted that there would be 'blood on the track' in the 5000 metres, where most of the adversaries would be meeting again, but there really were no grounds for that. Certainly it was the last thing I wanted; if I had, I'd have entered the boxing or wrestling ring instead. I had trained long and hard for these Games, and no on-track violence was going to affect that effort as far as I was concerned.

After seeing Dick Tayler win the 10,000 metres, the man I had to fear most, I felt, was another New Zealander, Dick Quax. Since I had finished behind him in the 1500 metres at Edinburgh he had also moved up to 5000 metres and had reduced his national record to 13:18.4, whereas my best was 13:23.8. He had been running very well recently, and the man who had coached Tayler, Arthur Lydiard, was widely predicting that Quax could break the world record of 13:13.0 by three or four seconds.

But while I did not underestimate Quax, he was being put under a tremendous amount of pressure in New Zealand, which could scarcely have helped him. In fact, he never made it to the starting line. A few days before he was due to run the 5000 metres heats he had to withdraw with a leg injury. In a sense, Lydiard was right, because Quax did eventually break the world record; but it was to take another three-and-a-half years. For the moment, he was on the sidelines.

There is no point in taking pleasure from other people's misfortunes. The real joy of success is when you perform better than your rivals, not when you win because your rivals are not there. So Quax's absence left a kind of hollowness over the race, or so I thought. There was still Dave Bedford and Dave Black of England, and the defending champion, Ian Stewart of Scotland, to consider, but as all three had run in the 10,000 metres, I knew they must have left something on the track in that race. Ian, particularly, was not at his mental or physical best.

I was totally relaxed during the build-up to the race, sharing Room 59 in the England team headquarters with steeplechaser Steve Hollings, a Yorkshireman whose frame was so light that when he got onto the top bunk bed above me he didn't even make a dent in it.

I had kept my training fairly low-key for the first week after we arrived, but a couple of track sessions after that told me I was going really well. I went down to QE2 Stadium, as we called it, to try out the Chevron all-weather track, and did a session of three times 1200 metres. The average of 3:01.2, with six minutes rest in between, was my best ever. Two days later I did two 800 metres with six minutes rest in an average of 1:53.8, again my best ever for that session. I knew I was in the form of my life, the opposition did not look too overwhelming, and at that point I really thought I was going to win.

However, I was reckoning without a superb Kenyan athlete named Ben Jipcho. He had already won the 3000 metres steeplechase, for which he held the world record, but when I had talked to him in the Games Village he seemed unsure as to whether he would run in the 1500 metres or the 5000 metres as well. As we began warming up for our 5000 metres heats on January 27th, it seemed clear that he had chosen the longer distance.

He qualified quite comfortably in third place in the first heat, and then it was my turn. Having not raced on a track since the European Cup final some four-and-a-half months before, I was quite keen to get some of the rustiness out of my legs, so after passing 1600 metres in 4:22, I went and stretched out a little. No one seemed anxious to come with me, so I ran hard for five laps, looking over my shoulder from time to time to check the situation behind me. I felt strong and relaxed, and towards the end of the race eased right off again to save something for the final. With the first six in the heat to qualify, I knew I was safe, and almost strolled round the last circuit as a group of four closed up on me.

No, we're not holding hands. Instead, Dave Bedford and I discuss his pace-making offer before the Commonwealth 5000m final in Christchurch. (Mark Shearman).

Some of the crowd may have thought I was tiring, but I was able to reassure them by putting on an expression of mock panic in the finishing straight and scuttling away from my pursuers in the last 50 metres. This moment of light relief was perhaps necessary after so many people had been wanting to see 'blood on the track'.

I knew now that in Jipcho I had a serious rival. Apart from his steeplechase world record, he was the second fastest-ever runner at one mile (3 minutes 52 seconds), and although he had not run a great many 5000 metres races, obviously thought he must be able to produce a good one here, even though he had never beaten 13 minutes 30 seconds for the distance.

Dave Bedford offered to lead the early laps, to make a race of it in the final, and he was as good as his word. He took us through four laps in 4:20, and then Dave Black went ahead for the next two. Jipcho, I later learned, had been content to run in the middle of the twelve-man field, but when I decided to make a move to the front, with just over five laps left, he immediately moved up to my shoulder and together we pulled away from the field. I eased a little on the ninth circuit, which allowed Dave Black to catch up with us, and in fact go into the lead for a lap, but with 800 metres left I knew that I could no longer delay my final effort. Jipcho was one of the world's greatest milers, but I hoped that a sustained drive would weaken him. With the sun beating down on us the race had turned into a two-man struggle, but hard as I pushed the pace I could still see Ben's shadow beside me.

The bell rang for the last lap, and still the shadow was there. Only when we came into the last home straight did he move alongside me and begin his own effort to the line. He moved slightly ahead of me, but I was still able to find a little more speed and gradually closed the tiny gap again.

I was gaining on him, and if I could sustain it for another 60 metres, I would be past him. I could almost see the line, we practically rubbed elbows in our effort to get there, but then about 30 metres from home he edged forward again and it was over. I had lost by a couple of feet. We went past the line suddenly divided at last by the result. Ben was elated; I staggered on a few more metres before having to rest my hands on my knees as I gasped in the warm air, trying to recover from the effort of that last lap. It took us 55.3 seconds, and Ben and I had become the second and third fastest-ever athletes at 5000 metres. Ben's time of 13:14.4 was a Commonwealth record, and only 1.4 seconds outside the world record. My time of 13:14.6 was a UK record, breaking Dave Bedford's mark by 2.6 seconds.

Ben came over and shook hands. I could scarcely rise to meet him as mixed emotions of disappointment and pleasure swept over me. I suppose at that moment it was mainly disappointment, because I had thought I had such a good chance to

So near, and yet . . . I break the Commonwealth 5000m record at Christchurch, but Ben Jipcho is there half a stride before me. (Mark Shearman).

win. But it was still a tremendous race to lose, the second fastest ever, and it taught me a lot about racing 5000 metres. Ben admitted to me afterwards that if I had started my effort one lap earlier he would not have been able to hold on. It gave me a lot of food for thought. Should I have had one or two sharpening races before the Games? Should I have started my bid earlier? It was too late to do anything but plan for the future, and acknowledge that Ben was a great champion, and an athlete I had underestimated before the Games. With two gold medals already in his pocket, you might have thought that he would be satisfied, but he was not. He announced his intention of trying for a third – the 1500 metres – so I would be racing him again very shortly.

'Racing him' is perhaps the wrong description, because the 1500 metres final on February 2nd was the greatest-ever mass race at the distance and if Jipcho was in the shadow of Filbert Bayi that day, I was in darkness! Bayi, the compulsive front runner, had dashed into the lead, as was his custom, and set a scorching pace – 54.4 seconds for the 400 metres, 1:51.8 at 800 metres – but the rest of the field ran together, some 30 metres down, convinced he would die in the last lap. Jipcho led the chasing group, and it was only on the final circuit that the crowd, and the rest of us, realised that Bayi was not dying.

As Jipcho was overtaken in second place by a young New Zealander called John Walker, who was just making his name, Bayi kept ahead all the way to the tape to win in a world record of 3:32.2, nearly a second faster than Jim Ryun's record set seven years earlier. Walker, who was as surprised as anyone to be running so fast as he had been basically an 800 metres runner, was also under the old world record in second place with 3:32.5, while Ben Jipcho just missed the mark by 0.1 second, running 3:33.2 in third place. I finished seventh in 3:37.6 which, regardless of the fact that I was never in with a medal chance, was still a UK record.

Many people still remember the 1974 Commonwealth Games for Bayi's world record, but for me Ben Jipcho was the man of the Games with his steeplechase and 5000 metres gold medals, and his bronze medal in the fastest 1500 metres event of all time. He later turned professional with the Los Angeles-based International Track Association, and competed regularly against his Kenyan compatriot Kip Keino and the American Jim Ryun. The ITA circus lasted four years, and as Keino and Ryun were probably past their best when they signed on as professionals, Jipcho was the greatest athlete they had at the peak of his career.

But what else could Ben have done as an amateur to surpass his running in Christchurch, at least until the next Olympics, which were still two-and-a-half years away? Athletics is not really that big a sport in Kenya, and earning a living and owning a farm are much more important.

I did not think that the ITA could last for long, anyway, because the money offered was not really that good, and there was the monotony of running against the same people every Friday and Saturday, or against electric pacer lights, or relay teams of shot putters and girl sprinters. I had been approached, along with Ian Stewart, about signing up for the ITA when we were on our indoor 'tour' in 1973, and I was asked again by Michael O'Hara, the ITA president, later in 1974 if I would join. I was even given a blank contract to study, and was asked to negotiate with them, but I was not really tempted, even though I was told I could make a quarter of a million dollars in a year.

To earn that, though, I would have had to race all over the world, and take part in all sorts of advertising promotion stunts, as well as winning races regularly. As I do not enjoy being away from home all that much, have a good job, and still nurse some Olympic ambition, it was never really possible that I would accept. Money is not everything, and I would have found it hard to muster the enthusiasm to train hard for a race against an electrically-paced spotlight.

I had underestimated Jipcho, whose two gold and one bronze medal made him my own choice as Man of the Games. (Mark Shearman).

I had a short rest when I came back from New Zealand before setting out on the build-up to the second half of the 1974 'double' – the European championships in Rome the following September. I finished third, behind Emiel Puttemans and Frank Shorter, in the Five Mills cross country race in Italy in late March, but could feel myself a little overweight. I was still putting in high mileages, over 120 a week, and had done so for four consecutive weeks when I had what I still consider one of my best-ever races.

It was in the AAA National twelve-stage road relay at Sutton Coldfield on April 27th. I ran the ninth leg for Gateshead Harriers around a hilly course of 5 miles 900 yards, and managed to move the club up from sixth to second place, one second behind the leaders. My time was 24:28.0 which was, I was told by athletics statisticians, equivalent to around 27:40.0 for 10,000 metres on the track, or less than 10 seconds outside the world record. (Ian Stewart often tells me that he knows where I took the short cut on that course!) Having someone to chase most of the way round was something of a help, of course, but what really pleased me was that it came on top of four weeks of really hard training, when I should have been extremely tired, but in fact found myself going well.

An emotional moment as I acknowledge the cheers of the Newcastle United fans at Wembley Stadium before the 1974 FA Cup Final. Boyhood memories flooded back.

The following Saturday was the day of my schoolboy dream come true when I won the special FA Cup Final 3000 metres race in front of 100,000 spectators at Wembley Stadium. It was marvellous to know that at least half of the crowd, the Newcastle United fans, were cheering for me, and even if they did not win the FA Cup that day, at least I managed to win the race, with Juha Vaatainen second and Tony Simmons third. I had obtained a black and white striped vest (Newcastle's colours) from Dave Bedford, because they are also the colours of his club, Shaftesbury Harriers, and after the race I threw it into the crowd. Years later I met a chap who told me that he had got it on the wall of the pub he ran in Newcastle, so it ended up in the north-east. The other great memory of that day was that I was able to take my Dad along to watch, recalling how he had tried in vain to get me a ticket when I was a kid in 1955.

It was that month, in May 1974, that a job advertised in the local paper was pointed out to me by Stan Long's wife, Joan. It was a new job, as Sports and Recreation Manager of Gateshead, and although I was quite happy teaching, I thought I would gamble a stamp on an application form and see what happened. I went for an interview, which consisted mainly of questions about what I thought

At my desk as Gateshead's new Recreation Officer in 1974.

A world record in Gateshead, a dream come true, but still not the end of the 1974 campaign.
(Tony Duffy).

could be done to make Gateshead have an impact in sport, and I answered them as best I could, with no real background to this sort of thing at all. They must have been the right answers, though, because I got the job, and was due to start in July, just before the opening of the new Tartan track at the Gateshead Stadium. One of my first tasks was to get involved with the organisation of the Gateshead Games, which had always been held but with which I had had little to do over the years. This time we wanted a big, spectacular meeting to open the new track with a bang, and apart from the remarks I had made about trying to break a world record, which I had spoken in a semi-intoxicated state at a civic reception some six months earlier, we had little to go on.

The next few weeks were the most hectic of my life, as I tried to train through

116

Relief, joy, satisfaction, elation . . . there are not enough words to describe how I felt after it was over.

a series of niggling injuries, organise the Gateshead Games, mark exam papers (I was still teaching at St Joseph's for the rest of the summer term), and try to interest sponsors and television in our meeting.

Finally, it all came right. Rediffusion came in as sponsors, ITV agreed to show the meeting live in their Saturday afternoon 'World of Sport' programme, I had a good response from a lot of internationals when I asked them to come and compete, on the day we had 10,000 spectators and I managed to break the world 3000 metres record for them. That would have been a good note on which to end the season locally, I suppose, but although that was Gateshead's highlight of the year (and the Gateshead Games has continued as a major international meeting), the European championships were still looming on the horizon. When I had broken the world two miles record, there was a niggle in my mind that someone else had run slightly faster indoors. That feeling was not removed until I set the 3000 metres record and had at last a record that was well and truly all my own.

It was the same with medals. I had been pleased to win bronze medals at Edinburgh and Helsinki, and a silver at Christchurch. I had come close to winning in the Commonwealth Games. I had world records, and I had won the European Cup final 5000 metres. But I had not won a title at a major Games, and more than anything I wanted to prove that I really could bring home a *gold* medal. If I did not do it in Rome, then I would have to wait another two years for the 1976 Montreal Olympics, and who could tell what would happen between now and then?

Rome, and the European championships, had been a long-term aim, but once the shouting had died down over the world record at Gateshead I had a little over a month to make final preparations. I had retained my AAA 5000 metres title in July, and won a 1500 metres race for Britain against Czechoslovakia at Meadowbank in July, so I felt that my place in the team for Rome must be fairly secure if a world record was not convincing enough that I was reasonably fit.

Almost inevitably, I felt a sense of anticlimax after the world record, and I was still training hard, trying to make up for time lost through those injuries earlier in the season. The following Saturday I had promised to run in the Emsley Carr Mile during an international invitation meeting organised by the British Amateur Athletic Board at Crystal Palace, and although I did not expect to run all that well I flew down to London from Newcastle early because I had agreed to help out with some pre-meeting publicity.

When I went to collect my expenses from the BAAB official concerned, he tried to insist that only a return train fare was due to me, and that if I wanted to fly I should have asked special permission. Now the train journey from Newcastle to London is a long one, particularly if you have to do it twice in two days, and if you are trying to get into top shape for a major Games, you try to smooth out every path. It would have been much easier for me not to come down to London at all, to stay at home training, but I had kept my word that I would come.

So when I was confronted with this problem I just about blew my top. 'Look,' I told the gentleman concerned, 'either I get my full air fare, or I don't run.' The official was adamant that I would only get my train fare, but eventually agreed to summon a higher authority in the person of the BAAB treasurer, Marea Hartman.

'What seems to be the trouble, Brendan?' she asked.

I explained, adding that 'there are a lot of spectators out there who are going to be disappointed if I withdraw from the mile today.'

I got my air fare. Now I don't like confrontations or threats, and I normally

118

get on quite well with the BAAB and its officers. I certainly don't think, 'I am Brendan Foster, therefore I should be treated differently from other athletes.' Next season I could lose form and be right at the back of every race. But I did feel strongly on that occasion that red tape was just overwhelming me, and I would seriously have pulled out of the race and gone home if I did not get the air fare.

An emotion-sapping argument just before a race is the last thing an athlete wants, and needless to say I never really got into the event. Frank Clement won it in 3:57.4 from Ray Smedley, with me third in 3:58.4. It was a struggle all the way, and the day totalled just three training miles instead of the twenty I could have covered at home.

To finish off my speedwork before Rome I ran in the Highland Games at Edinburgh the following Saturday and came fifth in the 800 metres in 1:51.4, and confirmed that I would not be challenging for a place in the 4 × 400 metres relay squad when I came last in the 400 metres in 52.6 seconds! However, it was a good day's speedwork, and placings simply did not matter. I had blown the tubes out.

On August 29th we flew to Rome, and as soon as we stepped off the aircraft we could feel the warm, humid air enveloping us like a blanket. Fortunately, I don't mind running in heat normally, but for some athletes their chance of doing well evaporated as soon as Rome was selected as the site for the championships.

The accommodation for the athletes in Rome was very poor. You normally expect to share a room on such occasions, but this time five of us were allocated to one smallish room, which at best was a twin-bedded room. My bed was not even a bed, it was a settee which folded out into a bed, and was not very comfortable at all. I am a bad sleeper when I am away from home, not only because of the strange surroundings, but because when you are close to a race you are easing down in training, and therefore not as tired as when you are running two or three times a day.

It was a real ordeal, and by no means confined to the British team, but every night I would be lying awake worrying about not sleeping. Or else I would drop off, only to be awakened by one of the other four coming into the room, and then not be able to get off to sleep again. I was not racing until over a week after we arrived, so it was not a very enjoyable prelude to such an important event. A group of us tried to solve the problem by booking rooms in an hotel just over the road so that we could sleep somewhere peacefully before our event, but that led to all kinds of problems with the BAAB who wanted to keep the team together. We finally tried out the new arrangement, and I was to share a room with Steve Ovett, but when we got there we found that the room backed on to a permanently broken toilet which made a constant noise because it never filled up, and had water running down the walls. It was equally hopeless, so I changed back from pyjamas to ordinary clothes to cross the road and return to the Black Hole of Calcutta, and I never used the room we had booked. The irony is that all year round when you are living at home you are quiet and comfortable, and then when the big test comes you are herded together like sheep in a pen to await your moment of truth in a kind of neurotic, communal claustrophobia.

To make matters worse, I had picked up a stomach bug, which is not unusual in Rome. This time it was a genuine bug, not my old trouble, and on the opening day of the championships I was in bed thinking my last hourhad come. I managed to get over to the stadium to watch the 10,000 metres final, in which Britain's Tony Simmons came within inches of beating Manfred Kuschmann of East Germany for the gold medal, but anyone who thought I should have been in that race, as some people suggested, should have seen me halfway through it – tottering out of the stadium to be sick!

The trouble quickly cleared, however, and by the 5000 metres heats on Friday I felt fine again. In my race I threw in a 59.1 seconds lap midway through, which stretched the field out, and then eased down before the finish, much as I had done in my Christchurch heat. Unfortunately, neither of the other British runners, Dave Black or Chris Stewart, made it through to the fifteen-man final. But among those who did were Manfred Kuschmann, the winner of the 10,000 metres, and Lasse Viren, the Olympic champion.

I had two days to think about the final, and how to run it. The time passed slowly, as I played music on my cassette tape recorder, read books I didn't really want to read, and made idle conversation with people I didn't really want to talk to. There was almost too much time to think. At home, with everyday things happening around you, you would not give more than a passing thought to a race some days off. But in a championship situation like Rome there was precious little hope of getting away from it. We knew why we were there, and that we would be judged as successes or failures on what we did.

I knew what I wanted to do. I wanted to win that gold medal, not in a last lap scramble, where it could go to any of half a dozen blokes, but by running 5000 metres hard all the way and being well clear at the end. 'Winning big', if you like. I did not want a repeat of my Commonwealth race against Jipcho, although I had learned from it. I thought about the great runners of the past, and particularly about the Soviet star, Vladimir Kuts, who won the European 5000 metres title in 1954 in such an overwhelming way that his victory will be remembered long after other, more recent, gold medallists are forgotten. I wanted to win like Kuts did. I knew that I might never be so fit and so ready again as I was at that moment.

120

On the Sunday, the day of the final, it was once again hot and humid. The temperature was nudging 80 degrees fahrenheit, and the white marble everywhere was scorching hot. I had met Kuschmann earlier in the day, and he said to me, 'Tonight you will be champion.' I wanted to believe him, I even thought he was probably right, but then cursed myself for such complacency. I had thought I was going to win in Christchurch, and I had lost, hadn't I?

The finalists, all of us looking gaunt and worried, filed into the huge Stadium where in 1960 the Olympic Games had taken place. It was here that Herb Elliott of Australia had launched an attack which will long be remembered for its daring and ferocity when he won the Olympic 1500 metres title from the front in a world record time. From the front. That was the way to run, just daring anyone else to come with you. I was just a soccer-mad schoolboy of twelve when Elliott was racing to immortality, but I liked to think that perhaps I could carry on a tradition.

In the crowd I could hear British voices shouting to me, and I could see huge banners painted with the words 'Howay Big Bren'. One of them, I later discovered, had been made by my younger brother Pete and his friend Dave Roberts, who had travelled to Rome and painted the slogan on a sheet from their Roman YMCA!

I am often asked just what 'Howay Big Bren' means, and the truth is that there is no literal translation, but to me it means 'go a bit faster'. It also meant I had some support in the Babel-like cheering which swept around the stadium. There was little cooling shadow; just a bit on the back straight. Otherwise the sun was on us. I gave a thought for the marathon runners, who had already set off, and wondered how they were coping with the conditions. But I quickly switched my thoughts back to my own race; that was enough to worry about.

I knew, and I think all of the other finalists knew, that I was going to lead and make a break. Exactly where the break would come they did not know; but they did not know that *I* did not know either, so they were two secrets away from what was to happen on the dark red track.

The gun fired, I went straight into the lead, and no one made any attempt to stop me. They just settled in behind me like a flock of sheep, which suited me perfectly. For seven uneventful laps we ran like that. I felt comfortable but wondered what effect the pace, with each lap between 63.3 and 66.0 seconds, was having on the others. Several times I thought, 'Right, I'll go now', but then changed my mind.

We were coming up to 2900 metres, and I knew I could not delay it any longer. Hesitation had cost me a Commonwealth title in Christchurch. So I got up on to my toes and started moving fast, my arms working harder, my knees coming up higher, my breathing harder, the pace faster. The crowd reacted, and I felt only

*As I try to get away from the field in the European 5000m final at Rome,
Olympic champion Lasse Viren matches strides and keeps me guessing about
his form.* (Tony Duffy).

one athlete had come with me as we went round that lap in 60.2 seconds. I turned
my head sideways slightly and I could see the sweating, almost haggard face of
Lasse Viren.

His ability to change his form drastically from race to race had given rise to all
kinds of allegations about his methods, none of which I believed, but for a fleeting
moment I just hoped that he had not suddenly found his Olympic form today.
Then a lap later he was gone, drifting back to the others, and the danger was
passed. I was on my own, in the lead, with three laps left. They seemed to take an
eternity, and I kept telling myself, 'Now get round this bend, and down that
straight and you'll only have two laps to go', and so on. It was hurting all over,
but I was controlled, not in a panic.

As I came up towards the bell I was 100 metres clear of the field, and, looking up at the giant clock on the scoreboard, I could see it said 12:14.0, which meant that if I could muster a 59 seconds last lap I would have Puttemans' world record as well. I thought 'Shall I have a go here?' but then I decided 'Oh, bugger it, I only want to win', so I took 62 seconds for the last lap instead, which gave me a little longer to savour the moment for which I had waited so long.

'You're going to win, you're going to be European champion,' I told myself. 'Just get round this next bend, because they're coming after you.' The chasing group was really too far back to catch me, but I was trying everything just to keep my legs going on that final circuit.

And then it was over. I looked round and saw half a dozen athletes sprinting down the home straight, with Kuschmann just beating Viren for the silver medal. But it was over. An Italian official tried to direct me down the athletes' tunnel but I broke away from him and jogged round the stadium, waving to the crowd, so many of whom had been vociferously encouraging me around those last lonely laps. My kid brother, Pete, was in there somewhere; so was a big party from *Athletics Weekly*'s tour. On the back straight a group of Finns were waving their national flags, but even though I had beaten Viren they were generous in their applause, and I was touched by their warmth. In their midst I saw Pekka Vasala, the Olympic 1500 metres champion who had earlier finished sixth in the 1500 metres here, and against whom I had run so often. We shook hands and then he faded back into the crowd. I have not seen him since.

Since that race I have had a great satisfaction about the run. I have often wished that I had gone a little bit faster and tried to break the world record, but on the day it was so hot and humid that I might have risked blowing up instead. The best tribute of all must be that of *Athletics Weekly*, which reported: 'Not since Kuts in Berne twenty years ago had a European championship field been humiliated in this manner.' They must have been reading my mind before the race.

The strange thing, though, is that immediately after the race, as soon as I had left the arena, I felt drained, tired, miserable, flat and disappointed, for no reason at all. Even when I went up for the gold medal, I felt nothing emotionally. I had always thought that to stand on the top step of a rostrum at a major Games would be terrific, but I don't even remember seeing the Union Jack flying, nor hearing the national anthem. It was a colossal anti-climax, because it was the last piece of the jig-saw. I had been running well, broken a world record, and now having won the European gold medal, that was the end. The final touch. Somehow the sparking challenge had been missing because everyone was expecting me to win, the other runners were all frightened of me, and I knew that I virtually just had to go out

A victory lap at Rome: Gold at last. (Mike Street).

there, run round, and the European title was mine. It was a strange, almost eerie, feeling.

A few minutes later I had to go to the medical room to give a urine sample for the dope test, and I remember sitting in this ultra-hygienic white-tiled room, waiting for the doctor, and thinking 'This is not all that glamorous, is it?' The crowd was outside in the stadium still talking about the race, millions of television viewers all over Europe, including my Mum and Dad and Sue in Gateshead, had seen it, and yet here I was totally depressed for no apparent reason in the medical room.

*1974: Veni, vidi, vinci? Wilf's view
of me in Rome.* (Wilf Wardle).

Ian Thompson came in, having just won the marathon gold medal for Britain, and he said, 'How did you get on?' I told him I had won, and he almost kissed me. Both of us were in a different world at that moment, totally removed from reality. I asked Ian how he felt after his twenty-six miles run in the torrid heat, and he replied, 'A little tired.'

We sat down together, I lent him my towel, and got him a drink, while in the stadium the British 4 × 400 metres relay team of Glen Cohen, Bill Hartley, Alan Pascoe and David Jenkins, were winning a third gold medal for Great Britain in one glorious afternoon.

But all the time I was totally depressed, thinking, 'Hell's bells, I never thought I'd feel like this.' Even at the press conference afterwards I was a bit flat. Someone asked to see my gold medal and I said, 'There you are, but that's history now. We've got to start planning for the next one.'

In the Press Box one of the British journalists let me use his telephone to ring home and talk to Sue, which made me feel a bit better, and that evening a group of us went out for a few drinks, which made me feel considerably better. Then next morning when I woke up my first thought was 'You're European champion'; and my second thought was 'But you're running at Crystal Palace on Friday night, so you had better get out and keep in shape.' I was still on the conveyor belt. So at 6.45 that morning, before we flew back to London, I was out running five miles around Rome. Nothing had changed.

Reunited with Sue at the airport after my return from Rome,
I seem to be demonstrating the art of medal levitation.

Ten

The events in Rome, widely covered by British television, had made much more of an impact than I had thought possible, and when the IAC–Coca-Cola meeting at Crystal Palace got under way the following Friday evening, traffic was jammed for miles around. An estimated 18,000 spectators watched the athletics that night, far more than the stadium held comfortably, and a long fence on the back straight collapsed under the weight of people climbing on to it to try to get a sight of the competition. All tickets had been sold, but the crowds kept pouring out of Crystal Palace station, off buses, and out of cars, and that evening was the first of the great 'atmosphere' meetings, which must have been what it was like at White City Stadium in the early 'fifties. Suddenly athletics was a booming sport again, and outside Crystal Palace ticket touts were doing good business. It contrasted vividly with the old joke about a spectator ringing up White City in its leaner days and asking what time the big athletics meeting started. Came the reply: 'What time can you get here?'

Lasse Viren was running with me in the two miles event that night, and we jogged together the mile down the hill from the Queen's Hotel to Crystal Palace. All the way down, people who were hopelessly stuck in traffic jams were sounding their horns and waving to us, and I assumed they were hooting at Lasse. But a few of them wound down their windows and were shouting, 'Good luck, Brendan', or 'Well done', and I realised that although I was jogging with a double Olympic champion, this time they were waving to me. It was very flattering, and an indication to me of the power of television coverage. When I had run my AAA road relay leg in April, in a time with which I was extremely pleased, few people even knew about it. Now, by winning a championship watched by millions of television viewers, in a time well outside my best, I was acclaimed.

127

The noise inside the stadium was terrific, and we sat in the changing rooms beneath the stands, guessing whether it was Alan Pascoe, or Ian Thompson, or any of the other British gold medallists, who were in action as the shouting reached a crescendo. Then it was time for the two miles, and as I stepped on to the floodlit track to have a stretching run down the back straight, the spectators gave me a marvellous ovation, which sent a tingle down my spine. It was the first time it had ever happened, when I had not even been announced; it was spontaneous, and a warming feeling swept over me.

Of the race itself, I remember little. The Australian, Graeme Crouch, led us round the first mile (4:11.5), and then on the fifth lap I put in a 60.8 circuit, which took me clear of the field. The talented young American runner, Steve Prefontaine, who was fourth in the Munich Olympic 5000 metres and was to die tragically in a car crash less than a year after this race, came with me briefly, but after five laps he stepped off the track. I felt flat as a pancake, but I got round the final laps to win what was, in all honesty, a rather insignificant race, in 8:23.4. Ray Smedley, Jos Hermens of Holland, and Lasse Viren had a great scrap for second place, and all three clocked the same time, 8:25.8, finishing in that order.

The season was over at last. I had run my last track race of the year, and the fact that the enthusiasm engendered at Crystal Palace that night was so vast helped me forget for a short while how tired I was. It was a great night for British athletics.

As I was to learn in the following months, my world record at Gateshead and my gold medal in Rome were the beginnings of what I call 'the world expects' syndrome. I had for so long wanted to be a gold medallist, number one in my event, but now that it had happened it brought with it a few pressures I had not anticipated. Whereas before I could spend the winter quietly training, I now found I was in demand for all sorts of functions, and it is a demand which seems to have continued ever since. Most certainly it is flattering in many respects, but you cannot get away entirely from the feeling that you are being 'used', and that by complying with too many of the requests you are actually jeopardising your future performances in the sport through irregular training or insufficient rest.

At the end of 1974 I was voted BBC Sports Personality of the Year, which is a great ego-tickler and a pleasant thing to win – for one night. You have to be very careful in your approach to such things because something like that has relatively little to do with what you achieve on the track. In 1971 Dave Bedford was runner-up in the BBC Sports Personality voting, and sixth in the European 10,000 metres. Yet if you asked him which he would prefer, I am sure he would say he would rather have been second in the European 10,000 metres and sixth in the BBC poll, because in a way such a poll is attempting the impossible. How could I be judged,

Attending dinners and presentations, such as this Vaux Awards dinner, is enjoyable, but I discovered early in 1975 that too many social events could affect my training.

as I was in 1974, alongside the world light heavyweight boxing champion John Conteh, who was second? In 1977, how could you really compare Steve Ovett with Barry Sheene, the world motor-cycling champion?

If anything, it added to the requests for my time, many of which have virtually nothing to do with my success in athletics. For instance, I have been asked to judge beauty contests, from Miss United Kingdom to Miss World, but I have always turned them down. I have never even judged Miss Gateshead! There are plenty of the lads in my club who run slower than I do who could be much better qualified to judge something like that; judging beauty contests simply has nothing to do with my ability to run fast, so I turn them down.

Occasionally I have presented prizes at a school or youth club, but sometimes people seem to think they own you. It is very flattering if a school names one of

Athletics can lead to many diverse honours, such as this honorary fellowship of Sunderland Polytechnic, which I received in April 1976. (Newcastle Chronicle & Journal).

its houses after me, or someone names an hotel after me, but it is not a thing I seek. Because when it happens they tend to assume that you are going to keep popping along there to give a talk or present prizes, which I would love to do if I did not have to run or work. But I've got to do both, so I cannot run, work *and* get involved in too much public relations work. If I was a professional sportsman, or someone whose living depended upon fame, like a singer, then it would be part and parcel of my life. But I am not, and it sometimes seems hard to get other people to understand that. For instance, a village flower-arranging society might decide to hold a competition with a sporting theme, so they write to me and say that they are going to do me the great honour of inviting me to judge their competition. But because it is their big night of the year, they assume it must be my big night of the year too, and sometimes they get upset when I say I cannot make it.

Recently a local variety club elected me as their Sportsman of the Year, and then started writing to me every couple of weeks saying, 'The Sportsman of the Year function this week is to go to so-and-so', and I had to say, 'Look, I'm not doing that.' So they said, 'But you're our Sportsman of the Year. Everyone else does.' And I had to point out once again that I had not *asked* to be elected as their Sportsman of the Year, and it was their problem, not mine. They seemed to think they automatically had me on permanent call.

Occasionally when I decline an invitation, the organisers come back and say, 'Well, if it's a question of money, we were going to pay you x pounds for expenses,' and I have to point out that as an amateur athlete I cannot receive any money anyway, and that the problem is simply time. And of course energy, because travelling is tiring, and the invitations come from all over the country. I simply cannot keep to the rigid training regime I need if I am constantly travelling, and in any case I simply enjoy being at home with my wife and young son.

Some of the letters I get are crazy ones, like that from the Irishman who wrote that he had this feeling that he could be the greatest runner in Ireland, but he did not know whether to tell anyone, and worrying about it had caused him to drink a whole bottle of cointreau in ten minutes every day. He wanted me to write back to him and tell him that *I* too thought he could be the greatest runner in Ireland!

Then there are the genuinely sad ones, where I am asked to visit people who are ill or house-bound. Or someone writes to say that if you don't go to their function, they will never get the roof on their scout hut because they need an attendance of so many thousands to ensure the money for their roof. I feel sorry for them, of course, as anyone would, but I have to face up to the fact that it is not *my* scout hut, and however much they try to make you feel differently it really is *not* my responsibility whether they get a roof or not.

This may all sound terribly callous, as if I have a heart of cold stone. Some of the letters do touch me very deeply. But I have to put everything into perspective. The way I do this is the way that I explain why I am turning down an invitation. I say, 'Look, you are inviting me to this because I am a well-known athlete. I am a well-known athlete because I train hard, and if I miss training to come to your function I'll be a less well-known athlete, because I'll be losing all the time. And in a year's time you won't even want me to come to your function.' Most people accept this when I have explained the situation.

A few, though, still believe that it is because I am simply rude, arrogant, heartless, and big-headed. I have had to come to terms with the fact that as I began winning more races and getting more publicity, there would be people shooting at me and sticking knives in my back for things I had never even thought of doing, let alone actually done.

Sadly, that has spilled over onto Gateshead Harriers, and although the club has built up to the point where we have won national cross country and road relay titles, and represented England in European competitions, as well as organising our own successful international meetings at Gateshead Stadium, in parts of the north and north-east we are hated. The trouble is that when other clubs see Gateshead Harriers turning up at a meeting, they know that half the prizes have gone straight away. Somehow our success is resented in certain areas, and although that is half understandable, as everyone wants to see their own club on top, it is also very small-minded because these people seem unable to comprehend the boost we are giving to athletics in the north-east as a whole, and that every club can profit from our success, as interest in the sport increases. Not everyone comes to Gateshead. There are plenty of other clubs in the area.

I used to worry about it when I overheard people talking about 'that bloody Brendan Foster, only out for himself', but now I don't. It is a fact of life, and I quite enjoy cocking a snoop at them, as long as my conscience is clear and I am doing it for a reason that is acceptable to me.

It was sad that after the 1977 National cross country championships in London, where Gateshead once again took the senior team prize as well as a collection of other trophies, there were sections of the audience at the presentation ceremony – people who live almost in Gateshead – who were booing when we went up for our prizes. The rest of the country seemed pleased for us, but a few misguided people seemed to think that anyone else's success had to be derided.

But that winter of 1974–75 was a time of adjustment for me, and the lesson that I learned was not to accept too many invitations. After Rome there seemed an endless number of dinners and similar functions to attend, and until that time it had never been a problem. But I began to lose sight of just how hard I had worked the previous winter to achieve that summer's success. Some of the functions would show a film of me winning comfortably in Rome, or setting the world record at Gateshead, and when I had downed a couple of glasses of wine and heard a bit of applause I would start thinking, 'Oh, it's easy. I could do that anytime'. The previous winter I had been piling in 120 miles a week, including speed work, all the time in preparation for Christchurch and the Commonwealth Games. This winter I was eating my way round the banquet circuit while trying to get back into shape from the long rest I had enjoyed after the summer.

The period between October and December when you are building up to a very high mileage is always a time when you need as few distractions as possible, just running and rest in great quantities of both. In fact, it is the least glamorous part of the yearly cycle, because there are no races of significance, but in many respects

132

A meeting of the Recreation Department's management team.

it is the most important part because what you do in the summer depends on the training 'base' you have laid down in the winter. As it was, my mileage was down, my weight was up, and I was rushing to get myself fit for a new event, a televised cross country race over a three-quarter-mile circuit at Gateshead Bowl, just behind the stadium. The late nights, early morning runs and niggling injuries did not help at all, and it is from this experience that I adopted my attitude towards functions. I was, I decided, an athlete first and a dinner guest second.

But some people still seem to think that my job is a sinecure. Nothing could be further from the truth and I have to apply myself as fully as anyone else. As Manager of Gateshead's Sports and Recreation Department, I have to report regularly to the town's Parks and Recreation Committee, and my responsibility covers nine swimming baths, umpteen football pitches, the Youth Stadium, the Indoor Bowls Centre and four recreation halls, as well as the development of sport generally, including grant-aid and coaching systems in the town.

A quarter of a million people live in the area, which covers 140 square miles, and they are not all athletics fans. So I have to ensure that their own favourite

*Rod Dixon leads Ian Stewart, myself, Tony Simmons, John Walker and
Emiel Puttemans in the Philips 2000m at Crystal Palace in 1975. I set a
UK record, but lost decisively to Walker.* (Mike Street).

recreational activities are available, and try to introduce them to new ones. The
work is complicated and tiring, and it is most certainly not a 'cover' for being a
full-time athlete. I sometimes wish it was!

The cross country race was televised on BBC 'Grandstand', and Ian Stewart
returned from a period of disillusion since Christchurch, during which he had taken
up cycling, and won the race from Knut Boro of Norway. I was fourth, behind
David Black, and it was very hard work in my semi-fit state. I felt, though, that we
had shown that cross country could be a good television spectacle, provided the
lap was short enough to be covered by cameras all the way round. The 1 in 4 hill

halfway round each lap certainly provided some good shots as we struggled up it six times, with only Stewart and Boro treating it as though it was little more than a molehill. The race, like our summer Gateshead Games, has since become an annual event.

It was not until the New Year that I really managed to pull myself together in training, but in March and April I had an ankle injury which reduced my mileage for seven weeks to an average of only forty-five. That, about a third of my normal load, plus the fact that I had done relatively little before Christmas, meant that I approached the summer far from my fittest. The few races I had that winter reflected this too. In March I ran in the Five Mills cross country race in Milan, but after a week in which I had been at a conference in Bournemouth and unable to get proper treatment for my ankle, I faded after the first mile and finished, extremely tired and disappointed, way down the field.

There was a bright note, though, when Gateshead Harriers won the AAA National twelve-stage road relay title for the first time, on April 26th at Sutton Coldfield. In the fortnight or so beforehand I had managed to get a little more training done, and in the race I took one of the shorter stages, the tenth, because I did not think I could manage one of the five-and-a-half miles long stages. Things went well, and although I felt tired after the first mile, my time of 13:58 broke the course record by 17 seconds and took us into a lead which we held until the end. It was great to be part of such a team success, which only a few years before would have been unthinkable.

On the track I still had some confidence left over from 1974, but my first serious race, a 2000 metres at Crystal Palace on July 4th, during the Philips Golden International, proved somewhat disastrous. John Walker of New Zealand won it in 5:00.6, a Commonwealth record, while I finished only fifth, just alongside Ian Stewart. I 'dipped' at the line, which got me the verdict over him, but we both shared a time of 5:03.0, which was a UK national record.

It was a race for which I had really been in the wrong frame of mind, because earlier in the week I had felt extremely listless, with my joints aching as though I was sickening for something. Only two days before the race I had dropped out of a track session of 10×300 metres when only halfway through because I felt absolutely exhausted, and so I was not exactly brimming with confidence.

Less than a fortnight later I ran for Britain in the European Cup semi-final at Crystal Palace. It was a relatively easy run, as I broke up the field with a hard third lap, and then steadied it down until the finish. My time of 13:30.4 left me twenty seconds ahead of the second man, Mikhail Ulymov of Russia, and everyone was saying, 'Oh, Brendan's back in good condition again.' But I knew I wasn't. That race had been against mediocre opposition, and I was trying to *force* the training to come, trying to get the training times I had managed the previous year to give me the confidence to race as I had the previous year. I was simply running too hard, a slave of my 1974 training diary in the 1975 season.

The next big test was to be the Gateshead Games on July 26th, where Rod Dixon of New Zealand would be my chief opponent in what, inevitably, had become heralded as a 'world record attempt', following my 3000 metres mark the previous summer. I suppose I did not really help, because I thought, 'Well, I did it last year, I can do it again this year', but I was in danger of becoming a machine. Although I had been mentally high after Rome, my physical condition had been deteriorating in the winter and now I was desperately trying to make up for lost time. The week before my race against Dixon I ran three times a mile in 4:09, my best ever, but they felt like three separate one-mile races. The previous summer I had managed three times a mile in 4:10, but felt fresh enough afterwards to have done three more. That was the difference, and looking back now I can see that my best action would have been to hand my 1974 training diary to someone and say, 'Hold on that for a couple of years,' so that I could not keep referring to it, and comparing what I had done twelve months earlier.

A word with Stan Long before the 5000m at the 1975 Gateshead Games. (Newcastle Chronicle & Journal).

136

The difference between a man who knows he is going to win, and one who knows he is going to lose. In some ways my defeat by Rod Dixon at the Gateshead Games helped me by demonstrating to the local population that I was not unbeatable. (Newcastle Chronicle & Journal).

The race with Dixon turned out to be a somewhat traumatic experience. He had run the distance only once before, and I felt confident that I could beat him through my still-limited but greater experience of the event. We had 13,000 spectators in the stadium, and a strong wind blowing into our faces on the back straight. Tony Simmons led the first five laps, when I moved ahead, and was followed immediately by Dixon. We were already outside world record pace, and with that wind it was out of the question now. Everyone, myself included, was wondering when I would throw in my hard lap. I kept putting it off, but then on the seventh circuit I put my head down and went as hard as I could. It was supposed to be a 59-seconds lap, but it was outside 62 seconds, and Dixon was still there, almost loping along as I screwed up my face; the pain was as much as it would have been for a 59-seconds lap. I was going to lose. I knew it from four laps out, and as we circled the track Dixon gained more and more confidence as I lost more and more. I was thinking, 'All right, you've won, why don't you just go by me and get it over?' But he stayed on my shoulder until, 500 metres from home, he swung wide and opened out for a final lap in under 60 seconds, to finish 40 metres ahead of me. The outcome had merely been a formality.

137

I congratulate Rod after the race. The following winter I played a videotape of that defeat regularly to remind myself how hard I had to prepare for Montreal. (Newcastle Chronicle & Journal).

It was a big disappointment, of course, to lose at Gateshead. The world record, I knew, was never on because I simply was not in condition to break records. Yet the event had its valuable side, because all the local people would now realise that I was not invincible, and that I could lose, even in Gateshead. It was disappointing to them too, perhaps, but at least it eased slightly the pressure I felt every time I stepped on that track. They probably believed that I could beat John Walker over a mile, too, so it was at least some consolation that the loss had not been entirely in vain.

The following day Sue and I went up to the Lake District for a week's holiday, and it was a time in which I did a lot of thinking and not a great deal of running.

When we arrived at our hotel I remember seeing a newspaper lying open, purely by chance, at the sports page, and a headline read 'Big Bren is only human'. I realised what the events of recent months had been telling me: that I was not a robot, programmed to run certain times irrespective of other considerations, and that I was not allowing my moods to dictate to me how I ran. I was becoming too regimented.

In that week I did quite a bit of walking around the beautiful Lakeland country-side, and only about five to ten miles a day of easy running – not really training at all. I also made some decisions. For a start, I was going to relax and not worry too much about the rest of the season, taking some pressure off myself. And secondly I would put everything into my preparations for the Montreal Olympic Games, where I would try to run both the 5000 and the 10,000 metres.

I came back feeling relaxed and refreshed, and my running showed an immediate improvement. On August 17th I won the European Cup final 5000 metres in Nice feeling well in control. I put in a burst after seven laps, and only Lasse Viren tried to come with me, as he did in Rome. A lap later he was ten metres adrift, and from then on the race was just a question of getting to the finish. I felt everything was coming right again, and that I had once more found the way of breaking the spirit of the opposition. Sadly, just before the race started, we heard of the death in Russia of Vladimir Kuts, the 1956 double Olympic champion, whose front-running had inspired me so much in the past. Our race was delayed for one minute's silence in his memory, but I like to think of my way of running it as my own small personal tribute to him.

Lasse Viren eventually fell back to finish fifth, but as we shook hands after the race he said to me, 'Don't worry. I'll be back next year!' Ominous words.

A week later I ran an 800 metres in the Edinburgh Highland Games, and managed to maintain my unique record of having finished last there almost every time out. This time my performance of 1:53.0 reached a new level of mediocrity, and there was no doubt that in whatever way my training was helping my 5000 metres running, it was not doing a lot for my 800 metres! But I had not entirely lost my speed because two days later I won the 1500 metres for Britain in their match against Russia at Crystal Palace. It was quite an exciting race, because there were three of us entering the home straight together, with me in third place, and I got up on my toes and managed to edge past Frank Clement and Vladimir Panteley before the line. The last lap took 55.9, the last 200 metres only 27.4 seconds, and one of my delights is playing a videotape recording I have of the race in which the commentator is saying '. . . and Foster is out of it now, he's got no speed'. For my next trick . . .

Only four days later I was back at Crystal Palace for a race to which I had really been looking forward, the 10,000 metres in the IAC–Coca-Cola floodlit meeting. As I was intending to run the 10,000 at Montreal, I knew I had to try the event at least once this season, and with a field which included all the top British boys – David Black, Tony Simmons and Bernie Ford – plus the Olympic marathon champion (and 10,000 metres finalist) Frank Shorter, and Holland's Jos Hermens, I knew that I could hardly have faced a stiffer test outside a major Games.

Once again recent British successes, including six wins in the European Cup final at Nice, had ensured a capacity crowd for the meeting, and although it was my first official 10,000 metres race it was not really new territory because I had run with most of the others on the roads or cross country. Still, I was a learner, so I decided that I would not lead an inch of the way, I'd just learn.

I started the race slowly, right at the back of the field, but when I looked up and saw Shorter, Simmons and company at the head of the field I thought I had better get up there too. So I did on the next lap, thus wasting about four laps of mental effort in doing so. One of the things I later discovered about the 10,000 was that you have got to get the early laps out of your system. There are twenty-five in all, and so there is no point in getting involved in the race early on. You just have to retain your confidence and keep calm. I purposely did not look at the lap indicator each time we came round, because I was afraid of the negative effect something like '19 laps to go' might have on me.

Being an evening meeting in late August, the weather was cool, and just right for such a race, and gradually the field was whittled down until at 6000 metres there were just six of us in the leading group. Shorter kept trying to surge away, and each time he did, I went with him, but I steadfastly refused to go in front myself until the moment I chose to make my bid with a long run for home.

I waited until just before the end of the twenty-first lap, then went as hard as I could. The burst stretched the bunch right out, apart from Hermens, who stayed with me. Black was not far behind either, and I knew that with twenty-two of the twenty-five laps gone my confidence was beginning to ebb. There I was in front, and my hard lap had not worked; the rest were beginning to close on me again. Fortunately, David Black made up the gap quickly, then went ahead, because he has little finishing speed and did not want to wait for a last lap dust-up. I moved onto his shoulder and when the bell clanged for the final lap, the noise from the crowd was almost rocking the roof as we weaved our way in and out of the lapped runners.

Only as we came off the final bend did I make my last effort to sprint, and managed to get clear of Black. I knew the race was mine, and as I neared the line

I turned to wave to the crowd in the main stand, who were on their feet. I did not realise until I saw a film of the race afterwards just how fast Frank Shorter, who had let himself fall too far behind, was finishing. He was sprinting much faster than me in the home straight, and there I was gaily waving to the crowd and almost losing the race as a result of it. Easing down before the finish is a terrible, schoolboyish habit of which I have tried to rid myself, but my pleasure in winning that race was complete at that moment.

My time of 27:45.4 was seventh on the world all-time ranking list, and the fastest-ever debut at the event. It was the fastest in the world in 1975, and earned me top ranking at the event in the prestigious US magazine *Track and Field News* for that season, which in a year without an Olympics is virtually the next best thing to an Olympic gold medal. I learned a lot from the race, though, and not simply about easing up at the finish.

Next morning, I could hardly walk. My feet were badly blistered from the race, and as I was out for a short hobble near the hotel, Frank Shorter, who had finished just 0.6 seconds behind me, sailed past on a training run. Just suppose, I said to myself, that the race last night had been an Olympic heat? There was no way that I could have run another 10,000 metres next day, as I would have to in Montreal. Yet I had been thinking about doing the double, and in Montreal the 10,000 metres came before the 5000 metres. Clearly there was more to consider than just form in one race. It would need a lot more thought. And possibly a spare pair of feet.

Eleven

The start of my build-up for the Montreal Olympics, due to be held in July 1976, began in the autumn of 1975. I could look back on a summer which had not been entirely successful, but in which I had learned a lot, and when you stop doing that, you stop making progress. Now as the nights drew in, and most people selected their favourite fireside television-watching chair, around the country a number of international athletes were beginning their own preparations. It meant night after night of running through cold, rain, sleet, snow and wind, so that as you reeled back indoors after yet another training run, your face tingled as icy skin was suddenly plunged back into warmth, and your pulse rate gradually came back down.

In many ways it is a masochistic existence, out into the cold night to run yourself into the ground, but I was motivated not only by the lads at the club who ran with me, but also by those I could not see. For I knew that down in Birmingham Ian Stewart and David Black would be piling in the miles, I knew that in Luton, Tony Simmons would be doing the same thing, and in Feltham, Bernie Ford was training hard. There were rumours that Dave Bedford would be recovered from injury in time to make a strong bid for a place in the British Olympic team. And, of course, there was always the unknown athlete who might be on the verge of a breakthrough, anywhere from Land's End to John o'Groats.

I was confident I could handle all of them on the day if I could get in a reasonable winter's work. But the great tradition of British distance running which has built up over the years means that you cannot take anything for granted when it comes to selection. The Kraft Games, on which Olympic selection would be based, were to be held at Crystal Palace in early June, and I knew that I would have to be in form then. If I was not, or if I had an off-day as I did in 1972, then my Olympic ambitions would get no further.

One of the advantages of being a runner in a country where there is such a vast reservoir of distance runners is that you can plan to reach your peak at the Olympics, and not have to worry about selection. In Britain, although you try to put it out of your mind and concentrate on the major Games, there is always a little speck of self-doubt when you suddenly remember 'but I've got to be selected first'.

Unfortunately in this country it seems as though you are never given any credit for your past record. In the winter of 1975 I could look back on being the first Briton home in every major championship I had run: 1970 Commonwealth Games (1500 metres, bronze medal); 1971 European (1500 metres bronze medal); 1972 Olympics (1500 metres, fifth in final); 1974 Commonwealth (5000 metres silver medal, 1500 metres UK record) and European (5000 metres gold medal). I had won the European Cup 5000 metres finals in 1973 and 1975. But I still had to go through the process of Olympic selection, which meant I was trying to aim for two peaks to the season: in early June for the selection trials, and in mid- to late-July for the actual Olympics. The two were not near enough to sustain one peak, which can last only a couple of weeks, not far enough apart to build up to separately.

But if I ignored the earlier one, I could find myself in good form at the time of the Olympics, but out of Britain's team. These were the twin problems which constantly went through my mind as I planned my preparation. Either way, I still had to put in a good total of mileage, and had a chance to see how I was progressing when I ran in the televised Gateshead cross country races at the end of November. This time I was better prepared than the previous year, and by the half distance in the International four-and-a-half miles race around the sharp hills, I had opened up a gap of 40 yards on the rest of the field.

I was feeling quite good up to then, but after four of the six laps had been completed I began to suffer a little. I also realised that the Dutchman Jos Hermens, who had recently broken the world records for ten miles, twenty kilometres and one hour, was closing on me. Halfway round the final lap we were together, and I had to put in two bursts to try to get rid of him. Even as we toiled down the long finishing straight, he was sprinting again, and I had to really dig deep to edge him to the line. We were both clocked at 22 minutes 41 seconds, and it was a good feeling to win in Gateshead again, only yards from the stadium where I had lost to Rod Dixon in July.

That day I had an extra reason to feel chuffed, because I received a letter in the morning indicating that I was to receive an MBE in the New Year's Honours list. Of course, I could not mention it to anyone, but it was a total and very pleasant surprise.

Sue and I flew to South Africa just before Christmas for the first of two one-month training trips at altitude which I had planned. We stayed in Johannesburg, and it made a pleasant change to be running in warm sunshine again instead of the sleet and snow which had been accompanying me on my last training runs in Gateshead. Lindsay Dunn came with us, so I had a training partner out there, and together we managed to put in a great deal of mileage.

On New Year's Day the Honours List was published, and my MBE seemed to cause a considerable stir in South Africa. We had photographers around to the hotel taking pictures of me running, walking, sitting down, standing up, having breakfast, and staring into space. But the whole time I was there, and during my second month's stay in May, I did not compete in any meetings, despite invitations, because none of them was multi-racial.

South Africa is a beautiful country, and we enjoyed our stay there, but I did not wish to compete in 'whites only' athletics meetings, despite the accusation from one leading athlete that I was scared to run against him. South African athletes have since been further isolated, because they had already been expelled from the Olympic Games, and in Montreal were to be voted out of the International Amateur Athletic Federation too. So I would not now be allowed to run in South Africa in any case.

We arrived back in London on January 13th, and four days later I took part in a cross country race in Glasgow. It was a course that suited me perfectly, and I won by nearly half a minute from Tony Simmons, who was running well himself at that time. I was very pleased with the race, but was beginning to feel a little jaded from the recent long spell of hard training. I had promised myself a break in the form of a very easy week, and I took it then, not before time. I just did a steady five miles each day, and the following week travelled with Gateshead Harriers to Arlon in Belgium, where I won the individual race in the European Clubs cross country championship. Our team was third overall.

In the middle of February I received my MBE at Buckingham Palace from Her Majesty the Queen, and it was nice that my mother and Sue were able to come too, and see the presentation. If I am quite honest about it, though, I suppose the actual decoration does not mean as much to me as it ought to, or as it perhaps will in future years. When you do not strive for a particular thing, you do not appreciate it if it comes your way. I have chased after records and medals and got as much, if not more, satisfaction from the struggle to achieve them as from actually reaching my goal.

The MBE was something about which I had never thought, and certainly never chased, and I know there was some feeling, especially in local government circles

144

With my wife, Sue, at the Buckingham Palace investiture in 1976. (Topix).

in the north-east, that I was much too young to receive such an honour. Was it jealousy? I don't know, but I do know that it was in recognition of my running, not my contribution to local government! It was flattering and exciting to hear I had been awarded it, and an honour to go to Buckingham Palace, but now it is in the past. I have almost forgotten it, except when someone puts 'Brendan Foster, MBE' on a letter. I have certainly never worn the medal at a function, nor do I intend to. But attitudes change, and I am perfectly willing to accept that in twenty or thirty years time I may value that MBE more than any of my athletics medals.

Soon I was back into the high training mileage, and by March I had reached my greatest-ever volume of around 135 miles a week. I also had my longest single run, a twenty-five-miler on a wet, miserable Sunday morning with Max Coleby, John

Caine and Andy Holden. We just went at a steady pace, around two-and-a-half hours for the distance, and I felt quite comfortable all the way round. I am often asked if I have thought about running a marathon, and my reply usually is 'Yes – when I've had a few drinks!' I know that I could run the 26 miles 385 yards if I had to, but the question is whether anyone would let me be satisfied with simply getting round the course. If I did run a marathon, everyone would be expecting me to race it, and indeed my own competitive instinct might force me to go a little faster than otherwise I should, so the real answer is that I have no plans for a marathon debut at the moment.

The daily grind of running about twenty miles a day every day of the week seemed a never-ending one. Only as we moved into April, and the buds and blossom everywhere reminded me that the summer was not too far away now, did it seem as though an end was in sight. The constant battering the body takes every day without really recovering from the previous one is considerable, and I noted in my training diary for April 8th:

> 'Am having to apply myself and in fact discipline myself very much to maintain this level of training. Am feeling extremely tired and low occasionally because of it. However, have the motivation to keep going, especially as it seems as if I'm running well. But I often think I'll never be able to do it again.'

That week I covered 131½ miles (even halves count when you are looking for bulk); the previous week I had run 123, and the following week I covered 136. At the end of April, after nearly three months of the hardest training of my life, I broke my own record for the short stage in the AAA National road relay by 21 seconds, and Gateshead Harriers once more completed the winter double of being national cross country team champions and national road relay champions.

The next day I wrote in my training diary:

> Have averaged 120 miles for ten weeks, and 126 for the last six weeks of intensive build-up. This is extremely high and I mustn't forget the effort that has gone into it. The cold, windy, dark nights running with Wilf (Wardle) when I was so tired from my morning run that I couldn't keep up; the hard stretches at the club when only my pride enabled me to pull away from the rest; the morning runs going past the Ravensworth pub to do 11 miles when I felt like turning back at the Ravensworth; the discipline that made me do two 10-mile runs in a day when I'd already done 80 miles in four days. When the track races approach it must be remembered how much effort has gone into obtaining a background.

146

Keeping an account of how I felt at the time not only was therapeutic then, but also valuable to me looking back. When things turn out well (or even when they don't) you can sometimes forget the moments when the future seemed hopeless, and when you were really down. I tend to think it is important to remember those moments as a spirit-strengthener for the future. I have many of my big races on videotape, and can re-live them whenever I want to, but the one I re-play most is not of a victory, but of Rod Dixon beating me over 5000 metres at Gateshead. You don't need to keep telling yourself what a great bloke you are; you need to remind yourself of what can happen if you do not prepare for the summer thoroughly.

Mick Channon and the rest of the Southampton soccer team joined me for a training session while visiting the north-east.

At the beginning of May, Sue and I went for our second combined holiday-cum-training trip to Johannesburg, and this time steeplechaser Andy Holden came with us, and acted as my training partner. We were there for three weeks, and again my notes at the time probably reflect my see-sawing spirits and doubts:

Friday May 6: Have been at altitude six days. Was struggling to begin with. Now running a bit better, but terribly stiff. Doubting my ability and worrying about form for racing. Must not allow myself to get into low spirits, worrying about my weight or my right-hand side back tooth.

Tuesday May 11: Seemed to take around seven days to be able to run well and confidently over ten miles. Now am able to run steady and relaxed and not worry about the altitude even though I'm very tired and usually stiff after a day's training. Have been training very hard and doing nothing else. This is obviously rather boring, as consequently I've been thinking about training and this is not a healthy situation since one gets a little down if too much thought is given to it, although resting between sessions makes it possible to run harder. I think the training will pay off. Confidence is growing slowly and I'm looking forward to getting back to England and into the races. It is almost essential for me to have someone to train with, and having Andy to run my morning ten-milers with has been great.

Saturday May 15: Been at altitude 15 days, am now going quite well and getting confidence in my ability to run out here, which is important. Am a bit fed up at times since all I seem to be doing is training; however, this is the most important time and I must keep at it.

Tuesday May 18: Have been running very well last two days, and good track session today. . . . Had a nice day today by breaking the routine of running ten miles every morning (good idea). Feel a little more confident about the 1500 metres, and really looking forward to the 5000 and 10,000 metres.

We got home on May 23rd, absolutely exhausted by an air journey which had taken us from Johannesburg to Dar es Salaam, Nairobi, Zurich, London, and then finally Newcastle. We watched the Britain v Soviet Union athletics international on television from Kiev, and then I went out and ran fifteen miles to get the journey out of my legs. That week I had two races in three days, one in London on Wednesday and one in Gateshead on Friday, so I wanted to get back to normal as soon as possible.

The first race was a 1500 metres during the AAA v Borough Road College match at Crystal Palace, and I felt full of running. Even on the last lap, covered in 55.6 seconds, I felt I was still holding something back, and I won the race in 3:40.2, ahead of the new Hungarian star, Janos Zemen.

The second half of the double was a mile at Gateshead two days later, which would re-match me with Zemen, plus the great Kenyan runner Mike Boit. It was a wet, chilly evening, but the meeting (known as the Superspike Classic, to raise money for the International Athletes Club) attracted 10,000 spectators, and the mile was supposed to be the highlight. We were confident that John Walker's track record of 3 minutes 57.6 seconds would be broken, but in the end it all turned out to be something of a damp squib, especially as far as I was concerned. The race started fast enough, but then slowed, and the big field were still together on the last lap. I found myself boxed in several times during the middle laps, but by the final circuit had moved out to a good position on the shoulder of the leader, Boit.

We came round the final bend and then suddenly I felt someone else's leg catch mine, and the next thing I knew, instead of launching my attack down the finishing straight, I was lying on the wet Tartan track with the rest of the runners belting past, and needle-sharp spikes zipping through the air, only inches away from my head. There was little I could do, except slowly jog down the finishing straight. Mike Boit won the race in 3:58.7, but the crowd were almost silent, not in deprecation of Mike's fine run, but simply at the shock of seeing me fall. Fortunately, the damage was no worse than a grazed shoulder, arm and leg, but it had not exactly been the finishing touch I had envisaged to my last race before the Olympic trial 5000 metres event, which was now little more than a week away.

It was a week of agitation, anxiety and nervousness, but not the usual sort. For I was getting nervous about a race which had nothing at the end of it, except sweat dripping onto the track. I was European champion, but if I had a poor day in the 5000 metres trial I could be out on my ear.

The athletes were, of course, told by the selectors that 'the whole season' and not just this one race would be considered when they picked the Olympic team. But I was cynical. I had to be, because Tony Simmons (13:21.2) and Nick Rose (13:22.0) had run the two fastest times in the world up to that point, representing Britain in Kiev, and I had done nothing recently at the distance.

As we gathered at Crystal Palace that weekend there was a very pronounced air of impending gloom in every athlete's face; there are few of us who don't believe the worst is going to happen, and the moments of worry are always heightened just before a race. When that race is (as ours was) an Olympic selection trial, that worry is particularly intense, and when our event got under way there was a great relief as the starter's gun sounded, and we headed round the first bend.

1976: Halfway to the Montreal Olympics after the selection trials. (Wilf Wardle).

I deliberately waited at the back, almost jogging the first 200 metres, so that I could keep an eye on everybody else, and give them a chance to wonder what I was up to. Five of the fourteen runners had personal bests superior to the Olympic record for the distance, and only three would go to Montreal. I held back, and the pace remained gentle. Only as we passed the '5 laps to go' marker did I make a move going to the front and putting in a 60 seconds lap which broke the field up. It was a familiar situation, and I was really feeling dead on the last two laps, with visions of the rest of them catching me, but they were engaged in their own battles. David Black finished second, and Ian Stewart third, while Nick Rose and Tony Simmons (fourth and fifth respectively) were to find that their fast times in May would not save them when it came to selection.

It was a hard race, but the tension was only half over. The 10,000 metres trial was to be held seven days later, and as I felt that this would perhaps be my better event in Montreal I still had that nagging uncertainty hanging over me. But at least I was sure of going to the Olympics now, at the shorter event if not the long one.

By the following Saturday I was even looking forward to the race, and was not too nervous as the cast of characters reassembled on the same stage. I wondered how some of them had spent the week. Tony Simmons, for instance, whose chances in the 5000 metres last week had been wrecked by flu. How many restless nights had he spent, knowing that he had to do well in the 10,000 metres this week if he was to go to Montreal? In Rome he had been just inches away from a European title less than two years earlier, but now we were all in the same boat. There was David Black, who knew he had probably got a place in the 5000 metres team, but would much prefer to qualify for the 10,000 metres. And Ian Stewart, who was telling everyone that the longer race was his better distance, although he had been a bronze medallist at 5000 metres in the Munich Olympics.

At the start it was Simmons who shot into the lead, apparently anxious to waste no time in staking his claim. He opened up a gap of some twenty metres in the first couple of laps, but we slowly hauled him back and by 3000 metres there were nine of us in contention. I shared the lead with Tony, but by 7000 metres Ian Stewart and I were beginning to pull away from Simmons, and the hot weather was taking its toll on the rest of the field. I decided that this was the moment to strike and I raised the tempo by several seconds on the nineteenth lap, covering it in 64.5 seconds. Unknown to me, several laps later Ian stepped off the track while in second place, a victim of bad blisters.

I pressed on to cross the line in 27 minutes 53.8 seconds, which was the second fastest time in the world at that point in the summer, but that did not really mean a great deal. At the Olympics we would all be back on the starting line together. Tony Simmons rallied to finish second in 27:56.4 and make up for his disappointment of the previous week, and Bernie Ford, who was on the point of dropping out of the race until he saw Stewart do so first, finished third.

All of us had suffered from blisters, and I had made an appointment to see a chiropodist next morning in case any treatment was needed. I remembered how bad I had been after the Coca-Cola 10,000 metres the previous season. But the damage was not too bad, and the day after the race I was able to run a steady twenty miles without too much trouble. The fact that I could, convinced me that I would be able to tackle both the 5000 and 10,000 metres at the Olympics, and the following day the team of fifty-five athletes was announced. I had been selected for both events, but in the 10,000 metres only Tony Simmons was named with me. The selectors decreed that Ian Stewart and Bernie Ford should race over 10,000 metres once more in Helsinki at the end of the month.

It seemed ironic to me that they should be asked to go to the same track where I had been asked to prove myself against John Kirkbride four years earlier, and Bernie Ford's subsequent decision to sit back on his previous performances of the year and wait to see what Ian could do in Helsinki must have taken a lot of courage. In the end Ian did not impress the selectors sufficiently by his race in Finland, and Ford got the third place in the Olympic team.

Ian had already been named for the 5000 metres, so he was not missing out on the Games, but both my partners at the shorter distance – Ian and David Black – would have preferred to have run the longer distance in Montreal. I could understand their feelings, but then making sure of your place in the team is half the battle. I remembered getting home to Gateshead four years earlier after I had messed up my own selection for Munich by a poor run, and sitting on a swing in the back garden, going to and fro, mulling over the situation and vowing I would never get in the same state again. It is not the sort of experience you ever want to repeat, because if you are only a borderline selection for your national team, it takes the devil of an effort to get up the confidence to run against the world without inhibition at the Olympics.

I was in the team safely, I seemed to be in good form, yet somehow things were still not quite right. I had trained so hard through the winter that when I started to ease down in the summer I had begun to feel a little guilty. Unnecessarily so, because I probably needed a recovery phase, but the Olympic pressure was hotting up. In Helsinki Lasse Viren had run a very fast 10,000 metres time, 27:42.9, which indicated that he would be in good shape to defend his titles in Montreal. I recalled his words to me in Nice the previous summer: 'Don't worry, I'll be back.' He was.

I just did not seem to be getting satisfaction from my running. I wanted everything at once – to win, to run good times, even break world records – but it was more important to wait the six weeks to Montreal. I took a break from racing, planning just two more before I left for Montreal. One would be the 1500 metres for Britain in their match against Poland and Canada at Crystal Palace, and the other would be the following day, in Stockholm, against a field which included John Walker, who was just rounding into top form. I felt the first race should be a mere formality, because my track training was going so well, and I was more concerned about getting in a very fast time in Stockholm. But I misjudged it, and found myself beaten at Crystal Palace by a Canadian I had never heard of, named Dave Hill. He jumped the field 200 metres out, and despite running the last lap in around 54 seconds, I could not catch him. I ran a stupid race, and had not done my homework properly; I had never even considered losing.

152

Then next day, in Stockholm, I found myself in a much faster race, and just got buried in the pack. Walker won in 3:34.2, just two seconds outside the world record, but I felt as though I was struggling early on and ended up in eighth place in 3:40.9. I would not have worried about the placing, but the performance was disappointing. Had I mistimed everything? It seemed as if I was going over the top, and I started to panic and worry a bit. I felt run down, and I had mouth ulcers.

A week later I went to Zurich for a two-miles race, secretly hoping that I might be able to improve on my own world record. But my confidence had been dented by my running in those 1500 metres races, and it was not until five of the eight laps had gone that I felt ready to take over the lead. I knew there was no chance of the world record, but pushed the final laps hard to clock 8:19.0, over five seconds outside my mark. I felt I could have run faster, but all the time I was too anxious. I was running better now, but not outstandingly so. If I had run, say, 27:45 in the Olympic 10,000 metres trials, instead of 27:53, then I might have been happier, more content. I needed a sign that I was not just fit, but at my absolute fittest, and it was not forthcoming.

Had I trained too hard? Was the balance of mileage and speedwork wrong? Had I neglected to give myself enough rest from the daily grind? These negative thoughts were ones I could not stop passing through my mind, hard as I tried. After all, my intention had been to prepare so thoroughly that I could go to the Olympics in a relaxed frame of mind, confident that whatever happened I could not have done more in my preparation. Yet here I was wondering if I had over-done it.

Whether I had or not, only time would tell. But even that was running out on me. On July 14th, 1976, I flew with the rest of the British team to Montreal.

Twelve

It would be a relief finally to get to the Olympic city, after the months and years of preparation. But before I left I made the rounds of people who had helped me and thanked them, promising to do my best to reward their time and effort. I had a farewell drink with a group of mates including Lindsay Dunn, John Trainor and Wilf Wardle, who had covered so many of the training miles with me in the past, and I reflected on how lucky I was to have such people not only as training partners, but also as friends. Because they understood what was involved in trying to succeed at the Olympic Games, they put no pressure on me at all. While the people who call out 'You'll win a gold medal for us, won't you?' do not realise it, they are actually increasing the pressure under which an athlete has to perform. 'Gold medal' is easy to say; I wish it was as easy to win.

I called over at Hebburn, to say goodbye to my Mum and Dad, and again the complete lack of pressure I felt in that visit was just what I wanted. I knew that my mother would be in a high state of nervous tension throughout the Games, watching it on television, and that the ordeal would be as bad, if not worse, for her than for me. But I felt reasonably relaxed, and as I walked down that garden path once more I could not help briefly remembering the hundreds and hundreds of times I had opened the gate to go out, or come back from, a training run when I was younger. Then I did not really know why I was opening the gate, or what I was training for. This time when I went through that gate I would be on my way to the Olympic Games.

I recalled the times when I had returned from races that had gone well, almost floating up that path. And times when it had all gone wrong, when I trudged up it. Or times when I had got home from school, or managed to get back for a weekend from university, and my Mum would say, 'You canna go out training in *this* weather, Brendan.' But I always did, because I knew, deep inside, that I had to. No matter how hard it was raining, or snowing, I knew that I must get out and put in a few more miles.

If you have a strong family background, as I have, it must be a great advantage when you go into the Olympic Stadium in pursuit of your life's ambition. For you know that even if you finish last you will retain the support of your family, who know that you have given all you could.

For my mother, my competitive move up to 5000 and 10,000 metres racing was worse than the 1500 metres, because her anxiety would last that much longer. But she is still not as bad as my Auntie Mary, who has to go down the bottom of the garden when I'm racing, and wait until someone rings up to let her know how I've got on!

I suppose it is part of a mother's natural instinct to worry about the possibility of her son suffering. Before I went to Montreal, my Dad was confident I would do well, but I think my Mum was far more concerned about how I would react over whatever I did out there than whether I actually won or lost. She realised I was under terrific pressure at that time, and her parting words to me reflected her feelings when she said, 'Go and enjoy yourself, and try to be satisfied with what you do.'

The whole family had seen me go through the mill before, and this time it was not so much a formal 'Good luck' from them, as a 'Go on, Bren, get out and show them!'

Sue was going to join me in Montreal later, so after saying goodbye to her I made the train journey down to London for the long flight to Canada. It was a strange time, with my confidence ebbing and flowing, as I thought back over my training and my injuries. I knew I should not think about negative aspects, but self-doubt is a constant companion to an athlete before a big competition, and this was the biggest of the lot.

The accommodation in the Olympic Village at Montreal was far from comfortable. The Village was actually two large blocks of flats, specially built, and twelve of us were assigned to share one three-roomed apartment. I knew from my previous experience at major Games just how claustrophobic this can become when athletes in a state of high tension are thrown together with a lot of time on their hands in not much space, and Sue and I had taken the precaution of booking a hotel room a mile or so away from the Village. For the first couple of nights I slept in the Village, but when Sue arrived in Montreal I was glad to be able to move into the hotel room.

I still used to spend all day in the Village because I felt some responsibility to the team to be seen around, and in between training sessions I would sit and chat, or play scrabble, or visit the Village cinema. I arrived every day about 9 am, but by 8 o'clock in the evening I was back in the hotel for some peace. Technically, I should not have done it, because the athletes were all supposed to be housed in the Village. But my main responsibility was to myself, because I was the one who had for years tumbled out of bed to go running before work, and again in the evening, and I was the one whose hard preparations would all be spoiled if, as had happened before, I could not sleep properly before the most important races of my life.

The heats of the 10,000 metres were to be held on Friday, July 23rd, which meant that I had about a week to wait, and in that time I went through the whole gamut of physical afflictions, some real and some perhaps psychosomatic. I had tight hamstrings, a bad back, and a stuffed-up feeling in my head, among other things, and one morning I was even woken up by an inflamed big toe throbbing. You cannot help being insular at a time like that, and if you are going to call upon your body to run harder than ever before you try to catch any possible physical problem as early as possible.

I saw the draw for my heat of the 10,000 metres, which did not seem too bad. None of the men I considered to be my main rivals were in my heat. Carlos Lopes of Portugal, a small, stocky man who had broken through by unexpectedly winning the International cross country championship the previous March, was in the first heat, while Lasse Viren, Emiel Puttemans and Dick Quax were all in the third heat. My heat was the second one, and I was not too worried about it.

In fact, it proved harder than I expected. I did not feel very nervous beforehand, because I felt I just had to go out and run round to get into the final, but as the race went on and there was still quite a large group of us together, I began to get a little worried. I was determined not to lead, so I just waited and waited, and did not feel very comfortable, because to run like that was not my style. Also my stomach, which had been a bit active in the previous couple of days, was beginning to play up and was sore during the race. When the bell sounded for the last lap, I kicked away from the group, and Marc Smet of Belgium came with me. We covered the last lap in 58.5 seconds, and crossed the line together in 28:22.2, over seventeen seconds slower than Lopes, who had won the first heat easily.

I came off the track feeling very low, despite the fact that I had just qualified for the final. There was no feeling of achievement at all, because it was a race run simply through necessity, and it had been harder work than I thought. My hamstrings were beginning to tighten again, and I was sweating a lot.

156

Steve Ovett, who had earlier won his heat in the 800 metres, came over, and I said to him, 'When you qualify for the final at the Olympic Games, you're supposed to be pleased, aren't you?' He said, 'I know exactly what you're thinking. You've got about ten minutes of satisfaction after the heat, and then you've got to start thinking about the next one.'

It is the sort of thing you never read about in coaching books. Coaches always say, 'Just get through your heat, and then do this and this in the final.' But no one ever says, 'Now you'll feel worse in the heats than the final, because you've got nothing to gain and everything to lose, and your body doesn't really want to go flat out until the race where it really means something.'

The third heat was won by Tony Simmons in the fastest time of all, 28:01.8, which I felt put him out of the reckoning in the final. He won by over ten seconds and seemed to have used up a lot of energy recklessly, while Viren had been content to qualify in third place. The real shock was Dick Quax, who faded in the middle of his heat and ended up ninth, out of the final. It transpired that he had been the victim of a stomach bug, and had lost ten pounds in weight the previous week because of it.

We had two clear rest days before the final, and I did very little running in that time. I just jogged a few miles to stretch my legs, and the doctors gave me some tablets for my stomach, which was still sore. In those days I went over the 10,000 metres finalists in my mind, and all the time I kept coming back to Lasse Viren. He had given little away in his heat, and he had an aura which none of the others possessed. But he was someone I had beaten in the past, and I wondered whether he was really hungry enough for success four years after Munich. There was Lopes, the Lisbon bank official, who could run strongly from the front but who had not really been tested in major track competition. And there was me, still a virtual novice at the distance, but with a solid training background and the determination to give everything I had.

Ironically, despite its great tradition in the events, Britain has never won the 5000 metres, 10,000 metres, or marathon events at the Olympic Games. As we warmed up for the final on Monday, July 26th, I thought I could, if all went well, be the first. But inside I could feel that all was still not well with my stomach, as the anxiety and the tension of the occasion swept over me.

As we finalists moved into the huge Olympic stadium, with its unfinished tower and building cranes, a constant reminder that these were the Games that at one stage seemed likely to be postponed or even cancelled because of the delays in building, we could see flags of every nationality being waved in the crowd. I could see at least a dozen Union Jacks draped over partitions, and as many flags with the blue cross of Finland. I told myself that this, at last, was the race that mattered, and that this was what all that work last winter had been aimed at. I'm not sure whether I was supposed to feel a great surge of patriotism, or of inspiration, at this thought. What I did feel was a sudden and urgent need to visit the trackside toilet again before the start, and so I hared off down the tunnel much more quickly than I had expected.

When I came to return to the track, just a couple of minutes before the start, a Canadian soldier tried to stop me, perhaps thinking I was an intruder, like the student who joined in at the end of the 1972 Munich marathon.

'You can't get through here!' he said.

'But I'm running in this race,' I shouted. 'Let me on the track!'

The moment of truth. Lasse Viren, Carlos Lopes, Jos Hermens and I stand on the line a few seconds before the start of the Olympic 10,000m final in Montreal. (Mark Shearman).

Finally, through desperation rather than brawn, I managed to push my way back onto the track, and join the others, who were just beginning to take off their tracksuits. I wondered how I would have been able to explain to all the athletics-mad lads back home, watching the Games on television, that I missed the 10,000 metres final because I found something more urgent to do!

There were sixteen of us in the final, and as the gun fired for the start I allowed myself to be swallowed up by the pack, just content to take it easy in the early stages. The pace was gentle in the opening lap, but by the second lap I knew I was going to have problems with my stomach. It was beginning to churn round, and as it did so my confidence was gradually being pulped.

There was little I could do except hold on and hope that it would improve, but it did not. The field was beginning to stretch out a little and on the ninth lap Lopes went into the lead and increased the pace. I moved up, and one by one the back-markers became detached from the leaders, until with seventeen laps gone there

Lopes leads the eventual winner, Viren, as I realize that they are pulling away from me. (Mark Shearman).

were just three of us left together in the leading group – Lopes, Viren and myself. I kept thinking I was about to be dropped, which had not happened to me since 1970, when I let the unknown Emiel Puttemans get away from me in his world record two miles at Edinburgh. Ahead of me I could see the slightly hunched shoulders of the long-striding Lopes, and the bony shoulders of Viren. At Nice the previous year, and in Rome the year before that, he had not been able to stay with me when I pushed the pace; now he was back in the driving seat, and I was suffering.

Never have I looked at the lap indicator board from so far out in any race. When it read '5 to go' I knew that Lopes and Viren were pulling away, and there was nothing I could do to stop them. I glanced back and thought, 'Thank God, we're clear of the rest', and I knew that if I kept going I could at least get a medal. But not the one I wanted.

It was a long, lonely trek around those last laps, if anyone can be lonely in an 80,000-seat stadium and watched by hundreds of millions of television viewers all over the world. I had given everything to try to stay with Lopes and Viren, but now my task was simply survival. When the bell rang for my last lap it was one of the most joyous sounds I had ever heard.

Already the crowd was standing as Viren had burst into the lead with 450 metres left and strode away with his second Olympic victory in the race. His time was 27:40.4, but the second half of the race had been much faster than the first. Lopes took the silver with 27:45.2, and even as I came into the home straight, struggling to find enough energy to get round, I could sense that something was happening behind me. Tony Simmons, who had lacked the confidence to come with the leaders earlier, was now in fourth place and coming at me fast.

If anything can illustrate how tired I was in that last lap it must be that I was unable to cover it in faster than 65 seconds. Normally you can raise some extra pace at the finish, and in these circumstances, with someone close enough to possibly take away my Olympic medal, I just could not produce any increase in speed. I crossed the line in 27:55.0, 1.4 seconds ahead of Tony, and never have I been so glad simply to finish a race. It was the hardest of my life.

Even now when I look back on that 10,000 metres I do so with mixed emotions. Frustration, naturally, because I know that if I had run normally I could possibly have beaten Lopes. As for Viren – well, I'll never know, because he has that certain Olympic magic about him. But I have also drawn a great deal of strength from that race inasmuch as I was satisfied that I could not have given another ounce. It was about the only time in my life when I did not race as much as simply run. I have lost races, but they *were* races. That day I was not able to race, but in athletics

160

it all comes down to how hard you can push your body, and I had successfully put myself on trial against myself. In one respect I was happy that I had succeeded, even if in another I was disappointed that I did not win the medal of which I thought I was capable.

There is a certain amount of truth in that Olympic saying about it being more important to take part than to win. If I had only to step out of the front door, run round the track, and win an Olympic gold medal for doing so, or if I was 7ft 6in tall with a 13-ft stride, then I would not appreciate any success. It would be nowhere near as satisfying as it was to win a bronze medal. 'Only' a bronze medal is how other people have described it, but it meant a lot to me, and I knew how hard it had been to get.

There was only one rest day until the heats of the 5000 metres, and at one point I thought I might not be able to run at all. My left hamstring was very stiff and sore, but I managed to get some treatment on it during the afternoon, which helped it a great deal. There were three heats for the 5000 metres, and Dick Quax

I could not have run harder, but Viren won, demonstrating once more his own brand of Olympic 'peaking'.
(Mark Shearman).

showed that he had recovered from his own brand of stomach trouble by winning the first in 13:31.0, with Lasse Viren again keeping a low profile by finishing a safe fourth. Carlos Lopes was due to run in the second heat, but withdrew because of blisters sustained in the 10,000 metres. My own heat was the third one, and I was running on anxiety again. But I had taken some stronger tablets, called Lomotil, after the 10,000 metres and these had helped a great deal, as they did in Rome. I had only refrained from using them before the 10,000 metres here because someone had told me they were on the list of drugs banned by the International Olympic Committee.

I felt quite comfortable once the heat got under way and put in less effort than I had in the 10,000 metres final. Only this time, because I was better, the running was much faster. A group of eight of us broke away, and I led through the first 3000 metres until Anicetos Simoes of Portugal went ahead for a couple of laps. Then I took the lead again on the last lap, and won in 13:20.4, which knocked six seconds off Lasse Viren's Olympic record, set in 1972. In fact, the first eight all beat the record, but only six went through to the final. Obviously I still had something there, and I felt I had re-established myself as a contender in the final.

I knew, though, that Rod Dixon, who was second in my heat, just 0.2 seconds behind me, would be a big danger because he had not run in the 10,000 metres, and his New Zealand compatriot, Dick Quax, would also have benefited from not having run the 10,000 metres final. And of course there was Viren, about whom nothing was certain.

On the morning of the 5000 metres final we slept until about 10 o'clock, and I remember dozing off again and dreaming very vividly that I was winning the race. I was slightly ahead of the field with 200 metres to go, and they were all chasing me, but I got across the line, waving like mad. I knew something was wrong, because it was on the training track, not in the main stadium, and when I awoke again and realised it was only a dream I was very disappointed.

I had decided to set the pace for the first five laps, and then take a rest, before making a big effort. The first part of the plan worked, as I led through 2000 metres in 5:26.4, before Viren came past me and slowed it down somewhat. With about five of the twelve-and-a-half laps left I went hard for about 200 metres, but it was only a half-hearted effort and then Quax came alongside and started leaning on me. I had to be careful as the field closed up on us because I could very easily run myself into the ground out in front, and then they could catch me at a low point and all come rushing past.

So I thought 'get out of this position', and managed to fade back into the field and let the West German, Klaus-Peter Hildenbrand, take up the pacemaking. I

At the bell in the Olympic 5000m final, as Viren leads from Ian Stewart, me, Dixon, Hildenbrand and Quax. There seemed no way that Viren could beat the kickers in such a situation . . . but he did. (Mark Shearman).

knew that I would not be able to break this field with a surge, and that it was going to be a sprint finish, so I tried to get myself into a position on the leaders' shoulders. But instead of running on their shoulders comfortably, I was hanging on, and when Viren made his run for home from the 4000 metres mark the race was on in earnest. His coach had told him to go ahead at that point and not let anyone past him, and that is exactly what happened. At the bell he led from Britain's Ian Stewart, me, Rod Dixon, Hildenbrand and Quax, all in a bunch. We were all on paper faster finishers than him and yet we could not get past.

As we moved into the final back straight, I suddenly began to run well and moved up just behind Dixon, as Stewart faded, and with 200 metres left both Rod and I were perfectly placed. But Rod decided to wait until the finishing straight to kick, and I began to run out of steam around that last bend of a lap that was covered in 55 seconds. Down the home straight Quax came wide, but he could not get ahead of Viren either and the amazing Finn won in 13:24.8 from Quax (13:25.2). Hildenbrand of West Germany threw himself across the line to snatch the bronze medal from Dixon in 13:25.4, and I was fifth in 13:26.2. Viren, this incredible competitor, had done it again. My only consolation was that my Olympic record of 13:20.4 in the heats remained intact, and giving me the unwelcome distinction, in more than thirty men's and women's events on the athletics programme, of being the only Olympic record holder who had not actually won a gold medal in their event.

I was not too disappointed, though. The 10,000 metres had been my better prospect, and the hard programme of four Olympic long distance races in eight days, including the illness, had taken its toll. But then what can you say about Lasse Viren, who became the first man to successfully defend the 5000/10,000 metres double in Olympic history? In that 5000 metres, when he was leading the last lap, there seemed no possible way he could win, and yet he did.

And as if that was not enough, the day after the 5000 metres final he ran in the longest Olympic event of all, the twenty-six-and-a-quarter miles marathon, for the first time ever, and finished fifth. And although he did not equal the 1952 feat of the great Czech, Emil Zatopek, by winning all three races in one Olympics, he came close at a time when international athletics had progressed so far in the quarter of a century since Zatopek ran in Helsinki. And Zatopek did not have to run 10,000 metres heats!

The fact that Viren had been so good in Munich, and again in Montreal four years later, after doing so very little of note in between, gave rise to all sorts of speculation about his training methods. No one seemed prepared to believe that he is simply an athlete to whom the Olympic Games and European championships mean a great deal, and everything else very little. The suggestion going the rounds in Montreal was that Viren had engaged in 'blood doping' to achieve his results.

Blood doping is not quite as sinister as it sounds, but nor does it seem as effective or even in use as much as some so-called experts claim. Basically, it entails removing blood from an athlete, storing the haemoglobin (the part that carries the oxygen around the system), and then when the body has made up the loss naturally, replacing the original haemoglobin so that the blood has a boost and in theory should be able to carry more oxygen than normal. But doctors say that it would only work on someone who is anaemic (and Viren is certainly not), and that if you pushed the level of haemoglobin too high, the blood would become too thick to operate properly, and illness could result.

Even if it did work for athletes, and if it had been used in an Olympic Games, it is hard to imagine what rules would have been broken. After all, there are a great many types of drugs which are banned from use by athletes in amateur competition, and every big meeting has doping tests to check on possible abuse of the rules. But blood cannot be banned, because everyone has got it!

Viren himself probably did not help matters by being very coy at the post-race Press conference. He has little time for journalists, especially those who seemed set on pursuing the blood-doping line instead of the athletic side of his successes, and he was virtually non-committal in his answers. At one point he even pretended he did not know what blood doping was, and ended up by saying that his secret was drinking lots of reindeer milk. It was his own way of having a little fun at the journalists' expense, but I thought he should have come out and denied it categorically there and then.

He did not have to convince me, though, because I feel certain in my own mind that Lasse Viren is simply a remarkable athlete, who needed no such aids as blood doping, even if it did work, to assist him. For a start, the supposed effects of blood doping only last a short time, and yet he was running brilliantly over 20 kilometres in May, and ran the world's fastest 10,000 metres before the Olympics in June. He has a brilliant knack of getting ready on the day that matters, and also a tremendous strength of character which is such that even if he finishes last in a race that is not important, then he genuinely does not worry. In many ways that is an admirable attitude, although if everyone was like him the sport would not be in a very healthy situation.

Viren is a 'one-off', a very private man who keeps himself to himself at home in his village of Myrskyla, sixty-five miles north-east of Helsinki. And anyone who is in the public eye but retains a deliberately low profile is bound to be the subject of speculation and rumour. The blood-doping stories were probably given more credence in Montreal because of accusations made by frustrated losers, who could not understand how the man could be so successful.

The losers, at a time of great stress after events for which they had prepared for years, were only seeking to excuse their inability to win by casting doubt on Viren, I am sure. After all, if you are a silver medallist, and you can make everyone believe that the gold medallist cheated, then that makes you the best after all, doesn't it? Jealousy was one of the factors behind those stories. It's only human nature. When I win, people don't accuse me of blood doping, but I bet they say something else like 'Oh, he's got it easy up there in Gateshead, he doesn't have to work for his living', or similar misunderstandings. We all want to believe, or get other people to believe, that we are the best. That is, after all, what motivates us into competition in the first place.

After Montreal I was able to visit Viren at his home, a beautiful lakeside house, which was built for him by the local people as a tribute to his running and because they wanted him to stay in the village, which has a population of only 2300. He works as a country policeman, patrolling the beautiful woodland near his home on foot, and as nothing much happens in the area, his training runs are seldom interrupted.

The difference is that in Britain if the local people did a similar thing for you, they would probably expect something in return. But Viren has educated the people there into realising that his preparation is a long and complex one, aimed at the next Olympics. There is no pressure on him to bring international stars to run in Myrskyla, and he has no desire to move to a big city. While I was there we ran together, swam in the lake, had a traditional Finnish-style sauna, and halfway through the evening he got out a little bottle of his illegally brewed local drink called Pontikka. It nearly knocked my head off.

I must admit I envy his set-up. Not only his specific way of life, but the way an athlete in Finland is treated. The Finnish federation looks after its great runners. In Britain we cater for *lots* of runners, not outstanding individuals. I wonder how Viren would run if he had to go through endless trials to get into his national team?

I talked to him about the Olympics, and he said he knew he was going to win the 10,000 metres, and the only person he had worried about was me. But in the race he realised that I was not running well, and that gave him extra confidence. I asked him about the 5000 metres, and said, 'Weren't you nervous with all those great athletes queueing up on your shoulder in the last lap?' He said, 'No, I never thought about it. I just had to get to the line first. My coach said, "get to the front with 600 metres left, and stay there." So I did.'

The difference was that he *knew* he was going to win, he really believed it. Quax *hoped* he could win, Dixon *thought* he could win, but Lasse Viren knew. He must be one of the greatest athletes of all time, and he is not yet as famous as I think he will become when people realise the full magnificence of his performances in the Olympic Games. I do not think he has finished yet either. We will see him again in Moscow in 1980, I feel certain, and by then he should be a real force in the marathon. He is running quite a few of them at the moment, and there is obviously a reason for that. He is not winning, but then that is Lasse Viren. There are plenty of lesser races to win, but only one Olympic Games.

166

Well, perhaps a bronze medal is not too bad. At least they still wanted to know me when I got back to Gateshead from Montreal. (Newcastle Chronicle & Journal).

I never really faced the decision of whether I would have retired from international athletics if I had won in Montreal. If and when I do make a decision to retire, it will be a hard one, because athletics is such a big part of my life. But when you line up for an Olympic final, you think, 'I don't want to go through all this again – ever.' It is not the actual running that is the problem, it is the nerves and worry and tension beforehand, which are heightened by the worldwide interest in the Olympic Games. Millions of people who, for four years, cannot tell a pole vault from a hammer throw, suddenly become glued to their television sets, urging on some British athlete who, more likely than not, is not going even to challenge for a medal. In fact, my bronze in Montreal was the only athletics medal won by a member of the British team.

When the Games are over, the casual viewer can switch his set off, and forget about athletics for another four years. But for the athlete there is a long period of deep thought as to whether it is worth embarking on the long road again. The Olympic experience is not all that pleasant. Usually, though, when your batteries are recharged you want to do it all again.

Within a few days of the Montreal Games ending, I was back on the track, running a two miles race in the Coca-Cola meeting which that year was held in Edinburgh. Six of the first eight in the Olympic 10,000 metres, including Viren and Lopes, were in the field and I won with a last lap effort, which took me clear of the rest, in 8:22.2. Lopes was fourth, and Viren was back in eleventh place. Such was the demand for his presence at international meetings, that he had already raced in Philadelphia and only arrived in Scotland a few hours before the meeting began.

Of course, it made a few headlines – 'Foster beats Olympic champion Viren' – but we both knew, and I think everyone knew, that it did not mean a thing. One athletics statistician even worked out that I had raced Viren eleven times in my career, and I had won nine of the encounters. Unfortunately, the two he won were both in Montreal! A few days later I beat him again in Helsinki over 5000 metres. I ran 13:26.4, and he finished seventh in 13:42.2. Then he came to my home patch, and I beat him again over two miles on a very windy day at the Gateshead Games, which made the score 11–2. But if I had beaten him a thousand times, it would still make no difference. He was double Olympic champion, and that was all that mattered. They did not take his gold medals away because I beat him after the Games.

I had never before tried to dash around Europe running races here, there and everywhere, as some athletes do, but I gave it a try that late summer and although I had a string of wins, they were all in relatively insignificant events, and I did not really enjoy the experience. I decided that my previous method, of building up to just a few races, suited me much better than forever packing bags and dashing to catch yet another flight. By the middle of September I was really ready for a long rest, and did not run again until October 1st. Even then the next three months still carried their memories of what had happened in Montreal, and I suppose it was not until Christmas that I was finally able to put 1976 firmly behind me and start thinking about races to come, instead of re-running those that had gone.

Thirteen

In any year when there is no major Games, the motivation and incentive for an international athlete is at its lowest, and in 1977, with Montreal still an anti-climax floating around my system, that was especially so. By December of 1976, when I would normally expect to be in reasonable shape after two or three months of winter training, I was still not really fit and training seemed to be a major task. The previous winter I had been able to constantly motivate myself by the thoughts of the Olympic Games, and missing any session made me feel exceedingly guilty. But in the winter of 1976–77 there was no such incentive. The Commonwealth Games and the European championships were not due to be staged again until 1978, and the Olympics until 1980.

It was just before Christmas when I forced myself to really get going again. I had run in the International Athletes Club cross country race at Crystal Palace, and expected to do quite well. In fact, I ran one of the worst races of my life, and I could not believe how difficult it was. I was just staggering along, and finished eighth in a race won by Bernie Ford.

Being hammered there was probably a good thing, though, because when I got home I told myself, 'You're not training properly, you're only messing around, and now look what has happened!' It was the turning point, and only then did I realise how long it had taken me to get over Montreal. In Christmas week I ran 100 miles for the first time that winter, and that was the start of my serious training. The break from the usual intensity of my regime was refreshing in its own way looking back, but it also reminded me that, Olympic medallist or not, I could not let up on the training if I wanted to keep my position. There were plenty of others waiting to take over.

From then on training went well, and I set my sights on the summer, when the

European Cup was due to be held at Helsinki in August, and a brand new competition, the World Cup, would be staged in Dusseldorf in September. Both of these were primarily team events, but they were to be the most important international meetings of the summer and so they became my targets for the year. It was extremely unlikely that Britain would qualify for the World Cup final, which included only two European national teams, but there was a third team, to be known as the Rest of Europe, and I reckoned that a good performance in the European Cup (where I had won the 5000 metres in 1973 and 1975) should see me into the Rest of Europe squad for the World Cup.

So, with a new horizon, the juices began to flow and my training perked up. I was averaging over 100 miles a week in January and February, with no intention of racing, although I felt I was running well again. We had just moved house, with all the chaos that entails, and Sue was expecting our first child in March. To have to worry about races at that time seemed an unnecessary burden, so I was quite content simply to run.

Then, one Tuesday night in mid-February, when I was covering a club night ten miles run with some fellow Gateshead Harriers, I could tell something was up. A lot of looks were being exchanged, and there were some mysterious asides, and I began to wonder what the big secret was. Eventually, Charlie Spedding, one of our best young prospects, was delegated by the others to approach me and ask if I would run in the National cross country championships at Parliament Hill on March 5th.

Until then, running that race had been the furthest thing from my mind. Gateshead Harriers had been national team champions for the past two years and as far as I was concerned were going to win again without any trouble, and without needing any assistance from me. But, explained Charlie, the lads were getting a little bit worried about Cambridge and Coleridge AC, who had finished second in 1976. They had not been far behind then, and had a considerable number of international class runners in their team, including Grenville and Graham Tuck, Kevin Steere and John Wild. Gateshead would be without Dennis Coates, the British steeplechase record holder, and they were afraid they could lose the title.

I was still convinced that Gateshead, who had won the Northern title easily the week before, were still good enough to beat any other club in the country, but I really had no option – unless I wanted to spend the rest of my running career changing on my own on club nights! So I noted in my training diary: 'Decided/persuaded by Charlie Spedding and the boys to run the National.' I did not mind really, of course, because I was quite curious as to how I was running. Also Gateshead Harriers have been a big part of my life since I first started running, and

In the autumn of 1976 I made a TV series about athletics for Tyne Tees Television, and here, high above the Tyne, I discuss jogging and 'fun runs' with my co-author, Cliff Temple. (Tyne Tees TV).

there was no way that I was going to be responsible for them missing out on a hat-trick of wins in the National cross country championships.

No one who has not been a member of a keen running club can fully appreciate just how much the 'National' means to the club man. All year round he may run in inter-club races, on track, road and cross country, but the nine miles English cross country championship gives him a unique chance to race alongside internationals and scrubbers alike in a field which is now well over the thousand mark every year. The start alone is the most spectacular you will see in Britain.

For the huge majority of distance runners in this country, the Olympic Games is something you read about, but the 'National' is something in which you run. And for Gateshead Harriers, that holds as true as for any other club. It is all they talk about for weeks beforehand, and weeks afterwards.

I thought I had better have some sort of a race having done nothing in terms of speed work or my normal preparation, because I had not expected to be running. So I took part in the Signals road relay, a local event on a trading estate at Gateshead, and had the fastest time for the two-and-a-half miles leg. It was 20 seconds faster than Chris Garforth, who was hoping to make England's team for the International cross country championships, so that was quite encouraging.

I met up with the rest of the lads at Newcastle Central station the night before the race, and we travelled down to London with all the youngsters who were representing Gateshead in the Youths and Juniors championships, plus the club reserves and supporters, who are equally a part of any success. We stayed overnight in a small hotel, and the whole atmosphere just overtook me. It was such a contrast to travelling and staying with an international team, where the athletes look gaunt and nervous. Everyone was speculating on our chances, guessing where every runner would finish, and we had quizzes about past championships. This was athletics at its most enjoyable, a world away from the Olympic Games, and it is where every athlete should spend part of his career. There is plenty of time for apprehension, tension and nerves if you reach the top, but the happy and relaxed atmosphere here was like a refreshing breeze. So much so that I did not even think about the race itself until the next morning; if it had been the Olympics, I would have been able to think about little else as soon as I reached the Olympic Village.

I considered the leading candidates for the individual title. There were three outstanding names – David Black, Tony Simmons and Bernie Ford, who had all been in good form recently, and had between them accounted for the national title in the past three years. My own chances, in the morning papers, were thankfully played down and it was emphasised that I was only turning out to help the club, which I was. But when people do not fancy me for a particular race, it often spurs

(left to right) Charlie Spedding, Max Coleby, Johnny Trainor, Lindsay Dunn, and Wilf Wardle relaxing after the Sunday morning ritual.

me on, and in cross country my chances are never rated too highly because I do not run well on heavy mud, which does not suit my style.

We set off for Parliament Hill with our brand new red and white tracksuits with 'Gateshead Harriers' on the back, and while we were warming up for the senior race we watched our juniors finishing second in their race, just twelve points behind the winners, Birmingham University. That in itself made us more determined to win the senior team race, because we thought how unfair it was that a university team – with athletes from different parts of the country – was allowed to compete against clubs who are much more restricted in their geographical areas.

The course for our race consisted of three laps, each of three miles, up and over Hampstead Heath. The start involves an uphill charge of nearly half a mile, and a

Half a mile gone in the 1977 National cross country championship as the huge field thunders over the first hill at Hampstead. (Peter Tempest).

fast getaway at that point is of extreme importance if you have any ambition of finishing high up, for otherwise you spend the rest of the race trying to overtake runners who tear up the hill and then 'die'. For once (and unusually for Parliament Hill) the ground was not too wet, and as I jogged round I reflected that I was in a position of not having prepared specifically for the race but knowing I was running well, and having no pressure on me.

There was a record field of nearly 1500 runners lining up in the special pens made of numbered stakes and rope, facing the long green hill, and with such a huge turnout the only way to start the event is for officials to explode a maroon which everyone can hear. But over the years, some runners have learned to anticipate the maroon and to move forward a few seconds early, knowing that it would be impossible to recall the 1500 runners for a false start. This time, though, the whole thing got completely out of control, as runners started edging forward well before the maroon was due to go off, and, rather like those mounted French knights in the Agincourt scene in Olivier's *Henry V* film, we seemed to be going faster until someone, somewhere along the line broke into a run and we all instinctively surged forward. The race was on, as angry officials stood helplessly on the line, and we must have been halfway up the long hill before the carefully timed maroon exploded beside the empty pens, half a minute too late.

It was a mockery of a start, as some runners fell, and others, caught unawares, angrily elbowed their way through the pack to get up the front. But I knew there was no point in standing around arguing, so I ran as hard as I could up the hill with the rest of them, and my experience of continental cross country starts was invaluable.

After the first mile I found I was running well, alongside Dave Black and Steve Ovett, and I put on a little pressure to open up a lead of about 20 yards. But the pack soon caught me, and I settled in with a group. I thought, 'If I'm going to win this race, it will have to be tactically. It's too far to lead all the way.' I kept pushing it along though, so that by the end of the first lap there were only five of us together: Black, Simmons, Ford, Mick McLeod of Elswick, and myself.

On the second lap, we were still in a group, but I made sure that I was fractionally ahead in order to dominate the race and dictate the pace. Bernie Ford kept trying to break away on the uphill stretches, and Tony Simmons tried to get away on the downhills, but I knew neither of them would make a clean break. Black and McLeod had dropped back, so there were just three of us left as we started up the hill for the final lap, with crowds of people lining the route. I was running comfortably, and it was then that I began to feel it was my race, and that if I ran the last lap properly I would win.

A new determination swept over me. It was a race in which I had run before but never come close to winning as the mud experts had always left me wallowing. 'This is the one I want,' I thought to myself. I caught sight of Bernie, with his long, jerky stride, on one side of me, and Tony, with his short, pattering stride, on the other. I knew they had both won the title before, and I was determined they were not going to do so again – at least this year.

The three of us approached a ditch halfway round the course, and I thought, 'I'll have to be careful here. I'm going to be the worst at clearing this, and I could

It's down to five of us out of nearly 1500 starters: (left to right) *Dave Black, Mick McLeod, Bernie Ford, me and Tony Simmons.* (Mark Shearman).

lose contact with them.' But instead all three of us jumped into it with both feet and climbed laboriously out of the other side, like a trio of carthorses going round Aintree, before carrying on running. It must have made an hilarious photograph if anyone had a camera there, because we had nearly 1500 runners chasing us, we were battling for the national cross country title, and yet there we were tackling a simple ditch with as much grace and agility as baby elephants.

At that point, I had visions of all three of us coming into the long finishing straight together, but Bernie stretched the pace a mile or so from home, and Tony dropped back. I knew then that all I had to do was to sit on Bernie's shoulder and outkick him, but I was going so well that I went ahead of him before I had to. Parliament Hill is an invigorating place to finish a race because you have a long downhill stretch in the last half mile, followed by a left-hand turn onto a virtually flat section, and then a right-hand turn into the final straight. The whole course was lined with spectators, and as I strode out the noise they made was tremendous.

By the time I turned into the last straight I thought I had dropped Bernie some way back, and began to wave to the crowd, but as the tape neared I heard the cheering turn into warning shouts, and as I looked round I could see him haring after me and closing the gap rapidly. Once again my habit of easing up too soon had nearly caught me out, and as I speeded up I just had time to cross the line a few yards in front of Bernie.

Tony had rallied in the closing stages too, as so often happens, and himself was only three seconds down on Bernie. But the fourth man, Dave Black, was nearly 40 seconds behind him, so we had really got clear of the field when the three of us were running together. It was not long before another Gateshead vest was coming down the finishing straight, with Chris Garforth inside it, in tenth place.

Six men score towards the team placings, and such was the determination of the lads to do well and retain their national title that our sixth and final scorer was only just behind Cambridge and Coleridge's *third* scorer. Dave Cannon (24th), Bryan Baggaley (an inspired 38th), Charlie Spedding (39th) and Max Coleby (43rd, realising a life ambition to finish in the first 50), followed myself and Chris Garforth home, and there was no doubt which team had won.

With 155 points we were well ahead of Cambridge and Coleridge AC, who were second with 338 points, and we were told that our total was the lowest score achieved since 1965. With finishing places being added together, the lower the score the better. And ironically I need never have run. Our next man home, John Trainor in 72nd position, would still have ensured a Gateshead win, even if I had not turned out.

But I'm glad the lads 'persuaded' me. It is not very often that I get excited about winning races these days, but that was one I really enjoyed. For days afterwards my first thought on waking up was 'You're National cross country champion!'

It really was a great day for the club too. Apart from our third successive team victory (and fourth in five years), we had finished second in the Junior championship, and we took the trophy as the club with the lowest aggregate points score in the three age groups. We also had another trophy as the leading Northern team, and I had a separate cup as individual winner. It was the first time a Gateshead Harrier had ever won the National title, and the man who had previously come closest, Bill Robinson (who was second in 1972), said to me afterwards, 'Trust you, you old bugger. You had to go one better, didn't you?' This time Bill had finished 220th.

One of the warming aspects of winning this race, for any athlete, is that so often clubmen all over the country tend to refer to 'Foster's National' or 'Bedford's National', instead of the year. Personally, I would not dare to assume that with 1500 others in the race it could be called after one man, but it is flattering to think that it might be!

It was a memorable day, if not quite as memorable for me as the following Friday when, in the early hours of the morning, Sue woke me up and said, 'I think we had better get to the hospital.' It seemed the baby was on its way. So we rushed off to the Queen Elizabeth Hospital at Gateshead, where nothing much happened, and the following afternoon I was still the expectant Dad, sitting at home watching 'Grandstand' on TV. They were showing a film report of the previous Saturday's National cross country event, so I was able to re-live the whole race again. Then, after it was over, the telephone rang.

If I live to be a hundred, I will always congratulate little Paul Brendan for his immaculate timing in allowing me time to watch the National again before his arrival. He weighed in at 8 pounds 9 ounces, to make Sue and I the proudest of parents, and more than one of the congratulatory cards we received contained a blank membership form for Gateshead Harriers.

The week after that I felt absolutely shattered. All the excitement had brought about a reaction, and for a short while I did not feel like training, let alone racing. The International cross country championships were due to be held in Dusseldorf the following week, and as it was an event I had never competed in before I had said I would run, providing Sue was out of hospital and everything was all right. But I was in no condition for racing after the heavy responsibilities of a week of fatherhood (looking after myself while Sue was in hospital!) had weighed me down, and I withdrew from England's team.

I had decided that my first track race would be a 5000 metres in the Debenhams Games at Crystal Palace on June 26th, because I wanted to be at my peak for the European and World Cup competitions in August and September. I first mentioned this publicly after running in the AAA National road relay in April (where Gateshead Harriers completed their third successive win in that event too), and it did not take more than a moment or two for someone to spot that this would be after a brand new meeting, called the United Kingdom Closed Championships, was to be held at Cwmbran in early June.

'Does that mean you're not running the UK Closed, Brendan?' I was asked, as a group of journalists came round me after I had just finished my lap in the relay.

'If they are before June 26th, then I'm not,' I replied. I knew full well they were before June 26th, but for a few moments I acted innocent.

A lifetime's ambition realized, as I win the National from fast-finishing
Bernie Ford and Tony Simmons. (Mark Shearman).

I also said a little more than my prayers about the new meeting, which was being organised by the British Amateur Athletic Board. I said that I thought the AAA championships had always been good enough in the past, and we did not need a new meeting like the UK championships. In retrospect, it might have been a little more diplomatic to have said nothing, and just thought that, but hopping about on one leg, trying to put on your tracksuit trousers, on a cold, damp afternoon in the middle of a park near Sutton Coldfield is perhaps not the best moment for rational thought. I said it, the national press heard me, and next day I picked up the papers and read headlines like 'I will not run, says defiant Foster'.

Despite several personal pleas from people closely connected with the new championships, I stuck to my guns and did not run in them. It was not that I was being bloody-minded. I simply knew that I could not start serious racing earlier than June 26th, a fortnight after the UK Closed championships, and still hope to be running well in September.

Even June 26th was a few days earlier than I would ideally have liked to start my season, but Rod Dixon, who had finished just in front of me at Montreal, was coming from New Zealand to run in the 5000 metres, and I thought it would be a good race.

My absence from the UK Closed championships did not cause the world to come to a halt, or the moon to turn into cheese, although both the 5000 and 10,000 metres were faster than I had expected. Ian Stewart led most of the way to win the longer distance in 27 minutes 51.3 seconds, his fastest time ever, and Nick Rose also set a personal best in the 5000 metres with 13 minutes 20.6 seconds, likewise doing all his own work. Both performances were the season's fastest in the world up to that time.

The 5000 metres at the Debenhams Games turned out to be something of a disappointment as a competitive race, though. I had planned to run three hard laps at the end of the race to try to beat Dixon, but the New Zealander was nowhere to be seen when it came to it. He had been suffering from travel fatigue and injury, and was almost a lap behind at the finish. 1 went into the lead around the halfway point, and won by 70 metres from Julian Goater, in 13 minutes 21.2 seconds. I was delighted with the time because although I had not been consciously aiming at a particular performance, it was still my fastest-ever opener to the season.

It was also, as several people were quick to point out, 0.6 seconds slower than Nick Rose's time at Cwmbran. But Rose was not in my race, having preferred to run the 3000 metres the previous evening. So the outcome was that when the British team for the European Cup semi-final, to be held at Crystal Palace on July 16th and 17th, was announced a day or so later, Nick Rose was picked for the

180

Sue and I with our son, Paul.

5000 metres in preference to me. I had a lot of phone calls from newspapers asking if I was angry or upset at being left out, as I had won the European Cup final 5000 metres for Britain on two previous occasions, but I was neither. Rose ran a faster time than me, so they picked him, and that was that as far as I was concerned. The semi-final was of less interest to me than the final itself in August, and I had by no means given up hope of getting into Britain's team for that.

In the event, Rose won the 5000 metres for Britain and Tony Simmons (replacing Ian Stewart, the original selection) won the 10,000 metres in the semi-final, and Britain duly qualified for the final in Helsinki on August 13th and 14th. A week earlier I had been selected to run the 5000 metres for Britain in their away match against Finland in Oulu, but turned it down because I wanted to concentrate on my preparations for the forthcoming AAA championships.

Only a handful of people knew I was going to have a crack at the world record in the 1977 AAA 10,000m championship. Josh Kimeto (40) led early on, but soon I was on my own. (Peter Tempest).

In these championships on July 22nd, I felt I could re-establish myself as a 10,000 metres runner in time for the European Cup final selection, so that if I did not get into the team at 5000 metres, as seemed possible, then I would have a second string to my bow. When I went down to Crystal Palace I did not say much to anyone, but I thought that I could come very close indeed to breaking the world record for the distance.

The record, which had been held by Dave Bedford at 27:30.8, had been beaten in Helsinki a month earlier by a little-known Kenyan, Samson Kimombwa, who had clocked 27:30.5. My target was to run 27:25.0, which I felt was on the cards. My training had been going well, and my only previous race of the season, a month earlier, had been a good one.

The AAA 10,000 metres, traditionally held on the Friday night of the championships when the weather is cool, has seen some great performances over the years, and it seemed to me that conditions would be ideal, just as they were when Bedford set his record on the same track at the same meeting four years earlier.

I had an arrangement with another Kenyan, Josh Kimeto, that he would try to lead through the half distance in 13:35.0, and I would take it from there. But at 4000 metres I could sense that he was slowing, and I moved ahead myself, feeling quite comfortable, almost floating along. I had never had anyone leading me for so long in a race of this type, and it made a great deal of difference. But then I was on my own, with fourteen laps still to run, and I knew it would be hard trying to maintain the same tempo. I went through 5000 metres in 13:38.9, which was faster than either Bedford or Kimombwa in their world records, and at 7000 metres I was still on schedule.

Then, in the eighth kilometre, I lost it. I suppose I was not prepared to dig deep enough, and at 8000 metres I had drifted some eight to ten seconds outside a world record schedule, preparing perhaps subconsciously to save something for the end. My laps were slowing to almost 70 seconds at one point, compared with the 66 seconds I should have been running, and when I finally crossed the line in 27:45.7 I knew I had been through a hard run. The lack of opposition had been disappointing, with the second man, Dave Black, finishing over half a minute behind me, and only three of us breaking 29 minutes. So many people ran below their best form in that race that the very high humidity that night, which everyone else had remarked upon but which I did not particularly notice until after the race, must have had a draining effect of some sort.

If it had been a little cooler, perhaps I would have broken the record. I will never know. But I do know that I could have run 27:45 with much greater ease on an even pace, and if I had run with the sole aim of just being the fastest man in Britain I could have achieved it much more comfortably. Tony Simmons had run 27:43.6 in Helsinki during Kimombwa's world record race the previous month, but in fourth place, even if it did put him fractionally above me in the UK rankings for 1977.

So once again I was in the situation of having run a very fast time on my own and found someone else slightly faster laying claim to the place in Britain's European Cup team. I knew I was going to have to wait some time to find out whether the selectors considered a solo 27:45 victory on a humid night was better

Drained by the humidity and the effort, I look up at my time on the scoreboard. There was no record and, although I did not yet know it, the run had also wrecked my hopes for the season. (Peter Tempest).

than a 27:43 in fourth place. I hoped that my racing record would hold up for me, and was surprised to read an interview with Tony Simmons in which he claimed that he was 'Britain's most consistent 10,000 metres man'.

I was not quite sure how he worked that out, as he had not beaten me over the distance in any of our three races (the Coca-Cola, the UK Olympic trial race, and the Olympic final). But before I had any chance to get involved in the controversy, something happened to take my mind off it anyway. Next morning, when I got out of bed at the hotel, I fell over.

My left leg simply gave way under me. I could not walk. The achilles tendon, just above the heel, was so stiff and sore that I could not put any weight on it. The tightrope an international athlete treads between fitness and injury is a thin one. On Friday night I had been attacking a world record; twelve hours later I could only hobble.

Later I was able to pinpoint the probable cause of the trouble. I had been walking around all day Thursday and Friday in a pair of flat training shoes, instead of shoes with a heel, and that had been stretching the tendons all the time. Running a hard race on top of that had been too much for them.

My training partner, Wilf, had come down from Gateshead to watch the race and he had shared a room with me that night. So I borrowed his street shoes, and gave him the flat shoes, saying that I never wanted to see them again. He has still got them. And I've still got his street shoes.

It was another salutary lesson in how you can become diverted from what common sense tells you to do. After the race I should have had a long jog to warm down and, to relax the muscles, perhaps some physiotherapy. But because it was the last race of the evening, and I was rushed to the Press Box for interviews straight afterwards, I found the stadium deserted and in darkness when I finished, so I skipped the warm down. It does not matter whether you are an international runner or a club-level beginner; you cannot cut corners like that with impunity.

The following Saturday I was supposed to be running 5000 metres at the Philips Gateshead Games against a field which included the Ethiopian Mirus Yifter. He was the one man many people felt might have beaten Lasse Viren in Montreal if the African nations had not staged their walkout, and he possessed a very fast finish. I had been looking forward to the race, because I knew I was in good shape, but early in the week I knew I could not run because of the leg.

Yifter won that race in 13:20.6, ahead of Steve Ovett, who made a great debut at the distance, but the pace had slowed with about four laps left, which would have suited me to make a break. I might not have beaten Yifter, but I know we would both have been well under 13:20.

The next three weeks were sheer misery. No athlete likes being injured, but when you have been in good form after a hard winter's training, and the season is reaching its peak, there is nothing worse than feeling your form (and your confidence) drain away as the days pass when you are unable to train faster than a jog-trot.

The British team for the European Cup final was announced, and Tony Simmons was preferred by the selectors to me, and it could not be because of my injury, as I was named as reserve. There was no point in my getting heated about it, because even if I had been selected instead of Tony, I could not run in the European Cup. It was a very depressing time because I would also miss out on the World Cup.

The Rest of Europe team was being selected from the European Cup results, so I did not have a hope, even if I recovered in time. The only glimmer at the end of the dark tunnel was the thought that there was one more attractive race – a 10,000 metres in the Coca-Cola meeting in which most of the big names were expected to compete, a few days after the World Cup.

My spirits still soared and fell though, as the stubborn injury made only slow progress. Some days I would say to Sue, 'I think I'll pack it up for the rest of the season.' And she would say, 'Why? You've trained all through the winter, and nothing is going to change if you run and don't win, is it?'

I had to admit she was right, and when the injury at last cleared, after three-and-a-half weeks of inactivity, I decided to run in a 5000 metres match event for Britain against the Soviet Union in Edinburgh late in August. It was not the sort of race I normally went looking for, and in fact I had never run 5000 metres in a two-a-side match for Britain, but I needed races to make up for lost time. I had ten days to prepare for it, and after six of them I went onto the track at Gateshead to run a ten-lap time trial. I was marginally outside 14 minutes pace for 5000 metres, more than 20 seconds slower than my *halfway* time in the AAA 10,000 metres, and I felt absolutely shattered by the effort.

Lindsay Dunn was there, holding the stopwatch, and I said to him, 'If I can't run faster than fourteen minutes, I'm not going.' He replied, 'You'll run better than that. It's done you a lot of good.' At least I was off the bottom, and a day or so later I managed a session of 10×400 metres in 60 seconds, which was not too bad. I still did not think I was in sufficient shape to win in Edinburgh, and when the two Russians went tearing off at the start I found myself dropped in the first 200 metres! But the pace slowed, I was able to catch them, and eventually win the race with a sub-60-seconds last lap, with my team-mate Dave Black second. The time, 13:42.4, may not have been sensational, but at least it was an improvement on my time trial a few days before. And I was delighted to be racing again with no ill effects, let alone winning.

Driving back from Edinburgh in the evening was a much livelier and relieved Brendan Foster than had travelled up in the afternoon with Wilf and Johnny Trainor. Both said that they hadn't seen me more nervous for years, and yet they knew that whilst I wasn't really fit enough, I would still win. I am glad someone had confidence before the race, but (after two pints of Scottish 'heavy' in a roadside pub in the borders) they admitted that they had been very worried for me early in the race. So had I.

I wanted one more race before the Coke 10,000 metres, which was now a fortnight away, and the only place I could find one was down in Leicester, at an inter-club trophy meeting, where they agreed to let me run as a guest in the 3000 metres. So the following Sunday, while everyone else was watching the World Cup from Dusseldorf on television, I was driving down to Leicester for this race. I am a great believer in the value of club athletics, and I was pleased that they were allowing me to run, but the meeting was so far behind schedule that I began to wish I had stayed at home. My race was due at 2.40, so I started warming up at 2.15, and was on the track, in my spikes, just before 2.40. The race actually started at 3.50!

It was cold and windy, and as race after race went off with no sign of the 3000 metres even being near, my legs were stiffening up. Stan Long had come down with me, and it was he who persuaded me to stay and run when I felt like getting in the car and going home. 'You've come all this way, you need the race, and you've missed watching the World Cup on TV, so it's silly to turn round and go back without running,' he pointed out. He was right, and I knew that he would much rather have been at home watching the World Cup on TV too, but he had given up his own time for me, so I owed it to him as much as anybody to run.

My time of 8:00.4, 25 seconds outside my world record, might not have seemed that encouraging on the face of it, but in the circumstances I was well pleased, because I knew I had run hard and that the conditions had been far from ideal. When, the following Tuesday, I ran four laps of jogging 50 metres and sprinting 50 metres in a total time of 4:06.9, I knew I was almost back, and not a moment too soon. The Coke 10,000 metres was only three days away.

The International Athletes Club, the promoters, and Coca-Cola, the sponsors, had gathered together a very strong field for the race. It included Samson Kimombwa, the world record holder from Kenya, Dick Quax from New Zealand, who had broken the world 5000 metres record earlier in the season, the strong Dutchmen, Jos Hermens and Gerd Tebroke, plus the British contingent of Ian Stewart, Tony Simmons, Bernie Ford, Dave Black and Co.

Once more the meeting lived up to its reputation of always attracting a huge crowd, and traffic seemed to be jammed around the entrance to Crystal Palace for hours beforehand. Floodlit meetings always produce an extra 'atmosphere', with fewer distractions outside the track, and seeing the coach-loads of spectators arriving from all over the country and the crowds pouring out of Crystal Palace railway station took me back two years, to my 10,000 metres debut at the same meeting. Would all these people expect me to be in the same form tonight?

There had been a lot of talk in the previous days about the world record being broken here. I was intrigued, and I must admit slightly amused, when I read Ian Stewart's headline-catching comments in that morning's newspaper: ' "We'll

At least I was able to end on a high note by winning the 1977 Coca-Cola 10,000m. Ian Stewart leads, Dutchman Gerd Tebroke and I follow. (Mark Shearman).

smash that record" vows gritty Ian.' I liked the reference to the plural! Whatever I was thinking about that night, it was certainly not world records.

This time I was simply going to race, and the past couple of weeks had given me a chance to pull myself together. I was not in the same shape as I had been for my AAA win, but I was prepared to have a go. Early in the race I found myself sharing the pace with Bernie Ford, but it was not until much later that the field began to string out. The first half (13:57.2) had been comfortable enough, and a relief, because if the others had blazed away from the gun it might have been too much for me.

Then, as the laps ticked off, the going got tougher, and with six laps remaining I was hanging onto the leaders, who included another strong Kenyan, Henry Rono, plus Tebroke, Ford, Hermens and Quax. Rono kept surging, and each time I thought, 'Well, I've had it now', but each time I got back with them. Then, with three laps left, Tebroke made a break which completely split up the leading bunch, and a burst of confidence hit me. The adrenalin was flowing, because Crystal Palace was bursting at the seams with 18,000 people in the stands, and they made the most ear-splitting noise as the race reached its climax.

I pulled Tebroke back gradually, as we weaved around the lapped runners, and Rono came with me. As the three of us went into the last lap, we could hardly hear the trackside bell ring above the crescendo of din in the stadium, and I decided I would wait until the back straight before beginning my last effort. I was going to wait until 200 metres were left, but with 300 to go I thought, 'Hell, let's make it now' and kicked as hard as I could. Rono responded, but Tebroke dropped back, and as I tried to lift my knees up to sprint round that last bend, I knew the little Kenyan was right behind me. I led into the home straight, and although it was certainly the longest finishing straight I've ever known, it was also one of the sweetest victories as I crossed the line first.

It was a marvellous feeling, because it was a race I really had no right to win after the time lost through the injury. I looked up towards the stands to give my usual victory wave, and to thank the crowd for their support, and I was greeted by the amazing sight of everyone in the main block up on their feet and waving programmes, scarves, coats and hats at me. It was a warming and emotional moment. At least they had not forgotten me, as I knew deep down they would not, even if the British selectors had decided I was over the top.

The local BBC 'Look North' TV programme had been along to interview me the day before the race and, with the goading of news editor, John Bird, and film cameraman, Dave Cox, fortunately both good friends of mine, the interviewer, Fiona Johnston, asked me: 'Do you not think you have been at the top too long, and are you not just a little past your prime?' I had managed to give a smiling, diplomatic answer on film, and promised John and Dave that I would show them.

To give them their due, they came back several days later to interview me again, and this time Fiona made a light-hearted public apology to camera for as much as hinting that I was over the hill, or past it. Then when she started the interview she asked: 'How did you feel on Friday night?' I couldn't resist answering: 'Past it!'

My time of 27:36.6 had put me third on the all-time world list, behind the world records of Kimombwa (who faded early in this race) and Dave Bedford, and I could not help wondering what I could have run if I had been in a race like that when I was in my AAA championships form. But then in athletics speculation is just part of the fun; actually getting on the track and doing something is the real meat.

I was repeatedly asked afterwards what I had felt about being left out of the European and World Cups, but the answer was that it did not really matter because I was injured when the European Cup final was held, and not properly in shape when the World Cup was on. I had only been back on form a week before the Coke race, but that week made all the difference, and I knew in my own mind that I was a better runner than Tony Simmons and Jos Hermens (who had been picked for the British and Rest of Europe team 10,000 metres respectively).

It would have been a good note on which to end a season of mixed fortune. But I had one more commitment, two days later, to run a 3000 metres race at Gateshead, in the Manitou Games. The aftermath of the Coke race, and being involved with the organisation of the Gateshead meeting, meant that I had not given the race any thought, other than to assume that I would just sit on Ian Stewart's shoulder and outkick him.

Only when we warmed up for the race did I notice that Mick McLeod had switched to the 3000 metres from the mile, and in the event he outkicked both Ian and I to win. It is never very nice to lose, especially for me in Gateshead, but I could reflect that McLeod had run well over a minute slower than me in the Coke race, finishing fifteenth, and so perhaps he was not as tired as me. However, all credit to him for becoming the first Briton to beat me over any distance further than a mile on the track – and, what's more, he lives in Gateshead too.

It had been a strange season, in which I had won races I could not have expected to win beforehand, like the National cross country title and the Coke 10,000 metres, and in which I did not even run in the races for which I had been peaking, the European and World Cups. But my form in my best races told me that I still had some improvement left in me, and that I should go on to the 1978 Commonwealth and European championships, and the 1980 Olympics. I might not get there, but I could not bear the thought of not trying.

Fourteen

One of the commonest questions I am asked by fellow athletes of all ages is 'What sort of training do you do?', but, as Eric Morecambe might say, 'There's no answer to that.' My training is of no specific 'type'; it differs according to the time of the year, and what major events I have planned in the future. The only common denominator is that the running I do is aimed at making me fast and strong, and at my fastest and strongest in the most important races of the year.

To do that, I have evolved my own particular balance of speed, endurance and strength work, built up over the years from a mixture of trial and error, research into what brought about past successes, and by constantly trying to learn more about myself and my body. For on the day you think you know it all and there is nothing more to learn, you might as well give up.

No two athletes are exactly the same, and even one athlete is different from one season to the next. The Brendan Foster who began his winter training in 1977 had run thousands more miles than the Brendan Foster who began his winter training in 1976, for instance. Therefore if I talk about my own training, and why I do it, you must realise that this is what suits *me*, and it is unlikely to be exactly right for another senior athlete and it most certainly is too much for a young athlete to copy.

You might think that goes without saying, but I am amazed how often young-sters follow someone else's published training schedule exactly, and are then surprised when they get exhausted, injured, or left behind in races. I recently received a letter from a depressed young athlete who could not understand why he was running so relatively badly, around 4:29 for a mile, when he was following the schedule which the former teenage prodigy Jim Ryun had used at the same age to become world mile record holder. But training follows certain patterns, which are fairly basic among international runners.

My year really starts in the autumn when, after a rest of about two weeks following the summer season, I begin building up my training mileage from early October until I am topping the 100 miles-a-week mark before Christmas. It is steady running for the most part, 6–6½ minutes per mile, usually twice a day, and this period builds the solid platform on which the rest of the year is based. It is not a glamorous time, because it is often cold, wet and windy, and there are no cheering crowds, but without this background there would be no summer success.

The steady running strengthens the heart and lowers the pulse rate at rest, so that when you start on your summer track work you will have the equivalent of an engine with an extra big capacity. The process cannot be rushed or skimped and it just becomes part of your daily routine. Apart from your heart, your legs obviously become very strong too, and the training gives you a great confidence boost when you have built up a backlog of training miles.

After Christmas, the heavy mileage continues, but I try to inject a little more quality into it, making some (but not all) of the runs faster. By March or April I am ready to try out my form in a road relay, usually after three months of particularly heavy mileage, where I have reached 120 miles a week, and from there I gradually move into track work.

Although I do run some cross country races in the winter for a little variety, you will have gathered that I do not make them the be-all and end-all of athletics, and prefer to sacrifice my chances of doing well on the country and concentrate on the more important business of training for the summer.

Before going onto the track, a month in which hill work becomes a part of training is valuable. You run repetitions hard up a hill of anything between 50 and 200 metres, and the slope ensures that you have to use a high knee lift and good arm drive to get up it. Both these aspects of fast running tend to become rusty in the long months of steady pace, but as with everything in athletics it is important to introduce it gradually at first. Three days a week of hill work is an absolute maximum, because the achilles tendons can become strained if you do too much.

Then I move some of my training sessions onto the track at the start of the summer. Not all, because again I feel that three hard track sessions a week are quite enough, and steady running for the rest of the week should enable you to recover. If you hammer away at the track every day the chances are that before long you will be injured, or that you will find your backlog of winter mileage running out on you in mid-season, leaving you fast but without much strength.

I have mentioned earlier the sort of track sessions I have done before major races, but the session with which I usually start off the summer is to run 10×400 metres in 60–61 seconds each. It has taken a long time to be able to start off that fast, and this makes me repeat my earlier point. Everything in an athlete's training programme is strictly relative to him or her, and no one else. Therefore it would be foolish for another athlete to say 'Brendan Foster runs 10×400 metres in 60 seconds at the start of the season, so I must try to do the same'. For a start, I have not told you what recovery I have between the runs; it could be 10 seconds jog, or one hour's rest in the changing room. In fact, it is 90 seconds.

The essential thing is just to come onto the track without trying to break any records the first day you put on your spikes. Instead the aim should be to gradually increase over a period of weeks the intensity of your track interval sessions, to improve your tolerance of oxygen debt. Gradually you are moving towards a 'peak' of fitness, which should coincide with the race you most want to win that year.

The whole thing is really very simple in concept. A long period of steady running in the winter to build up strength, followed by a sharpening up spell in the summer before the main races. But you cannot have one without the other. Without the strength, the track sessions will be too hard. Without the speed, you will run on strongly but no faster. A middle-distance runner needs speed *and* strength at the same time.

What every athlete should also have is a training plan and a racing plan. On these he or she should plot out the whole year, deciding at which point they are going to be training hard and not worrying too much about racing, and at which point they want to be at their absolute fittest. There are plenty of athletes who can run well from time to time, but it is those who know *why* they have run well in a specific race who will progress. If you manage to improve your mile time from five minutes to four-and-a-half minutes, then you should look back in your diary and see what kind of training brought about that improvement. If it worked before, it will work again; far more so than by blindly copying a training schedule of, say, Alberto Juantorena, published in an athletics magazine. You can learn from that sort of thing, certainly, but the schedule published is one which suits an Olympic champion and has been designed and tailored for him, not you.

You have to get to know yourself, and be realistic in your ambition. It is no good aiming to be an Olympic champion yourself without first becoming club or county champion. They are stepping stones, and they cannot be missed out. Training for distance running is hard work, and if you are going to be successful there will be a lot of times when it is uncomfortable.

By having a definite plan to follow, you feel that each ten-mile run through the rain is a specific piece of the jig-saw, and not just 'another' run. Without a sense of purpose, you are more likely to miss sessions when the weather is bad, and if you do that then you most certainly will never make it as a successful distance runner.

*A training night with some of the Gateshead Harriers lads:
the greatest bunch in the world.*

More than that, if you have to get up in the morning to run for an hour before work, and then have to do a full day's work, and then go running for another hour in the evening, you have to got *know* that it is doing you good and helping you towards your goal.

My own routine each day starts around 7.30 am when I get up, have a cup of tea and some cornflakes, put on my tracksuit, and then run a long route of between five and ten miles to work. I get changed there, work until 5 pm, and then run home by the same circuitous route. Occasionally I go out training again later in the evening. I have got a responsible administrative job in Gateshead Council and I work hard at it, but although I live only three miles from work I can honestly say that in the past four years I have only taken the direct route back twice.

Obviously, running so much means that a good night's sleep is important and I try to be in bed by 10.30 or 11 pm at the latest when I'm training hard. Often I am so tired that it does not need much effort to go to bed even earlier.

For, if we are talking about any athlete who wants to be an international, then I would say that they would have to accept that their life will be planned around their training, and not the other way round. The regularity and the quantity of it is so important that it has to take precedence if you are ambitious. Any male athlete over the age of eighteen, who sees himself as a potential international, should be running at least twelve miles a day at the very minimum in my opinion.

Standards are getting tougher all the time, and while I do not envisage endless bulk mileage as the answer, I think the future will see new balances between mileage and speed work to produce tomorrow's athletes. We have already seen world-distance running records being crushed since the post-war years, and many top internationals now do more training in a single day than some internationals did in an entire week twenty-five or thirty years ago. And you do not see them collapsing after races now, as you did then.

As far as food is concerned, we have a fairly balanced diet in Britain. Many of us eat too well in many cases, but for an athlete there is no point in carrying any excess weight. Racehorses have to do so as a penalty, but that has not spread to athletics yet, so why lug a few extra pounds round with you? You would soon notice if they were potatoes and you had to carry them.

I am always being asked if I eat any special food, but the answer is simply that I eat the same as my wife, though perhaps just a little more. The greatest fallacy of the lot, however, is people's tendency to say, 'It must be great to be fit!'

Apart from the obvious benefits to your long-term health, the remark could not be further from the truth. When you are fit for international running, most of the time you are tired, sleepy and more susceptible to colds and flu than most people. You never feel fit when you are training hard, so in all honesty there is not a great recommendation in international running to keep you sprightly, wideawake and active all day in the same way that there is for recreational running and jogging, which really does tone you up.

The limitation of training for international athletics is simply to allow yourself, grudgingly, enough energy to get you through the rest of your daily life. It's training, recovery, training, recovery, all the time, and you spend every day either tired or recovering from being tired, which is why manual work is absolutely out for a distance runner with ambitions. Your body really needs to sit at an office desk and recover.

If I have made it sound a daunting prospect, that is not my intention. There are many thousands of club athletes who enjoy weekly competition and regular training without ever experiencing the fatigue to which I have referred, and for athletics' sake, that is a great thing. But I am trying to paint a realistic picture of what it is like to be an international distance runner, and my definition is someone who starts the morning tired and ends the day even more tired.

For youngsters, of course, that should be a world away. My advice to them is simply to train regularly and often, but also to enjoy as much competition as possible. There will be plenty of time for 'peaks' later in their career; but when you are twelve or thirteen there is nothing so important as next Saturday, whatever it is.

Whenever I hear about a twelve-year-old boy who is 'building up for the 1988 Olympics' I almost despair, because at that age they cannot possibly know what they want in terms of challenge. More likely it is some grown-up, a parent or coach, who has their eye on 1988 on his behalf, and such ultra-long plans seldom come to anything.

It is far more important at that age to instil the basic essentials of training, such as warming-up. Lots of youngsters (and some seniors who should know better) often go straight into a training session without bothering to jog a few laps and do some exercises as a warm-up. But to skip the warm-up is to invite injury, and it is not a corner to be cut.

Neither is there any benefit in training in just vest and shorts on a cold night, as I see so many youngsters doing. Some people think that such a Spartan approach adds something to the value of the training, but the opposite is true. Muscles work far more efficiently when they are warm, and there is no stigma in going out in a tracksuit and jumper if you feel you want to. It is not soft to do so, just common sense. I often wear gloves and a hat, in addition to two tracksuits, on really cold days. It is difficult enough to get out sometimes without having to freeze as well!

So for youngsters taking up athletics, I would offer the following points:

1. Decide what you want to do next season, but make it a realistic target.
2. Decide the level at which you are willing to train, and stick to it.
3. Be progressive about your training – but make sure it is *your* training and not someone else's.
4. Don't be frightened or unwilling to be satisfied with your own performances. If you run 5 minutes 20 seconds for 1500 metres, and it is *your* best time, then it simply does not matter how many other people have run faster. Athletics is all about individual progress, and there is as much satisfaction in this as in winning an Olympic title, if you look for it.
5. Rome wasn't built in a day. Be patient.

Excerpts from the Training Diary

The following excerpts are really to illustrate the daily breakdown of my training at different times of the year, and at different stages of my career.

FEBRUARY 1968

(My 'blue' period in Brighton, when things were going badly.)

Sun Feb 11: 16 miles steady run. Felt very tired.

Mon Feb 12: (am) Repetition hills. Total 6 miles.

                  (pm) 7 miles steady. Felt v. tired.

Tue Feb 13: (am) 4 miles jog.

                  (pm) 11 miles run, Stanmer Village to Saltdean. 1hr 20mins.

Wed Feb 14: (am) 4 miles Stanmer Village. Felt tired.

                  (pm) 4 laps of football pitches in Stanmer Pk. Total 7 miles.

Thu Feb 15: 4 miles easy, preparation for race.

Fri   Feb 16: 4 miles easy.

Sat   Feb 17: Hyde Park Relay. Started off hard, legs and thigh muscles very sore. Couldn't run properly. Bad run, felt really tired. $2\frac{3}{4}$ miles lap in 16 mins 40 secs.

                                  Week's total: 69 miles in 10 sessions.

Sun Feb 18: Fed up. Decided to have a day off.

FEBRUARY 1969

(Twelve months later I had found out about my iron deficiency anaemia and corrected it.)

Sun Feb   9: Easy run 13 miles. Ankle sore.

Mon Feb 10: 14 × hills very hard. Total 11 miles.

Tue Feb 11: 8 miles steady run.

Wed Feb 12: Hills flat out again. Total 13 miles.

Thu Feb 13: 6 miles.

Fri   Feb 14: Steady jog, 4 miles.

Sat   Feb 15: Hyde Park Relay. Flat out from start, very good run, felt very tired. $2\frac{3}{4}$ miles lap in 13 mins 33 secs (8th fastest time of the day).

                                  Week's total: 64 miles in 7 sessions.

MAY–JUNE 1972

(I was one of at least half-a-dozen contenders for Britain's Olympic 1500 metres team at Munich.)

Sun May 28: (am) 10 miles steady/hard run.

(pm) Speed work. 10 × 120m, 10 secs rest between.

2 × 100m flat out. V. hard session, important to do it regularly.

Mon May 29: 4 miles easy run.

Tue May 30: (am) 4 miles easy run.

(pm) 800m time trial at Meadowbank. 1:52.3 (55.5 + 56.8). Then 6 × 200m, with 200m jog. Average 25/26 secs. Going okay.

Wed May 31: (am) 4 miles easy run on golf course.

(pm) Track session at Meadowbank. 12 × 400 metres with 90–95 secs rest. Average 58.4 secs. Very hard session, legs tired from yesterday, unable to relax at this speed. Total 6 miles.

Thu Jun 1: (am) 10 miles easy run.

(pm) Track session. 8 × 200m with 25 secs rest, quite hard.

10 × 100m turnabouts, going hard.

3 × 100m flat out. Total 7 miles.

Fri Jun 2: (am) Easy run. Total 4 miles.

(pm) Easy run. Total 6 miles.

Sat Jun 3: (am) Easy run with Wilf, 6 miles.

(pm) At Usworth track (ran over and back). 2 × 600m with plenty of rest: 89.0 and 88.3 secs. Trying to pick it up was difficult. 4 × 100m flat out. Total 10 miles.

Week's total: 80 miles.

Sun Jun 4: 12 miles easy run. Foot sore.

Mon Jun 5: (am) 4 miles easy run. Felt a bit rough.

(pm) Fartlek (speedplay). 2 × 1 mile, 3 × 500m, 6 × 100m. Felt lethargic at first, felt v. tired throughout, especially hamstrings.

Tue Jun 6: (am) 4 miles easy run.

(pm) Track, 10 × 300m, 45 secs rest. Average 44.2 secs. Rather windy. 4 × 100m sprints. Felt rather hard for what it was. Total 7 miles.

Wed Jun 7: (am) 4 miles easy run.

(pm) Easy run though rather tired, with Wilf. Total 6 miles.

Thu Jun 8: (am) 4 miles easy.

(pm) 4 miles easy.

Fri Jun 9: (am) 2 miles easy jog.

(pm) 2 miles easy jog.

Sat Jun 10: Emsley Carr Mile at Crystal Palace. Finished 2nd in 3:55.9
             (personal best).

Week's total: 62 miles.

DECEMBER 1973

(I was trying to prepare for the Commonwealth Games in New Zealand the following month.)

Sat Dec 15: (am) Track session at Usworth. 8 × 400m, 90 secs rest. Average
             60.2 secs. Good session in fourth lane, driving snow, and
             wind, full tracksuit and tights.
             (pm) Easy run, 5 miles.

Sun Dec 16: 20 miles steady run. Right heel very sore. Could hardly walk
             afterwards.

Mon Dec 17: (am) Steady run to school, 5 miles. Heel too sore to run properly.
             (pm) Treatment from physio Norman Anderson. Heel badly
             bruised.

Tue Dec 18: Treatment.

Wed Dec 19: Treatment.

Thu Dec 20: Treatment. Norman said heel nearly okay.

Fri Dec 21: 4 miles steady run on school field.

Sat Dec 22: Steady run, 10 miles.

Sun Dec 23: Steady run with Lindsay, 16 miles.

Mon Dec 24: (am) 7 miles steady.
             Delayed journey to Malaga. 12 hours travelling. Very tired.

Tue Dec 25: (am) Steady run, 10 miles, in hills at Malaga. Met Juha Vaatainen
             by chance.
             (pm) Steady run in woods. 3 × 700m, 3 × 200m. Total 7 miles.

Wed Dec 26: (am) 10 miles on road. Tired. Quite hot.
             (pm) Steady run in hills, v. tired, 7 miles.

Thu Dec 27: (am) Set off for steady run, but after about one mile had to stop
             because of bad stomach. In bed all morning. Thought I might
             not run in afternoon.
             (pm) Track session at Malaga with Vaatainen. 10 × 300m, 45 secs
             rest. Average 42.8 secs. One of best ever? Felt OK, legs stiff
             with hard track. Total 8 miles.

Fri Dec 28: (am) Steady run in wind and rain, 10 miles.
             (pm) Steady run with Vaatainen to Los Pacos. Felt tired for last
             4 miles. Total 13 miles.

Sat   Dec 29: (am) Steady run 7 miles. Felt tired to begin with.

(pm) In woods – 2 sets of 8 × 200m (18–20 secs rest). Seemed to be going okay. Faster on second set. Seem to go best when I've warmed up a bit. Total 7 miles.

Sun   Dec 30: Steady run by myself along seafront. Quite warm, felt okay, until last few miles. Total 20 miles.

Mon Dec 31: (am) Steady run along the beach for 7 miles. Felt okay, as though I was running again.

(pm) Track session at Malaga. Warm day, slight breeze in back straight. 6 × 800m 4 mins rest. Average 2:01.5. Best session ever!

JULY–AUGUST 1974

(Preparing for European championships in Rome.)

Sun Jul   21: 20 miles steady run.

Mon Jul   22: (am) 10 miles steady to work.

(pm) 8 miles steady run.

Tue   Jul   23: (am) Steady 5 miles.

(pm) Steady 5 miles.

(pm) Track 7pm. 3 × 800m (4–4½ mins rest). Cold windy night. Average 2:01.3. Very hard session, needed it. Ran 4 × 100m on grass afterwards.

Wed Jul   24: (am) Steady run to work, 9 miles.

(pm) 2 sets of 8 × 200m quite hard (20 secs rest). 4 × 100m. Quite a tough session. Total 6 miles.

Thu Jul   25: (am) Steady run, 6 miles.

(pm) Steady run, 5 miles.

(pm) Steady run, 5 miles.

Fri   Jul   26: (am) Steady run to work, 6 miles.

(pm) GB v Czechoslovakia 1500m race in Edinburgh. 1st 3:41.2. (2nd F. Clement 3:41.7.)

Sat   Jul   27: 15 miles with Mike Baxter, quite fast.

Week's total: 110 miles.

Sun Jul   28: (am) Track at Gateshead. 3 × 1600m. Nice day. Average 4:10.18 secs; equals best ever. Very hard.

(pm) Steady 10 miles run. Very tired, but felt better than I thought I would.

Mon Jul 29: (am) 10 miles steady.

(pm) 10 miles steady.

Tue Jul 30: (am) 6 miles steady run.

(pm) Track at Gateshead, lunchtime. 10 × 400m (90 secs rest). Average 58.49 secs. Quite hard throughout.

(pm) 8 miles steady run.

Wed Jul 31: (am) Steady run, 7 miles.

(pm) 2 sets of 8 × 200m (20 secs rest). Recovering well.

Thu Aug 1: (am) Steady run to work, 6 miles.

(pm) Steady run, legs sore, 8 miles.

Fri Aug 2: (am) Steady run, 5 miles.

(pm) Steady run, 5 miles.

Sat Aug 3: Gateshead Games. 3000m in 7:35.2. World record. Quite pleased with last lap.

(pm) 4 miles steady run.

APRIL 1976

(The bulk work for Montreal had gone on throughout the winter, and was reaching its highest level.)

Sun Apr 4: 20 miles easy run, quite comfortable.

Mon Apr 5: (am) 10 miles steady.

(pm) 10 miles hard with Wilf.

Tue Apr 6: (am) 10 miles steady. Quite tired from last night. Worried about knee injury.

(pm) 10 miles steady, with three hard stretches. Only ran steady because of knee, felt a little discomfort after 7 or 8 miles. Very tired tonight.

Wed Apr 7: (am) Seemed very tired when I got up, had to persuade myself to go running. My knee was worrying me and the fact that I'm not sure if I'd be able to complete 10 miles doesn't help. Had to work hard to keep going all the way, suffering for it. 10 miles.

(pm) Steady run with Wilf, 10 miles. Very tired, in fact could hardly keep going over the last few miles. Knee not too bad.

Thu Apr 8: (am) Steady 10 miles, going okay.

(pm) Steady 10 miles, seemed to be going well, even though very tired indeed, very fatigued over last few miles.

Am having to apply myself to maintain this level of training. Am feeling extremely tired and low because of it occasionally, however have the motivation to keep going, especially as it seems I'm running well.

Fri Apr 9: (am) Steady run 5 miles.
(pm) Steady run 5 miles.
(pm) Steady run 5 miles.

Sat Apr 10: (am) Track. Nice day. 10×400m (90 secs rest). Average 61.26 sec. Pulse 172 15 secs after last one. Total $5\frac{1}{2}$ miles.
(pm) 10 miles steady by myself. Felt stiff, possibly because of track session, but going okay when able to concentrate properly.
Week's total: $131\frac{1}{2}$ miles.

Sun Apr 11: 20 miles steady run.

Mon Apr 12: (am) 15 miles steady.
(pm) Steady run up hills and in woods – 7 miles.

Tue Apr 13: (am) Steady run, 11 miles.
(pm) Club run, 12 miles.
Feeling as though I'm doing as much running as I possibly can, getting sick of all the running without variety, and hope racing and track training will release the boredom. Would be worse if I wasn't running well.

Wed Apr 14: Feel like taking an easy day.
(am) Steady run, 10 miles. Made little effort.
(pm) Steady run with Wilf, 10 miles, going quite strong.

Thu Apr 15: (am) 10 miles steady.
(pm) 10 miles steady. Felt tired nearly all the way. First time this week that the tiredness has really caught up with me.

Fri Apr 16: (am) Steady run. Tired. 5 miles.
(pm) Easy run on football field, 5 miles.
(pm) Steady run with Lindsay, 5 miles.

Sat Apr 17: (am) Track. 5×600m (2 mins rest). Average 91.9 secs. Quite hard. Felt stiff. Total 6 miles.
(pm) 10 miles steady run with Pete. Felt stiff to begin with and rather stiff and tired when I finished.
Week's total: 136 miles.

Sun Apr 18: (Last three weeks average $131\frac{1}{2}$ miles p.w.)
(am) 20 miles steady run. Quite stiff to begin with, but very tired from halfway.

202

Mon Apr 19: (am) 11 miles steady.
            (pm) 10 miles steady. Warm day, nice for running, felt very tired, especially later on. Legs feeling the pressure.

Tue Apr 20: (am) 15 miles steady run by myself.
            (pm) Steady 7 miles with Mike Tagg. Got going after halfway, running quite strongly.

Wed Apr 21: Only 7 hours sleep.
            (am) Steady 6 miles with Mike Tagg.
            (pm) Easy slow run with Lindsay, 10 miles.

Thu Apr 22: (am) Steady 10 miles.
            (pm) Steady 7 miles.

Fri Apr 23: (am) 5 miles steady.
            (pm) 5 miles steady.
            (pm) 5 miles steady.

Sat Apr 24: (am) Steady run with Wilf. Felt tired and short of breath. 3 miles.
            (pm) National Road Relay, Sutton Coldfield.

            Felt lethargic warming up, but determined to beat record. Didn't feel as though I was running fast but quite hard, and not getting particularly tired until I finished. Time: 13:37 for 3 miles 100 yards. Course record by 15 seconds.

Week's total: 126 miles

And For The Future . . .?

Sometimes when I feel miserable about the amount of training I have to do to remain an international runner, I reflect how much more comfortable it might have been twenty or thirty years ago, when everyone trained less – and times were consequently slower. But then again, those of us running internationally in the 'seventies may be fortunate that we do not find ourselves training even harder, to the exclusion of virtually everything else, as I feel may be the case in the not-too-distant future.

So, purely as a daydreaming exercise, I have compiled what I think might be a typical week's training for an athlete of the future – in the year 2000, for instance. In the Olympic Games of that year (to be held in Gateshead perhaps?) I estimate that the winning times in the 5000 metres and 10,000 metres will be around 12:50.0 and 26:40.0 respectively.

Training for those Games will, I suspect, be much more scientifically monitored, if not programmed. It could possibly include extra activities like gymnastics, yoga or weight training, plus an enormous amount of running. Quite probably there will be no time for a job too, so therefore less chance for the British athletes to succeed in the face of competitors given full government backing. The schedule could be something like this:

Sunday	(am)	Long run: 25 miles in 2½ hours.
	(pm)	Exercises, then technique running on the track, followed by massage.
Monday	(am)	10 miles run in 60 minutes.
	(lunchtime)	5 miles run in 30 minutes, plus 30 minutes yoga.
	(pm)	15 miles run in 1½ hours.
Tuesday	(am)	10 miles run in 60 minutes.
	(lunchtime)	Weight training, then easy 30 minutes run.
	(pm)	15 miles run in 1½ hours.
Wednesday	(am)	20 miles run in 2 hours.
	(lunchtime)	Weight training (1 hour)
		Two hours sleep in afternoon
	(pm)	7 miles run in 45 minutes; exercises; gymnastics.
Thursday	(am)	15 miles run in 1½ hours.
	(lunchtime)	Massage and hypnosis, then rest.
	(pm)	Track session: 2 × 5000 metres in 13:30.0.
Friday	(am)	10 miles run in 60 minutes.
	(lunchtime)	Medical check-up by doctor, and run 30 minutes.
	(pm)	30 minutes run, then 1 hour weight training.
Saturday	(am)	20 miles run in 2 hours.
	(afternoon)	Sleep or rest 2 hours.
	(pm)	Run 10 miles in 60 minutes.

In order to carry out a training regime like this it would be necessary to sleep about nine hours a night, and about two hours in the afternoon. The diet would have to be controlled by sports medical experts, and a whole back-up team of physicians, physiotherapists and psychologists would be essential. These services already exist in countries like East Germany.

However, sleeping will take up eleven hours, eating about two-and-a-half hours, running about three hours, extra training, such as weights, about one-and-a-half hours, which only leaves six hours a day free. Obviously this is not the training system of a British amateur athlete, but will be the sort of system used in the year 2000 to run 5000 metres in 12:50.0.

Fifteen

Something which perhaps I do not do often enough, amid the constant training grind and preparation for the next race, is to stop and analyse deeply the answer to one specific question: *Why?* Probably there is no single answer anyway, and my motivation for wanting to continue at a high level of competition is extremely complex. But threaded through it is this need I feel to keep proving myself to myself. I just cannot be satisfied resting on old laurels, because whatever has gone in the past cannot help you when you step up to the line for the next competition. They do not give you a start because you have won before; it is the others, who are hungry to win, who often benefit from what has happened in the past. As far as I am concerned, I may have some medals at home somewhere, but it all starts again fresh on Saturday. Medals don't help you. You still have to go out there and do it again.

And because I doubt my own ability from time to time, I have to try to prove I can still do it. It may be that, deep inside, I am always afraid that I may one day return to being the slow runner I was at university, and that the dream will end. If I was injured tomorrow and could never run another step, I have some good memories of athletics on which to look back. But while I can race, I want to convince myself that I can still reach out for new horizons.

Sometimes, when I start training again with just a slow, solitary mile at the end of my two or three weeks break in the autumn, and I find how hard it is even to go faster than a jog, I worry whether or not I will ever get my form back. Even after all these years, I cannot help wondering if each season will be the one where my ability suddenly leaves me.

Yet as the training gets under-way, and my legs regain their strength, back comes the confidence and I know that there is life in the old boy yet. Whether I will still be turning up at the AAA championships when I'm ninety-six to see if I can run as fast as I could at ninety-five remains to be seen, but my enthusiasm is strong. I have no plans for running a marathon because I think I can run faster yet at 5000 and 10,000 metres, and the inner me wants to prove it, not just think it.

For there *is* an inner me whom very few people know. Sue says that at university I was always the life and soul of the party, taking the mickey out of other people, cracking jokes, and generally carrying on. But I think that was just a front to disguise my shyness. For some people think I'm tough and hard, and certainly the job I have does call on me to make decisions which are not always popular. They think, 'Oh, he doesn't care' when I make an unpopular decision, and occasionally I suppose I rub people up the wrong way when I'm under pressure. But I have to keep up this front, like a sort of shield, because I like a degree of privacy, a world into which I can retreat when I feel the need. Sue says that I have an invisible line which is as far as I will let people come, and perhaps that sums it up best.

There are, though, a very few people who see behind that shield because they are the closest friends who, over the years, have shared so many of my ups and downs. I would like to mention three of them here, apart from my own family who are, and always have been, a tremendous support, because without them I would never have had a story to tell.

First there is the man who is so much of the driving force behind Gateshead Harriers, Stan Long. He is someone who has a passionate love affair with distance running, and his enthusiasm just envelops you. It is as great now as it was when I was a kid, when he first began to build up the club's youth section. Then he was a welder by trade, although it was simply a means to earn his living and he turned down the chance of overtime because he wanted to spend every available minute with athletes, talking about athletics.

Stan is a great motivator, a man who gets on with people, which is a rare gift. I am sure he would talk in exactly the same way to the Queen as he would to a shop floor worker in Gateshead, and I am sure that both would be bowled over by his genuine enthusiasm for helping young people. But every time he tried to get a job in youth work his absence of 'paper qualifications' let him down.

Now he works in my Recreation Department at Gateshead, and he is in his element. He coaches the youngsters, and encourages the vast hordes of joggers we now have at lunchtime in the stadium, keeping them at it. He is also an inspiration to me, because he makes me determined to be as fit and active at the age of forty-seven as he is.

Our relationship has changed over the years, from the days when I was a raw beginner and he was telling me what to do at each training session, until now, when I formulate most of my own programme and he comments on it and suggests possible variations. He is very much a simple approach coach, always there to lend a hand, pat you on the back, hold a stopwatch, or cheer you up when you are low.

Sometimes I may not see him for a couple of weeks, sometimes I'll see him every day, and sometimes we will run together, just chatting things through. I always remember one summer evening in 1972, when I had run badly in the AAA championships 1500 metres final and jeopardised my chance of going to the Olympics. Stan and I had just heard that I was going to have to run that special trial race against John Kirkbride in Helsinki to decide who would fill the third spot in Britain's team, and we went to the Gateshead Stadium for a special track session. There were just the two of us, and we had to climb over a wall because the stadium was locked up. But after the session we walked and walked for miles, just talking the whole thing over. Stan had come straight from work, and was wearing his boilersuit and big boots, and I remember him saying finally, 'Well, if you canna beat Kirkbride in Helsinki, you don't deserve to go to the Olympics.' That, perhaps more than anything else he said, struck home.

The only time we have had a sticky patch was in 1976, before the Montreal Olympics. He had come to work in my department, and the situation where I was his boss, but he was my coach, was not really an ideal one. We were also both under a lot of pressure at the time. Stan had been named as one of the British team coaches for the Games, a great honour for him, but one which was spoiled by jealous coaches who wrote some unkind letters to him, suggesting that he was lucky to be going to Montreal at the 'expense' of others. At the same time I was under pressure as one of the Olympic favourites, and the result was that we were arguing quite a lot about small, unimportant things. But that was all sorted out when the pressure relented, and perhaps we both learned from the experience.

The second member of the trio is motor insurance manager Lindsay Dunn, who spends all of his spare time either running or thinking about running. Lindsay reads everything printed on athletics, and he is the one who is always weighing up past and present, comparing different athletes' strengths and weaknesses, and he is the suggester of new ideas. He puts forward possible racing programmes and thinks about the technical side of my running, as well as sharing many of my training miles.

He is quieter than Stan by nature, and not a motivator in the same way. But he has his own subtle way of goading me into action, asking things like, 'I suppose you're happy with finishing second now, are you?' in just the right tone of voice to have an effect. Between them, Stan and Lindsay are a real strength behind me, and their contributions are complementary, not overlapping. We work together as a team and if, for instance, Lindsay suggests a session of eight laps of alternately sprinting and jogging 50 metres at a time, then I can rely on Stan to help me get through this exhausting effort on the track by his encouragement.

The three of us do not get together as much as we used to in the old days. It was while sitting round a pub table that we hatched out the idea of the world two miles record in 1973. But now each of us has greater commitments. Stan is coaching over forty young athletes at the club as well as supervising many more and is deeply involved in his Recreation Department work; Lindsay is also coaching youngsters and running himself; and the demands on my time seem to be increasing every year.

The name of Wilf Wardle may not be a very familiar one to athletics fans, but he is the only runner in Britain who can thrash me regularly, and as such plays just as important a part in my preparation as Stan and Lindsay.

Wilf is an art teacher who lives just a short distance away from my parents' home in Hebburn. He is also the man who drew the excellent cartoons which are reproduced in this book, and which were executed after each of my major championship races (had you noticed I get progressively uglier in each one?). But he has an equal talent for running, which is very rarely seen, even though he covered about the same training mileage as me – over 4000 miles – during 1977. He simply does not like competing, because he gets exceptionally nervous before races, so he contents himself in the main with running for the pure love of it.

I meet him about twice a week to train, and we don't hang about, because he is a hell of a runner. I can recall one particular session we did back in 1972, when we put in a very hard three-quarters of a mile stretch at the end of a road run. We were absolutely racing it, and about 300 yards from the end I kicked and went ahead of him, going absolutely flat out. A moment later he came whistling past me! I simply could not stay with him, and I am convinced that we covered that last three-quarters of a mile in around three minutes. A week later I ran my best-ever mile, 3:55.9.

But Wilf could never have matched his run on the track; it was only because we were running on country roads with no one around that he was able to let himself go like that. Physically he is a very talented athlete, with best times of 51.0 for 400 metres and 1 hour 49 minutes for twenty miles, so there ought to be some good track performances in between. He has recently joined Gateshead Harriers, and we hope we might be able to persuade him to turn out for us in races more often, but I would not be surprised if he was satisfied simply to run for fun – and there is nothing wrong in that. He often reminds me, though, that he is one of the very few

British runners to have beaten me on the track. It was in a mile race when I was about eighteen, and he was twenty-one, but he doesn't let me forget it!

Training partners like Wilf are the great unsung heroes of international athletics, because he makes it so much easier for me to train. I am sure Steve Ovett would say the same about Matt Patterson in Brighton, and Lasse Viren about Seppo Tuominen in Finland. There are occasions, particularly in the dead of winter when I am putting in my highest mileage, when I can hardly run faster than a jog, and it is only by having someone like Wilf alongside me, encouraging me to keep going, that I get round at all. In return, he gets very little out of it, other than involvement, and I find that extremely flattering, especially when I know that before I have run an important race on TV, Wilf has been out in the garden, unable to watch, because of nerves. And when I won the Coke 10,000 metres in 1977, after so many frustrations in the summer (which he shared), he was actually crying. He is a hell of a bloke to have as a friend and training companion, and Sue and I often go on holiday with Wilf and his wife, Margaret.

There are, of course, many others who have helped in varying degrees and varying ways. People like PE teacher George Felton, who started me running at school, John Trainor, who grew up with me, John Caine, who first showed me what hard training was all about, and marathon runner Max Coleby, all have a lot of good ideas about running. So does Charlie Spedding, who often comes with us on our Sunday morning twenty-miles training runs. It is really a source of strength and reassurance to have such a nucleus of people around me who can enthuse about running in the same way that I do. It gives me an extra dimension, and the fact that they don't worship plastic gods, and that I know they will soon chop the legs from under me if they think I am getting big-headed, is of great value.

They have known me all along, from the schoolboy soccer player, to the struggling university student, to the international athlete. And I know, as well as they do, that if you let up on the training, even for a short while, you are soon off your cloud and back down to earth with a bump.

In athletics, you have to work hard to stay in the same place, because there are always others coming up behind you. As an example, let me mention a road race I won in Barrow-in-Furness in March 1977. It was a ten miles event, and I did not really want to take part because after my National cross country win and the birth of our son I was suffering a 'reaction', and had not run for a while. However, the organisers had been let down by some other athletes who had pulled out at the last minute, and they offered to *fly* me down before the race with some of the other lads from Gateshead to Barrow (which is not that far). At the airport we were met by a Rolls-Royce and taken to the course in real style. It made us feel like royalty.

I won the race in 47:16, which was quite pleasing, but just four seconds behind me came a young student from Ranelagh Harriers, Hugh Jones. There had been no plane and no Rolls-Royce for him. Instead, he had travelled up to Barrow the previous evening, been unable to find anywhere to stay, and eventually spent the night in a bus shelter, while I was peacefully at home in bed.

Ironically, he had run the previous day for the British Universities in their annual match against the ECCU and Combined Services, finishing a creditable seventh. It was the same match which, eight years before, I had won as a BUSF representative myself, and made what I felt was my big breakthrough in athletics. Was his run at Barrow an omen, or a nudge that I had better get back into hard training again pretty soon?

Howay Big Bren!

Appendix

In the following compilation of my racing record since 1962 we have tried to include, where possible, the following information about each race: date, meeting, venue, distance, my position and time, plus any other relevant details, such as the winner and winning time if I lost, and the runner-up if I won. Some of the details in my earliest races have unfortunately been lost, but we have included everything available to try to give as comprehensive a record as possible.

The following abbreviations are used:

CC = cross country   h'cap = handicap   ht = heat   m = metres
M = mile(s)   s.f. = semi-final   y = yards

Date	Meeting	Venue	Distance	Position and time	Other positions
1962					
Dec	Catholic Diocesan Schools CC champs	Sunderland	2½M	2nd	1st J. Trainor
1963					
Feb	Hebburn District Schools CC champs	Hebburn		2nd	1st J. Trainor
Mar	Durham County Schools CC champs	Stanley		10th	1st J. Trainor
May		North Shields	440y	1st 59.7	
		Blaydon	440y	1st 59.5	
		Silksworth	440y	1st	
	District champs	Hebburn	440y	1st 56.5	
June		Durham	440y	4th (55.5 in heat)	
		Brinkburn	880y	1st 2:09.0 (disqualified)	
	Diocesan Schools champs	Billingham	440y	1st 50.5	
	Durham Schools champs	Houghton	440y	2nd 54.8 (54.4 in heat)	
Jul 19	English Schools champs	Chelmsford	440y ht	4th 55.5	

Date	Meeting	Venue	Distance	Position and time	Other positions
Oct	Harrier CC League	Houghton		18th	1st J. Bulman
Nov 9	Road race	Heaton	1½M	5th 8:00	1st J. Trainor 7:37
Nov 16	Road race	North Shields	2½M	2nd 13:09	1st J. Trainor 12:38
	Tyneside Grammar Schools CC champs	Monkwearmouth		8th	1st J. Caine
Nov 30	Road race	Bedlington		2nd 8:45	1st J. Trainor 8:25
Dec	Inter-county CC match	Middlesbrough		3rd	1st J. Trainor
	Harrier CC League	North Shields		9th	1st J. Foley
Dec 26	Congers road race	Gateshead		2nd	1st J. Trainor

1964

Date	Meeting	Venue	Distance	Position and time	Other positions
Jan	Sherman Cup Boys CC race	North Shields	2M	3rd 9:34	1st J. Trainor 9:15
	Harrier CC League			10th	
Feb 1	North-East Boys CC champs	West Hartlepool	2¼M	2nd 10:35	1st M. Coleby 10:24
Feb 15	Northern Boys CC champs	Middlesbrough	2¼M	10th 11:13	1st D. Brennan 10:32
	Royal Signals Boys road race	Gateshead		4th	1st J. Trainor
Mar	Durham Schools Intermediate CC	Houghton	4½M	2nd	1st M. Coleby 26:27
	Triangular CC match	Carlisle		9th	1st B. Louden
Mar 21	English Schools CC champs	Leicester	4M	64th	1st T. Simmons, 19:26
	Benwell Boys relay			3rd leg, winning team 6:40	
Jun 5	Tyneside Grammar Schools champs		440y	6th 58.8	
	Durham Schools champs		880y	7th	
	Diocesan Schools champs		440y	1st 55.1	
	St Joseph GS sports		1M	1st 4:54.0	

1965

(Injury and exams precluded competition in the summer)

Date	Meeting	Venue	Distance	Position and time	Other positions
Oct	Harrier CC League	South Shields		5th	
Oct 23	Road race	Bedlington		7th 15:37	1st J. Trainor 14:41
Oct 30	Gateshead road relay	Gateshead	3 × 2¾M	1st Gateshead H (ran 2nd leg)	
Nov 13	Road race	Heaton		7th	1st B. Mileson
	Road race	North Shields		8th	1st B. Mileson
Dec 26	Congers road race	Gateshead		6th	1st B. Mileson

1966

Date	Meeting	Venue	Distance	Position and time	Other positions
Jan	Sherman Cup Youths CC race	North Shields	3M	1st 18:38	2nd B. Louden 18:40

Date	Meeting	Venue	Distance	Position and time	Other positions
Feb 10	Northern Youths CC champs	Huddersfield		31st	1st B. Mileson 16:47
	Royal Signals Youths road relay	Gateshead		1st Gateshead H	
Mar 5	National Youths CC champs	Sheffield	3½M	10th 15:47	1st B. Mileson 15:10
Mar 12	Inter-Counties Youths CC champs	Leicester	3¾M	20th 18:20	1st T. Simmons 17:25
Mar 19	Road race	South Shields	3M	2nd 14:39	1st B. Mileson 14:07
Mar 26	Road race	Jarrow		8th 21:22	1st J. Trainor 20:36
May 10		Newcastle	1M	2nd 4:26.1	1st W. Wardle
May 14		Billingham	1M	4th 4:24.0	1st M. Benn
Jun 11		Billingham	880y h'cap (off 43y)	1:51.0	
Jun 13		Sunderland	2M	4th 9:29.0	
Jun 15		Gateshead	1M	4th 4:15.8	1st K. Carr
Jun 20		South Shields	880y	2nd 1:59.0	
		,,	1M	2nd 4:26.0	
Jun 25		South Shields	880y h'cap (off 38y)	1:56.0	
Jul 2	Northern Junior AAA champs	Middlesbrough	1 M ht	3rd 4:20.0	
		,,	1 M final	6th 4:28.8	1st C. Mason 4:15.7
Jul 9		West Hartlepool	1 M h'cap (off 22y)	4:17.0	
Jul 13		Huddersfield	1M	3rd 4:17.0	1st C. Mason
Jul 20		West Hartlepool	1M	1st 4:19.4	2nd B. Mileson
Jul 23		Houghton	880y	2nd 1:57.6	
Aug 3			880y	1:56.0	
Aug 13	AAA Junior champs	Hurlingham	1M ht	5th 4:25.0	
Dec 3	Portsmouth relay	Portsmouth		3rd fastest lap 11:44	
1967					
Jan 14	Harrier CC League	Bedlington		3rd	1st D. Cockburn
Feb 4	British Univ CC champs	Parliament Hill	6M	163rd	1st R. Robinson 30:26
Apr 20		Brighton	1M	2nd 4:37.0	1st C. Carter 4:07.0
Jun 10		Eastbourne	1M	2nd 4:34.8	
Jun 18		Eastbourne	880y	2:02.0	
Jul 12		Jarrow	2M	9:45.0	
Oct 4	Sussex Univ CC trial	Brighton		4th 35:04	
Oct 7	Sussex Univ CC trial	Brighton		2nd 34:05	
Oct 19	University Coll CC relay	Parliament Hill	1½M	8:38	
Oct 21	Reading Univ v Sussex Univ	Reading	5M	30:00	1st M. Tagg 26:41
Oct 28	Inter-college CC match	Brighton		2nd 33:44	1st J. Ledbury 31:39
Nov 18	Southern Univ CC champs	Reading		dropped out	
Nov 25	Bristol Univ v Sussex Univ	Bristol		21st	
Dec 2	Portsmouth relay	Portsmouth		12:02	

Date	Meeting	Venue	Distance	Position and time	Other positions
1968					
Jan 27	North-East Junior CC champs	Darlington	6M	13th 35:49	1st B. Mileson 30:19
Feb 17	Imperial College road relay	Hyde Park	2¾M	16:40	
May 11		Hurlingham	880y	2:08.0	
May 29		Brighton	880y	2:07.0	
		,,	440y	55.8	
Jun 6		Bognor	880y	2:10.0	
		,,	440y	56.2	
Oct 12	University College relay	Parliament Hill	1½M	8:35	
Oct 26	Road race	Southwick		8th	1st R. Roseman
Nov 2	Inter-College CC match			1st	
Nov 9	Inter-college CC match	Brighton		1st 29:56	
Nov 16	Southern Univ CC champs	Bristol		4th	1st M. Tagg
Nov 30	Inter-club CC match	Brighton		6th	1st F. Stebbings
Dec 4	Osterley Park relay	Isleworth	2½M	15:23	
Dec 7	Bexhill CC match	Bexhill		7th	1st P. Standing
Dec 26	Congers road race	Gateshead		3rd	1st J. Hillen
1969					
Jan 11	Sherman Cup CC race	North Shields	6M	3rd 31:46	1st W. Robinson 31:26
Jan 25	CC match	Parliament Hill		13th	1st J. Valentine
Feb 1	British Univ CC champs	Sheffield	7½M	9th	1st equal, A. Holden, M. Thomas 39:09
Feb 15	Imperial College road relay	Hyde Park	2¾M	8th fastest lap 13:33	
Feb 22	Sussex CC League			4th	1st D. Bedford
Mar 2	Bognor College road relay	Bognor	1⅛M	fastest lap 5:47	
Mar 5	Essex Police v Sussex Univ	Chelmsford		1st	
Mar 15	British Univ v Combined Services v ECCU CC match	Fareham	6M	1st 30:45	2nd G. North 30:52
Mar 22	Sussex CC League	Brighton	5½M	1st 26:50	2nd R. Roseman 27:19
Apr 4	Elswick road relay	Elswick		equal fastest lap 10:10	
Apr 12	Road race	Jarrow	6½M	4th 32:16	1st J. Caine 31:07
Jun 4		Crawley	800m	1st 1:56.7	
Jun 14	British Univ champs	Motspur Park	800m ht	1st 1:53.0	
			800m final	3rd 1:52.6	1st A. Carter 1:51.5
Jun 16	PE Colleges v UAU v Southern AAA	Crystal Palace	800m	9th 1:56.0	1st A. Carter 1:49.2
Jun 23		South Shields	440y	1st 51.4	
			1M	1st 4:16.8	
Jun 25	Gateshead Games	Gateshead	1500m	1st 3:48.4	2nd R. Bell
Jul 5	Open track meeting	West Hartlepool	1M	1st 4:05.6	2nd M. Baxter 4:06.8

Date	Meeting	Venue	Distance	Position and time	Other positions
Jul 9	Jarrow & Hebburn Sports	Jarrow	2M	1st 8:48.8	2nd E. Pomfret 8:48.8
Aug 1	AAA champs	White City	1500m ht	7th 3:51.0	
Aug 16	Invitation race	Middlesbrough	1500m	4th 3:47.1	1st J. Boulter 3:43.3
Nov 29	National PE Colleges CC champs	Richmond Park	5M	1st 28:59	2nd J. Bicourt 29:14

1970

Date	Meeting	Venue	Distance	Position and time	Other positions
Jan 17	Inter-Counties CC champs	Derby	7½M	32nd 38:46	1st R. Taylor 36:45
Jan 24	North-East CC champs	Morpeth	9M	4th 48:43	1st J. Adler 46:12
Feb 4	Univ of Salford road relay	Salford	3¼M	fastest lap 16:02	
Feb 14	Imperial College road relay	Hyde Park	2¾M	12th fastest lap 13:50	
Feb 28	International Students CC race	Berne		10th	
Mar 21	Gosforth relay	Gosforth		fastest lap 20:20 (course record)	
Mar 27	Elswick relay	Elswick		fastest lap 10:04 (course record)	
Apr 18	William Hall road race	Jarrow	6½M	1st 30:51	2nd W. Robinson 31:01
Apr 25		Keighley	3000m	2nd 8:30.0	1st M. Baxter 8:23.0
Apr 29		Durham	800m	1st 1:57.4	
May 5		Stretford	1M	1st 4:07.1	2nd A. Birks 4:11.6
May 10	BMC Mile	West London Stadium	1M	1st 4:06.6	2nd M. Benn 4:11.8
May 17		Keele	800m	2nd 1:52.7	1st C. Moreton 1:51.1
May 24	Inter-Counties champs	Leicester	1M ht	1st 4:08.3	
May 25	Inter-Counties champs	Leicester	1M final	4th 4:06.0	1st J. Whetton 4:04.2
Jun 6	Commonwealth Games trials meeting	Leicester	1500m	2nd 3:42.8	1st J. Whetton 3:41.5
Jun 14	PE Colleges v UAU v Southern AAA	West London	800m	1st 1:53.3	
Jun 28	International track meeting	Brussels	1500m	2nd 3:42.9	1st F. van Zyl
Jul 5	Sward Trophy	Crystal Palace	2M	2nd 8:30.8	1st K. Keino 8:29.0
Jul 18	Commonwealth Games	Edinburgh	1500m ht	2nd 3:43.8	
Jul 22	Commonwealth Games	Edinburgh	1500m final	3rd 3:40.6	1st K. Keino 3:36.6
Aug 1	European Cup semi-final	Zurich	1500m	3rd 3:48.6	1st J. Wadoux 3:44.4
Sep 2	World University Games	Turin	1500m ht	3rd 3:45.0	
Sep 3	World University Games	Turin	1500m final	10th 3:59.7	1st F. Arese 3:52.7

Date	Meeting	Venue	Distance	Position and time	Other positions
1971					
Jan 9	Sherman Cup CC	North Shields	8M	3rd 40:04	1st J. Alder 39:36
Jan 16	Inter-Counties CC champs	Leicester	7½M	18th 35:48	1st T. Wright 35:04
Jan 30	North-East CC champs			3rd	1st J. Alder
Feb 20	Royal Signals road relay	Gateshead	2½M	fastest lap 10:37 (course record)	
Mar 6	National CC champs	Norwich	9M	22nd 49:23	1st D. Bedford 47:04
Mar 20	Ashbrooke Relay			8:40	
Mar 27	Southern Games	Trinidad	5000m	2nd 14:36.0	1st K. Keino 14:04.0
Mar 28	Southern Games	Trinidad	1500m	3rd 3:50.4	1st K. Keino 3:40.6
Apr 3	Southern Games	Trinidad	1M	3rd 4:04.6	1st K. Keino 3:58.3
Apr 7	Easter Games	Barbados	1500m	1st 3:44.1	
May 23	International track meeting	Lodz	800m	16th 1:52.7	
May 30	Inter-Counties champs	Leicester	1M ht	4th 4:06.7	
May 31	Inter-Counties champs	Leicester	1M final	3rd 3:58.5	1st W. Wilkinson 3:56.6
Jun 12	Emsley Carr Mile	Edinburgh	1M	4th 4:01.8	1st P. Stewart 4:00.4
Jun 26	Track meeting	South Shields	800m	2nd 1:52.6	
		,,	2M	1st 8:53.0	
Jul 1	International track meeting	Milan	1500m	4th 3:39.4	1st M. Liquori 3:36.0
Jul 10	UK v France	Portsmouth	1500m	2nd 3:40.6	1st J-P. Dufresne 3:40.6
Jul 17	Handicap track meeting	Whitley Bay	800m	2nd 1:52.0	
Jul 23	AAA champs	Crystal Palace	1500m ht	1st 3:43.3	
Jul 24	AAA champs	Crystal Palace	1500m final	3rd 3:40.7	1st T. Polhill 3:40.0
Aug 13	European champs	Helsinki	1500m ht	4th 3:42.8	
Aug 15	European champs	Helsinki	1500m final	3rd 3:39.2	1st F. Arese 3:38.4
Aug 21	Highland Games	Edinburgh	2M	2nd 8:24.8 (UK rec)	1st E Puttemans 8:17.8, world rec
Aug 30	UK v W. Germany	Crystal Palace	1500m	3rd 3:45.1	1st H. Norpoth 3:43.9
Dec 11	North-East CC champs	Middlesbrough	9M	1st 47:18	2nd J. Alder 47:37
1972					
Jan 8	Sherman Cup CC	North Shields	6½M	1st 34:01	2nd J. Caine 34:11
Jan 15	Inter-Counties CC champs	Derby	7½M	15th 41:15	1st Gren. Tuck 39:18
Feb 19	Royal Signals road relay	Gateshead		fastest lap 10:35	
Mar 4	National CC champs	Sutton Coldfield	9M	14th 48:44	1st M. Thomas 47:27
May 13	Northern League	Gateshead	400m	2nd 53:4	1st M. Riddell
May 20		Newcastle	400m	1st 51.2	
Jun 10	Emsley Carr Mile	Crystal Palace	1M	2nd 3:55.9	1st P. Stewart 3:55.3
Jun 16	UK v Poland	Edinburgh	1500m	1st 3:43.7	2nd A. Kupczyk 3:45.1
Jul 3	International track meeting	Oslo	1500m	2nd 3:40.7	1st G. Larsen 3:39.9
Jul 5	International track meeting	Stockholm	1M	1st 3:57.2	2nd P. Vasala 3:57.2

Date	Meeting	Venue	Distance	Position and time	Other positions
Jul 14	AAA champs	Crystal Palace	1500m ht	2nd 3:42.7	
Jul 15	AAA champs	Crystal Palace	1500m final	4th 3:39.3	1st P. Stewart 3:38.2
Jul 25	Finland v UK v Spain	Helsinki	1500m	2nd 3:42.0	1st P. Vasala 3:41.2
Aug 5	International meeting	Crystal Palace	800m	4th 1:51.1	1st J. Abidoye 1:49.5
Sep 8	Olympic Games	Munich	1500m ht	4th 3:40.8	
Sep 9	Olympic Games	Munich	1500m s-f	3rd 3:38.2	
Sep 10	Olympic Games	Munich	1500m final	5th 3:39.0	1st P. Vasala 3:36.3
Nov 11	IAC/Findus CC race	Parliament Hill	8000m	21st 22:58	1st D. Black 22:07
Dec 9	North-East CC champs	Whickham	9M	1st 46:44	2nd J. Alder 47:06

1973

Date	Meeting	Venue	Distance	Position and time	Other positions
Jan 12	Indoor meeting	College Park, Maryland	1M	3rd 4:01.9	1st B. Wheeler 4:00.5
Jan 13	Indoor meeting	Uniondale, New York	2M	1st 8:38.6	2nd R. McAfee 8:45.4
Mar 3	National CC champs	Parliament Hill	9M	17th 45:00	1st R. Dixon (guest) 43:42
Mar 25	Five Mills CC	San Vittore Olona	9500M	2nd 31:05.8	1st F. Shorter 31:00.8; 29th L. Viren 33:36.2
Apr 7	Northern road relay	Morpeth	4½M	fastest lap 18:46	
Apr 14	Road races	Jarrow	6½M	1st 30:19 (course record by 62 secs)	2nd D. Slater 31:36
Jul 1	Vaux track meeting	South Shields	1M	1st 3:59.2	2nd C. Spedding 4:04.0
		,,	Paarlauf	3rd	with Wilf Wardle
Jul 14	AAA champs	Crystal Palace	5000m	1st 13:23.8	2nd I. Stewart 13:31.0
Aug 18	Highland Games	Edinburgh	1500m	3rd 3:42.0 (tripped at start)	1st R. Dixon 3:40.0
Aug 25	UK v Hungary	Crystal Palace	1500m	2nd 3:38.5	1st F. Clement 3:38.5
Aug 27	International meeting	Crystal Palace	2M	1st 8:13.8 (world record)	2nd C. Stewart 8:33.0
Sep 9	European Cup final	Edinburgh	5000m	1st 13:54.8	2nd M. Kuschmann 13:55.3; 5th L. Viren 14:18.2
Dec 2	International CC race	Vanves	8000m	2nd 23:51	1st E. Puttemans 23:34

1974

Date	Meeting	Venue	Distance	Position and time	Other positions
Jan 27	Commonwealth Games	Christchurch	5000m ht	1st 13:45.6	
Jan 29	Commonwealth Games	Christchurch	5000m final	2nd 13:14.6 (UK record)	1st B. Jipcho 13:14.4
Jan 31	Commonwealth Games	Christchurch	1500m ht	4th 3:44.9	
Feb 2	Commonwealth Games	Christchurch	1500m final	7th 3:37.6 (UK record)	1st F. Bayi 3:32.2; world record
Mar 24	Five Mills CC race	San Vittore Olona	9500m	3rd 31:34.8	1st E. Puttemans 31:08.6; 7th L. Viren 32:32.0
Apr 20	Nysgardparkenrundt CC	Bergen	4000m	1st 11:35 (course record)	

Date	Meeting	Venue	Distance	Position and time	Other positions
Apr 27	AAA National road relay	Sutton Coldfield	5½M	fastest lap 24:28 (course record)	
May 4	FA Cup Final race	Wembley Stadium	300m (grass)	1st 8:05.0	2nd J. Vaatainen 8:13.0
Jun 30	Track meeting	South Shields	2M	1st 8:42.4	2nd D. Bedford 8:57.6
		,,	2M Paarlauf	1st	with D Bedford 7:57.0
Jul 13	AAA champs	Crystal Palace	5000m	1st 13:27.4	2nd J. Hermens 13:53.2
Jul 26	UK v Czechoslovakia	Edinburgh	1500m	1st 3:41.2	2nd F. Clement 3:41.7
Aug 3	Gateshead Games	Gateshead	3000m	1st 7:35.2 (world record)	2nd D. Black 7:51.0)
Aug 10	Emsley Carr Mile	Crystal Palace	1M	3rd 3:58.4	1st F. Clement 3:57.4
Aug 17	Highland Games	Edinburgh	800m	5th 1:51.4	1st M. Winzenried 1:48.6
Sep 6	European champs	Rome	400m 'B'	8th 52.6	1st R. Jenkins 47.5
		,,	5000m ht	1st 13:37.0	
		,,	5000m final	1st 13:17.2	2nd M. Kuschmann 13:24.0; 3rd L. Viren 13:24.6
Sep 13	IAC–Coca-Cola meeting	Crystal Palace	2M	1st 8:23.0	2nd R. Smedley 8:25.8; 3rd L. Viren 8:25.8
Dec 14	International CC race	Gateshead	4½M	4th 23:37	1st I. Stewart 23:21

1975

Date	Meeting	Venue	Distance	Position and time	Other positions
Jan 25	Royal Signals road relay	Gateshead		fastest lap 10:38	
Mar 8		South Shields	5½M	1st 24:54 (course record)	
Mar 23	Five Mills CC race	San Vittore Olona	9500m	18th	1st F. Bayi 30:18
Apr 26	AAA National road relay	Sutton Coldfield	3M	fastest lap 13:58 (course record)	
May 23	Standards track meeting	Gateshead	800m	2nd 1:53.6	1st A. Asgeirsson 1:53.5
Jun 8	Pye Gold Cup 1st round	Gateshead	1500m	1st 3:43.6	
Jun 26	World Games	Helsinki	1500m	7th 3:40.3	1st J. Walker 3:36.3
Jul 4	Philips International meeting	Crystal Palace	2000m	5th 5:03.0 (UK record)	1st J. Walker 5:00.6
Jul 13	European Cup semi-final	Crystal Palace	5000m	1st 13:30.4	2nd M. Ulymov 13:50.8
Jul 26	Gateshead Games	Gateshead	5000m	2nd 13:33.0	1st R. Dixon 13:27.4
Aug 17	European Cup final	Nice	5000m	1st 13:36.2	2nd E. Selik 13:42.8; 5th L. Viren 13:49.8
Aug 23	Highland Games	Edinburgh	800m	6th 1:53.0	1st M. Winzenried 1:48.1
Aug 25	UK v USSR	Crystal Palace	1500m	1st 3:42.2	2nd V. Panteley 3:42.5
Aug 29	IAC–Coca-Cola meeting	Crystal Palace	10,000m	1st 27:45.4	2nd F. Shorter 27:46.0
Sep 1	Greenham Games	Gateshead	2M	1st 8:29.8	2nd J. Brown 8:33.2
Nov 15	Road race	North Shields	5M	1st 23:33	2nd C. Garforth 23:46
Nov 29	International CC race	Gateshead	4½M	1st 22:41	2nd J. Hermens 22:41

Date	Meeting	Venue	Distance	Position and time	Other positions
Dec 20	International CC race	Crystal Palace		4th 26:46	1st J. Hermens 26:30; 25th L. Viren 28:31
1976					
Jan 17	Home countries CC international	Glasgow	6M	1st 29:33	2nd T. Simmons 29:57
Jan 25	European Clubs CC champs	Arlon	10,000m	1st 30:23	2nd M. Haro 30:36
Feb 21	Royal Signals road relay	Gateshead		2nd fastest lap 11:23	fastest, C. Garforth 11:21
Mar 7	Five Mills CC race	San Vittore Olona	9500m	3rd 30:48	1st F. Bayi 29:55
Apr 3	Northern road relay	Gateshead	2¼M	fastest lap 10:03	
Apr 23	AAA National road relay	Sutton Coldfield	3M	fastest lap 13:37 (course record)	
May 26	Borough Road College meeting	Crystal Palace	1500m	1st 3:40.2	2nd J. Zemen 3:41.3
May 28	Superspike meeting	Gateshead	1M	12th 4:14.3 (fell at last bend)	1st M. Boit 3:58.7
Jun 5	Kraft Games	Crystal Palace	5000m	1st 13:33.8	2nd D. Black 13:35.4
Jun 12	Kraft Games	Crystal Palace	10,000m	1st 27:53.8	2nd T. Simmons 27:56.4
Jul 4	UK v Canada v Poland	Crystal Palace	1500m	2nd 3:42.9	1st D. Hill 3:41.9
Jul 5	International track meeting	Stockholm	1500m	8th 3:40.9	1st J. Walker 3:34.2
Jul 9	International track meeting	Zurich	2M	1st 8:19.0	2nd B. Malinowski 8:26.4
Jul 23	Olympic Games	Montreal	10,000m ht	2nd 28:22.2	
Jul 26	Olympic Games	Montreal	10,000m final	3rd 27:55.0	1st L. Viren 27:40.4
Jul 28	Olympic Games	Montreal	5000m ht	1st 13:20.4 (Olympic record)	
Jul 30	Olympic Games	Montreal	5000m final	5th 13:26.2	1st L. Viren 13:24.8
Aug 6	IAC–Coca-Cola meeting	Edinburgh	2M	1st 8:22.2	2nd N. Rose 8:23.0; 11th L. Viren 8:35.4
Aug 10	International meeting	Helsinki	5000m	1st 13:26.4	2nd K. Kvalheim 13:26.8; 7th L. Viren 13:42.2
Aug 14	AAA champs	Crystal Palace	5000m	1st 13:33.0	2nd N. Rose 13:37.0
Aug 22	Rediffusion Games	Gateshead	2M	1st 8:36.2	2nd K. Kvalheim 8:36.6; 3rd L. Viren 8:40.2
Aug 26	International meeting	Lappeenranta	5000m	1st 13:47.4	2nd L. Viren 13:51.4
Aug 30	Emsley Carr Mile	Crystal Palace	1M	3rd 3:57.7	1st D. Moorcroft 3:57.1
Sep 1	International meeting	Cologne	3000m	4th 7:46.3	1st R. Dixon 7:43.6
Sep 13	Bell's Whisky Games	Gateshead	2000m	1st 5:07.2	
Sep 17	Debenhams Games	Crystal Palace	2M	2nd 8:24.7	1st R. Dixon 8:24.0
Sep 19	Invitation CC race	Loughrea		1st	
Oct 16	International road race	Amsterdam	10M	4th 48:40.2	1st K. Lismont 47:31.4
Oct 24	International road race	Rennes		6th 24:35	1st T. Simmons 24:11

Date	Meeting	Venue	Distance	Position and time	Other positions
Nov 21	Grenoble CC race	Grenoble		3rd 22:59	1st J. Boxberger 22:48
Dec 4	North-East CC champs	Framwellgate Moor		1st 34:17	
Dec 11	IAC/Philips CC race	Crystal Palace	5M	8th 26:52	1st B. Ford 26:20
Dec 28	Gateshead H Club	Gateshead	Paarlauf	1st	with J. Foley
1977					
Jan 15	International CC race	Belfast	5M	2nd 28:11	1st G. Deegan 28:00
Jan 23	International CC race	Augsburg	10,500m	3rd 32:39	1st H-J. Orthmann 31:38
Feb 19	Royal Signals road relay	Gateshead	2½M	fastest lap 12:20	
Mar 5	National CC champs	Parliament Hill	9M	1st 43:49	2nd B. Ford 43:50
Mar 27	Chas Kendall road race	Barrow-in-Furness	10M	1st 47:16	2nd H. Jones 47:20
Apr 16	Conoco-Lanes road race	Londonderry	5M	1st 23:47	2nd G. Deegan 24:03
Apr 23	AAA National road relay	Sutton Coldfield	3M	fastest lap 13:48	
Jun 8	Track league	Gateshead	800m	2nd 1:53.8	
Jun 15	Track league	Gateshead	800m	2nd 1:53.6	
Jun 26	Debenhams Games	Crystal Palace	5000m	1st 13:21.2	2nd J. Goater 13:30.0
Jul 8	Track league	Gateshead	800m	1st 1:54.5	
Jul 22	AAA champs	Crystal Palace	10,000m	1st 27:45.7	2nd D. Black 28:19.0
Aug 26	UK v USSR	Edinburgh	5000m	1st 13:42.4	2nd D. Black 13:43.8
Sep 4	Boot Trophy	Leicester	3000m	1st 8:00.4	
Sep 9	IAC–Coca-Cola meeting	Crystal Palace	10,000m	1st 27:36.6	2nd H. Rono 27:37.1
Sep 12	Manitou Games	Gateshead	3000m	2nd 7:49.6	1st M. McLeod 7:49.1
Sep 14	Jarrow Paarlauf	Jarrow	3000m	1st 7:54.2	with A. Amos
Sep 18	Navan Carpets International road race	Loughrea	4M	1st 18:05	2nd N. Cusack 18:12
Nov 26	Schweppes International CC race	Gateshead	4½M	16th 22:47	1st N. Muir 22:13
Dec 31	Sankey road race	Ipswich	4M	1st 19:12	2nd K. Penny 19:13
1978					
Jan 23	International CC race	Vilamoura	10,000m	3rd 30:11.1	1st G. Meyer 29:44.4
Jan 29	International CC race	Fermoy	10,000m	1st 29:11	2nd D. Black 29:15
Mar 11	Open road race	Windermere to Kendal	10M	1st 47:54	2nd J. Calvert 49:55
Apr 9	Chas Kendall road race	Barrow-in-Furness	10M	2nd 46:17	1st M. McLeod 45:44